Foundations of Pastoral Counselling

Foundations of Pastoral Counselling

Integrating Philosophy, Theology and Psychotherapy

Neil Pembroke

scm press

© Neil Pembroke 2017

Published in 2017 by SCM Press

Editorial office
3rd Floor, Invicta House,
108–114 Golden Lane,
London EC1Y 0TG, UK

SCM Press is an imprint of Hymns Ancient & Modern Ltd
(a registered charity)

Hymns Ancient & Modern® is a registered trademark
of Hymns Ancient and Modern Ltd
13A Hellesdon Park Road, Norwich,
Norfolk NR6 5DR, UK

www.scmpress.co.uk

British Library Cataloguing in Publication data
A catalogue record for this book is available
from the British Library

978 0 334 05535 8

Typeset by Regent Typesetting
Printed and bound by CPI Group (UK) Ltd, Croydon

Contents

Foreword

Well-digested, enduring and practical insight and wisdom are in short supply in the contemporary world, even in the spheres of pastoral and practical theology. There is a tendency for contributions to be either enormously practical, but light on theory, or theoretically sophisticated, but deficient in practical applicability.

In this context, *Foundations of Pastoral Counselling* is a welcome, important and mature contribution from one of Australia's leading and most prolific pastoral theologians. Neil Pembroke manages both to draw insightfully on his extensive experience of pastoral care and counselling and to bring this into critical dialogue with sophisticated philosophical and theological theories, lightly but clearly presented on their own terms. The book is an education in complex theories, used with great effect to illuminate everyday practice and experience. Readers cannot but go away from this volume with a renewed sense of the value of pastoral practice and the importance of philosophical and other theories as a real source of insight and stimulus for developing their approaches and skills. I hope it will be read by experienced pastoral *and* non-religious counsellors as well as by students of ministry and pastoral care in training. I have no doubt that the range of thinkers and ideas it covers will assist the latter in their wider theological and philosophical studies, as well as in becoming more pastorally aware and responsive.

One of the real strengths of this book is the love and deep understanding the author has for his practice and for the thinkers, ancient and modern, that he draws on. It is this love or desire (as Simone Weil, one of Pembroke's interlocutors, would say) that communicates itself in his beautifully clear expositions of complex thought. If you have heard of Levinas, Buber and Kierkegaard, but have been bemused or defeated by the complexity and incorrigibility of their writings, or been fobbed off with tokenistic inclusion of key ideas in practical text books ('I-Thou' as a basis of all kinds of relating), then here you will find clear, critical and sympathetic expositions of their thinking. This from an author who has clearly immersed himself in their texts so that he can explain and interpret their thrust and significance for counselling practice 'in his own words'. Quite apart from the application of their thought to pastoral counselling, readers will acquire a substantial education in important aspects of philosophy and theology.

The expository clarity Pembroke applies to philosophical thinkers is also typical of the range of psychotherapeutic and counselling theorists whose work he uses. Heinz Kohut's work, for example, is as complex and difficult to grasp as it is significant. Pembroke, nothing daunted, retrieves insights that are immediately applicable in pastoral counselling dealing with issues of shame and self-worth. So here again there is wider gain for readers.

A particularly important aspect of the book is that it also finds space for critical and creative insights from the theological tradition, often neglected as a source of wisdom even within pastoral counselling. For Pembroke, the word 'pastoral' means something distinctive and important in the quest for helping individuals to flourish in all aspects of their lives. So he does not hesitate to draw on the Bible, on theologians like Aquinas and Karl Barth, and on spiritual writers such as Thomas Merton and Henri Nouwen. This allows him to find space for discussions on, for example, the empathic or passionate nature of God amid wider conversations on issues arising in pastoral counselling.

A further strength of this work is that it is full of wise and insightful comments and illustrations from the author's own experience, as well as from the work of other therapists. A particularly rich discussion illustrating this is in the chapter about facilitating self-change indirectly using the inspiration of Kierkegaard's philosophical positions. But throughout the book, there is constant earthing of theory in practice. Even particular phrases stick in the mind, like the idea that the counsellor must manage the 'empathic dance'.

Pembroke's clearly written chapters typically start with a particular fundamental framing, or substantive issue in pastoral counselling, and then go on to identify and expound theoretical and philosophical resources that illuminate it, moving then towards the application of these ideas. This measured and clear pattern allows readers to cover a lot of ground with ease, if not without effort. While this may look at first sight like the application of theory to practice, it is clear that this is just a way of structuring a mutual learning conversation between different perspectives on pastoral counselling. This conversation is invariably enriching.

This book will not tell you how to become a pastoral counsellor or provide you with basic technical information and skills. It is likely that some of the issues and thinkers addressed in it will not be of the same level of interest for all readers. My advice would be to start where you find something of interest and read outwards from there. I am pretty sure that you will not only want to read all the remaining chapters, but will also want to follow up the references and thinkers to whom Pembroke points and whose work has inspired his own thought. The book will not yield up its riches without some work on the part of its readers, but if you follow the author where he gently leads, you will find that your practice and thought will be much enriched. You will acquire critical horizons and resources that will sustain and stimulate you for a long time to come.

Pastoral counselling, once central in practical theology and ministry, has tended to become rather peripheral to these disciplines in recent years, particularly outside the USA. It is really good to see a major, critical, interdisciplinary contribution to this field that is intellectually challenging, rigorous and practically insightful. I salute its author for all the work that has gone into thinking through and writing a book that is unique in its scope and depth and will have enduring value. I commend it to what I hope will be a very large readership over time.

Stephen Pattison
University of Birmingham, UK

Introduction

There are specialist pastoral counsellors and there are those who counsel as part of general pastoral ministry. This book brings together both categories in addressesing foundational issues of pastoral counselling. The intended readership is primarily those beginning their exploration of the complicated and delicate art of counselling, but experienced pastors, chaplains and counsellors may also find insights and methods that are fresh and add value to their established ministries.

The aim is to offer a concise treatment of the *foundations* of pastoral counselling, which means there are some significant issues that the book is unable to cover. Having said that, the issues selected for treatment are to my mind the absolutely central ones:

- the nature and scope of pastoral counselling
- respect for the freedom and individuality of the counsellee
- attentive listening and empathy
- embodiment and the counselling relationship
- the authenticity of the counsellor
- inclusion in the inner world of experience of the counsellee
- confirmation of counsellees in their God-given potential
- guided discovery in addressing faulty lines of cognition
- social justice counselling
- facilitating self-challenge
- working with metaphors used by counsellees
- reframing thinking
- using ritual in a communal witness to hope
- the spirituality of the counsellor.

Pastoral counsellors who are able to fully embrace all the attitudes and values offered in the book, and artfully enact all the skills and interventions discussed, are in excellent shape for their ministry.

The discussions in the book have the particular shape of a three-way conversation involving philosophy, theology and psychotherapy. A hallmark is the inclusion of a significant philosophical discussion in each chapter. It is a natural move in a work on counselling to draw in various insights from philosophy. After all, a number of the founders of leading counselling/psychotherapeutic approaches have taken this line. Carl Rogers referred to Martin Buber as his 'favourite philosopher'. Rogers saw strong connections between his own ideas of acceptance and empathy and Buber's notions of confirmation and inclusion. Albert Ellis and others in the cognitive therapy movement drew on the ideas of the Stoic philosophers and utilized a Socratic method. Michael White and David Epston engaged with the poststructuralist thought of Foucault and Derrida[1] in developing narrative therapy. And, of course, existentialist therapies are informed by the thinking of Kierkegaard, Heidegger, Marcel and others.

Not only is it a natural move, it is also a most fruitful one. When it comes to thinking about counselling, there are enormous riches to be mined from the work of some of the truly great thinkers in human history. I have learned more from Emmanuel Levinas on acknowledging otherness, more from Simone Weil concerning deep attending, more from Martin Buber about a genuine meeting with another person, than I have from all of the writers on counselling and psychotherapy taken together.

Though philosophical input often comes first in a chapter, this should not be taken to mean that it is assigned primacy over theology – far from it. Don Browning, Don Capps, Elaine Graham, Stephen Pattison, Bonnie Miller-McLemore and Daniël Louw, to name just some of the leading voices, have taught us well concerning the need to avoid uncritical borrowing from other disciplines in developing our pastoral psychologies. The book aims to establish a correlation between the two disciplines.

I want to state clearly at the outset that although most of the issues addressed crop up in any form of counselling, this is very definitely a book about *pastoral* counselling. When I did my basic training in pastoral counselling with Homer Ashby at McCormick Theological Seminary in Chicago in the early 1980s, Homer required us all to write a major paper entitled 'What's "Pastoral" about Pastoral Counselling?' It presented itself to me then as a vitally important question, and it still does today. There are some elements that come immediately to mind in contemplating an answer to the question. First, pastoral counselling needs to integrate into its therapeutic ministry the spiritual therapy of the Church. Pastoral counsellors have available to them the rich resources of the Church: the Bible, the classic spiritual writings, prayer and worship. There are many very helpful works available on this theme, but it is not necessary to expound them here.[2]

Second, pastoral counsellors demonstrate their theological commitments by engaging in reflective practice that draws not only on psychology and counselling theory, but also on the Christian heritage. When it comes to this type of reflection on practice, the process is often referred to as the 'pastoral cycle'. This term reminds us that theological reflection is a cyclical or, better, a spiralling process (we want our practice to progress, not to go around in circles!). Fresh insights are generated through theological reflection on current practice and a revised approach to pastoral counselling is developed. But as soon as this new practice is set in place, it becomes the subject of fresh theological analysis, leading to more revisions. And so the process spirals on.

The most well-known and widely used process model is probably the one developed by James Whitehead and Evelyn Eaton Whitehead. Their book *Method in Ministry* was first published in 1980 and revised in 1995.[3] The Whiteheads' method of theological reflection involves three stages:

- The first attends to the information available from the faith tradition, personal and communal experience, and contemporary culture.
- The second is a vigorous conversation set up among the sources. The aim in this dialogue is to struggle with the diverse views until consensus emerges.
- This leads to the third stage – generating a model for renovated pastoral practice.

We find the same basic elements of lived experience, exploration of and reflection on that experience, and pastoral response in the more recent work of Emmanuel Lartey.[4] Lartey presents a five-phase process. Particularly helpful is the way in which Lartey discusses the capacity of a situational analysis[5] to critique theology. The phases in his pastoral cycle consist of attending to experience, situational analysis, theological analysis, situational analysis of the theology (correlation is a two-way street), and response (a new approach to practice emerges).

These and similar methods are inspired by the approach to reflective practice taken in healthcare, the human services and education. However, they incorporate the all-important theological dimension. Theological reflection needs to be employed regularly by pastoral counsellors if they are to be true to their vocation. The aim, as in all forms of ministry, is to develop within one's personhood and pastoral effectiveness.

The third element in my response to Homer Ashby's question is that pastoral counselling is a work both of the individual pastor and of the community of faith. The secular counsellor works most often in isolation. Pastoral counsellors are blessed with having (ideally) a supportive and nurturing community as an additional resource. The communal dimension of pastoral counselling features in Chapter 9.

The final point in response to the question is that pastoral counselling differs from its secular counterpart in that its major focus is supporting people on a journey of transformation or ongoing conversion to Christ.[6] The three domains in which this transformation takes place are personal psychology, spirituality and the moral life. Clearly, these are not three watertight containers standing side by side; they leak into each other. For this reason, naming the three domains in this way is not entirely satisfactory, and certainly does not imply that spirituality is a discrete category, and that one's psychological life and personal ethics can somehow be neatly separated out from it. Having acknowledged this shortcoming, it is also true that each area has its own specific focus. When it comes to the psychological, we are concerned with intrapsychic and interpersonal dynamics. The spirituality area involves us in reflection on prayer and meditation on God's Word, images of God and the God-relationship. Finally, in the ethics category we concentrate on moral principles and rules, on virtue and character, on what is right and good.

With these categories in the foreground of their thinking, there are those who want to mark out three distinct and discrete areas of ministry. Proponents of the three silos approach aim to ensure that a particular ministry does not get 'contaminated' by extraneous concerns. There are some pastoral counsellors, for example, who seek to follow quite closely the path mapped out by their secular counterparts. In this approach, moral issues are bracketed out, because the primary responsibility is construed as helping people deal with their intrapsychic and interpersonal dysfunction and the pain associated with that.

The well-known spiritual theologians William Barry and William Connolly are representative of the silo approach in their particular field of spiritual direction. In their view, the focus of spiritual directors is on helping directees mature in their God-relationship. Attention to moral issues represents a distraction. They present a case in their widely read book *The Practice of Spiritual Direction*[7] to make their point. A married woman with two young children comes for spiritual direction to a nun who is a member of the parish team. Prayer is important in the woman's life and she values being close to God. However, she finds herself facing a moral dilemma because she has fallen in love with a divorced man. On several occasions recently they have come close to making love. She cannot make sense of what is happening to her. She feels more energized and vital than she has for a long time, and even finds that her prayer life has deepened. She also feels guilty. The desire that she expresses to the director is to relate to God in a deeper way and to discover God's will.

In response to the question of whether or not the director should pick up on the moral issue, their answer is nuanced, but the bottom-line is that it is better to leave it alone. Barry and Connolly put it this way:

> In the first place, the directee usually knows that there is a discrepancy. In the example, the married woman was disconcerted by the exhilaration she felt when she also felt guilt. Secondly, spiritual direction is only one of the many ministries of the church. We can presume that sermons, articles, newspaper items, pastoral consultations are also part of the religious ambience of a directee. Thirdly, the issue is not whether the director should or should not remind the directee of her obligations, but what the director's primary purpose is in any intervention she makes. We believe that her primary purpose is to foster the directee's relationship with God.[8]

We have seen a strong and, to my mind, very welcome reaction against the compartmentalization approach from some in the field of pastoral care and counselling. For example, in the mid-1970s Don Browning and others started a movement to restore the moral context of pastoral care.[9] Also significant is the argument put by Jean Stairs, that a comprehensive approach to caring for others requires the integration of theological and psychological insights with wise teaching on the spiritual life.[10] Stairs discusses the nature of the close relationship between pastoral care and the ministry of spiritual direction.

My book *Moving Toward Spiritual Maturity*[11] argues for an approach that includes all three areas. Growing in the way of Christ requires careful and sustained attention to the psychological, spiritual and moral domains. In his pastoral theology, Daniël Louw similarly rejects a compartmentalized view of ministry.[12] Louw construes the work of pastoral counselling as helping people correct unhealthy personal schemas.[13] He points out that the categories that make up a schema are psychological, spiritual and moral in nature. Len Sperry tackles the issue in his own particular way in his book *Transforming Self and Community*,[14] but he ends up at the same place that Louw, I and a number of other pastoral theologians do. Helping people move towards spiritual maturity involves engaging them at all three levels. I construe pastoral counselling as an integrative ministry that encompasses intrapsychic, interpersonal, spiritual and moral issues and concerns.

Having discussed the vitally important question of what distinguishes pastoral from other forms of counselling, there now follows an overview of the book. In Part 1, the theme is fundamental attitudes and skills; and in Part 2, it is fundamental interventions and strategies.

In Chapter 1, attention is given to the crucially important attitude of respect for the uniqueness of the counsellee. It begins by acknowledging that it is a good thing for the counsellor to make judicious use of one or more of the available psychotherapies. They offer a variety of interventions that in many cases prove efficacious in facilitating healing and growth. However, I go on to suggest that it is vitally important for the counsellor to be aware of a potential problem associated with counselling and psychotherapeutic systems – the totalizing impulse. 'Totalizing' is a central term in the philosophy of Emmanuel Levinas. He defined this destructive tendency as colonizing the 'other' with the themes and categories in one's theoretical model. Levinas attempted to counter the totalizing impulse in Western philosophy through arguing strongly for respect for absolute alterity. Tuning into the language of 'the wholly other' suggests a correlation with Barth's approach to God-talk. The great neo-orthodox theologian launched an attack on what he construed as the attempt by nineteenth-century liberal theologians to close the infinite gap between time and the eternal God in order to advance their anthropocentric and humanistic project. Barth finally recognized, however, that it is wrong to view God and humankind as completely isolated from each other (in Christ, God and humanity meet). Is it therefore reasonable to expect that a similar move would provide Levinas's extreme formulation of alterity in human relations with much needed nuancing? After all, the difference between God and humankind is massively larger than anything that might exist between two human beings. Though smoothing off the hard edge in Levinas's extreme language may seem a reasonable move, maintaining the absolute distinction between the 'I' and the 'other' is essential to Levinasian ethics.

Levinas's insight concerning the totalizing tendency in Western philosophy has something very important to say to counselling theory and practice. It alerts us to the fact that counsellors may fail to recognize the imperialist tendency in the systems they employ. When this is the case, they unwittingly dominate and oppress the counsellee through imposing its tightly prescribed theoretical constructs.

The absolutely fundamental topic of empathy is the concern of Chapter 2. It begins by suggesting that thinking about the nature of empathic relating benefits from engagement with the philosophical conversation on social understanding. Also significant is the fact that some philosophers accent the role of embodiment in the interactive process of social cognition. In the discussion, these two aspects of the philosophical conversation are brought together. In developing these facets, I draw from a theory of social cognition called 'participatory sense-making' (PSM).

When it comes to reflecting on empathic relating, we will take particular note of the fact that for PSM theorists social cognition involves the moments of attunement and alienation. Drawing also on the dance metaphor that these theorists employ, there is a discussion on the therapeutic value of being slightly out-of-step (subtly altering counsellees' expression of their inner state may lead to new insights), falling into missteps (in certain therapeutic contexts empathic failures are positive), and taking the lead (a highly empathic counsellor can grasp something that is outside the counsellee's awareness). The theological reflection centres on whether or not there is a biblical and systematic theological justification for the notion of an empathic God.

In Chapter 3, we discuss the skill and discipline of deep listening. To help us in our exploration, we will draw on Simone Weil's profound thinking about what she calls 'attention'. The first insight that we gain from Weil is that attention flows from desire and an experience of joy in being with another. 'Muscular effort' is no substitute for being led by desire. Attending to the other does, however, require effort. Weil refers to the need for negative effort or passive activity. It is counterproductive to force oneself to be attentive. Genuine attention is spontaneous and instinctive; it emanates from a deep desire to know, to understand, and to support the other. It is both dispositional and a free gift of grace. We cannot make ourselves good listeners simply by an exercise of will.

The second connection that is made is that attention requires the stance of waiting. Pastoral counsellors need to listen with openness and expectancy. They are aware that they must not attempt to wrestle meaning from what the counsellee is saying. The patterns in the counsellee's story must be allowed to unfold. An attempt to force the process will derail it.

The final insight offered is that attention is founded on self-emptying. If the ego fills the interpersonal space, there is no room for the communications of the other. Weil's notion of 'decreation' is helpful in this context, but the way she articulates it is less so. The language she uses sounds nihilistic. For this reason, I turn to the thinking of Thomas Merton on the true and false selves to shape the discussion. It is clearly not the self *in toto* that needs to pass into nothingness, but rather the false self. Pride, hard-heartedness and selfishness all militate against attention. It is these, along with other similarly sinful tendencies, that need to be emptied out.

Chapter 4 takes up the question of how to engage in a genuine dialogue. We begin by surveying the way various psychotherapists have been inspired by Martin Buber's dialogical philosophy. These therapists cover virtually the entire spectrum of psychotherapeutic approaches. What unites them is their conviction that while theories of personality and particular therapeutic interventions play an important role, the really decisive factor in the healing and growth process is the quality of the relationship developed between therapist and client.

In reviewing Buber's dialogical philosophy, I identify three central elements in establishing a genuine meeting with the counsellee. The first is *offering a genuine presence to the counsellee.* To be authentically present to the other involves a willingness to drop image and pretence. Buber refers to this as relating to the other in the 'being' mode rather than in the 'seeming' one. The second element is *inclusion in the life experience and view of life of the counsellee.* For Buber, including oneself in the world of another involves a bold 'swinging over' into the lifeworld of the other. In terms of a correlation, some theologians have made a plea for an approach to the incarnation that focuses on categories such as empathy with, and attunement to, fundamental human experience. The last of the crucial elements identified in Chapter 4 is *confirmation of counsellees as the people they are at present and the ones they have the potential to become.* Buber envisions a more active role for counsellors than does Carl Rogers. A pastor counsellor struggles with counsellees to help them grow into their God-given potential.

Chapter 5 signals a shift in gears from attitudes and skills to interventions and strategies. The particular interventions we focus on here are those associated with action for social justice. In the early part of the book, an important aim is the provision of a comprehensive model of what John Patton calls 'relational humanness'.[15] While this is the cornerstone of pastoral counselling, over the past 30 years we have witnessed a growing awareness that a comprehensive ministry of care includes a commitment to 'relational justice'.[16] In this chapter attention is given to three major issues: the conceptual history of social justice (we need to know what we mean when we say we are working for justice), the thinking associated with the emergence of this new paradigm, and the way leading proponents discuss engaging in relational justice. The aim is to show that relational humanness needs to be complemented with relational justice.

In Chapter 6, the comprehensive approach outlined above – one in which the domains of psychology, spirituality and the moral life are all included – is applied to the task of developing a strategy for helping counsellees revise faulty ways of thinking. The aim is to show how the Socratic method can be effectively used to support counsellees in doing their own therapeutic work on what I like to call belief-sickness. In the philosophical tradition such an approach is referred to as facilitating 'self-doctoring'; in contemporary psychotherapy it is called 'guided discovery'. A belief-sickness here is defined as a take on self, others, life or God that is unrealistic, unhealthy or unfaithful, and that causes significant emotional and spiritual distress and/or militates against personal well-being, positive interpersonal relating, and movement towards spiritual maturity.

Chapter 7 is on the blind-spots that we all suffer from. There are certain things – our faulty self-interpretation, our unrealistic thoughts, our self-deception, and certain moral inferiorities – that we just do not see. Søren Kierkegaard picked up on what he saw as a rather large blind-spot in the vision of his fellow Danish Christians in the Golden Age. In their eyes, they were genuine Christians. He, on the other hand, viewed this as simply illusion; and believed they were a long way from engaging in a serious manner with the demands of authentic Christianity. In his writings, Kierkegaard took an indirect route to challenging the cosy Christianity that he claimed he could see all around him. Through the use of polyphony and irony, he created an ambiguous communication that forced his readers to figure it out for themselves, thus aiming to stimulate their subjectivity and personal appropriation.

While it is clear that a relatively straightforward and direct approach to challenging a counsellee is useful, and the option that most pastoral counsellors probably choose, it is suggested here that there are three potential advantages associated with the *indirect* method. First, the creativity and playfulness associated with an indirect mode of communication resonates strongly with the inclinations and abilities of certain pastoral counsellors. Second, it is less likely than a direct approach to trigger defensiveness, opposition of the will, and stubborn refusal to open the eyes to see what the counsellor is seeing. And finally, there is the potential for greater impact. This is so because the counsellor creates the conditions for personal discovery rather than simply inviting an endorsement of a plain statement of the blind-spot.

The theme in Chapter 8 is working with counsellee images. It is now clear, thanks to the philosophers, that the use of metaphor is not simply a means of adding colour and interest to our conversations. It is essential to human thought and language; it is not an optional extra. We need metaphors to think and to express ourselves.

Given the indispensable role metaphorization plays in human thought and expression in general, it is to be expected that it will feature in counselling conversations. Helping counsellees unpack the images they use connects us with absolutely core issues in counselling. These issues include understanding of and talking about affect, empathic attunement, making tacit awareness of issues explicit and, finally, reframing a situation and finding new possibilities.

Though working with counsellee images (and with counsellees in general) requires art, intuition and flexibility, there is value in using a step-by-step procedure – especially when one is learning the process. It is crucially important to recognize that the method is not intended to be employed in a rigid, mechanical and inflexible manner. The steps are these:

- write it down
- invite exploration of the image
- invite reflection on the metaphor as a sensory image
- ask for a description of feelings/experience associated with the metaphor
- encourage changing the metaphor
- invite counsellees to make connections between the image and the problem situation
- ask if the way in which counsellees changed the image suggests any changes they might make.

We have already noted that pastoral counsellors have the asset of being connected to a supportive and nurturing community, and in Chapter 9 we take up this theme. In the Western world, there is a tendency to think of hope as something that an individual is responsible for. In the *Ubuntu* philosophy of sub-Saharan Africa, in contrast, hope is viewed as a work of the people as a whole. This connects with the biblical vision; the worshipping community serves as a witness to hope. Everything that happens when the community comes together for worship points to the source of Christian hope: the grace of our Lord Jesus Christ, the love of God, and the communion of the Holy Spirit. However, there is also the possibility of developing personally tailored rituals that employ Christian resources.

In the discussion in Chapter 9 on rituals for building hope, the term 'ritual' is defined thus: a communal action that has form and structure, incorporates the elements of words, Word, action and symbol, provides a safe space for expression of thought and feeling, and aims to connect the suffering person to human and divine witnesses to hope. In such a healing ritual, people in distress are offered a safe and loving space into which they can communicate their personal stories, their deep desires, and their hopes for a brighter future in word and in symbolic action. The witnesses participating in the ritual not only listen, but also offer the Word, words of prayer, and their personal words/actions of empathy, love and acceptance.

In the concluding reflection, I argue that what we bring as people contributes at least as much to the quality and effectiveness of our counselling work as does our skilful technique. The conscientious and faithful counsellor constantly works on enhancing knowledge, skill and technique. But just as importantly, and probably more so, counsellors continually open themselves up to the Spirit of God in the journey into stronger faith, deeper compassion and firmer character.

Now that we have a map of the territory to be traversed, we are set up for our journey. It begins with a discussion of how to avoid the totalizing impulse so as to ensure proper respect for the uniqueness and individuality of the counsellee.

Notes

1 The emphasis was much more on Foucault than Derrida.

2 On the topic of utilizing spiritual resources in pastoral care and counselling, see D. Capps, *Biblical Approaches to Pastoral Counseling* (Louisville, KY: Westminster John Knox Press, 1981); R. L. Underwood, *Pastoral Care and the Means of Grace* (Minneapolis, MN: Fortress Press, 1993); E. P. Wimberly, *Using Scripture in Pastoral Counseling* (Nashville, TN: Abingdon Press, 1994); D. Lyall, 'The Bible, Worship, and Pastoral Care', in P. Ballard and S. R. Holmes (eds), *The Bible in Pastoral Practice* (Grand Rapids, MI: Eerdmans, 2005), pp. 225–240; and N. Pembroke, *Pastoral Care in Worship: Liturgy and Psychology in Dialogue* (London: T&T Clark International, 2010).

3 See J. D. Whitehead and E. E. Whitehead, *Method in Ministry: Theological Reflection and Christian Ministry* (New York: Seabury Press, 1980), and their rev. edn of this (London: Sheed & Ward, 1995).

4 See E. Lartey, 'Practical Theology as a Theological Form', in J. Patton, J. Woodward and S. Pattison (eds), *The Blackwell Reader in Pastoral and Practical Theology* (Oxford: Blackwell, 2000), pp. 128–34.

5 Lartey uses this term to indicate that social and psychological analysis, along with any other relevant analysis, is required to adequately understand a pastoral situation.

6 In making this point, I have not lost sight of the fact that pastoral counsellors often work with people of another faith or even of no faith.

7 W. Barry and W. Connolly, *The Practice of Spiritual Direction*, rev. edn (San Francisco, CA: HarperOne, 2009). The case study begins on p. 150.

8 Barry and Connolly, *The Practice of Spiritual Direction*, p. 151–2.

9 See D. Browning, *The Moral Context of Pastoral Care* (Philadelphia, PA: Westminster Press, 1976); G. Noyce, *The Minister as Moral Counselor* (Nashville, TN: Abingdon Press, 1989); R. Miles, *The Pastor as Moral Guide* (Minneapolis, MN: Fortress Press, 1998); D. Capps, *Life Cycle Theory and Pastoral Care*, reprint. edn (Eugene, OR: Wipf & Stock, 2002), ch. 2.

10 See R. W. Fairchild, 'Guaranteed Not to Shrink: Spiritual Direction in Pastoral Care', *Pastoral Psychology* 31, no. 2 (1982), pp. 79–95; J. Stairs, *Listening for the Soul: Pastoral Care and Spiritual Direction* (Minneapolis, MN: Fortress Press, 2000); G. W. Moon and D. G. Benner (eds), *Spiritual Direction and the Care of Souls: A Guide to Christian Approaches and Practices* (Downers Grove, IL: IVP Academic, 2009), chs 9–12; and D. J. Louw, '"Habitus" in Soul Care: Towards "Spiritual Fortigenetics" (*Parrhesia*) in a Pastoral Anthropology', *Acta Theologica* 30, no. 2 (2010), pp. 67–88.

11 See N. Pembroke, *Moving Toward Spiritual Maturity: Psychological, Contemplative, and Moral Challenges in Christian Living* (London: Routledge, 2007).

12 See D. J. Louw, *A Mature Faith: Spiritual Direction and Anthropology in a Theology of Pastoral Care and Counseling* (Leuven: Peeters Publishers and Grand Rapids, MI: Eerdmans, 1999); and Louw, 'Philosophical Counselling: Towards a "New Approach" in Pastoral Care and Counselling?' *HTS Teologiese Studies/ Theological Studies* 67, no. 2 (2011), 7 pages. DOI: 10.4102/hts.v67i2.900.

13 See Louw, 'Philosophical Counselling'.

14 See L. Sperry, *Transforming Self and Community: Revisioning Pastoral Counseling and Spiritual Direction* (Collegeville, MN: Liturgical Press, 2002).

15 See J. Patton, *Pastoral Counseling: A Ministry of the Church* (Nashville, TN: Abingdon Press, 1983), ch. 1.

16 The term is Larry Graham's. See L. Graham, 'From Relational Humanness to Relational Justice', in R. Hunter and P. Couture (eds), *Pastoral Care and Social Conflict* (Nashville, TN: Abingdon Press, 1995), pp. 220–34.

PART I

Fundamental Attitudes and Skills

Respect for the Uniqueness of the Counsellee, or Resisting the Totalizing Tendency

An essential aspect of learning the art of counselling is gaining mastery of basic skills such as deep listening, empathic relating, the use of questions, problem-solving interventions and confrontation. Naturally enough, these skills will be covered in the chapters that follow. Beyond gaining facility with the basic techniques, there is also the challenge of learning to use some of the more advanced techniques associated with the various psychotherapies. In particular, facility with Rogers's person-centred approach provides the basic building blocks for effective counselling. Other commonly utilized methods are drawn from schools such as Gestalt therapy, transactional analysis, cognitive-behavioural therapy (CBT), narrative therapy and existentialist psychotherapies.

It is beneficial for the counsellor to make judicious use of one or more of these therapies. They offer a variety of useful interventions that in many cases prove efficacious in facilitating healing and growth. However, it is also important for counsellors to be aware of a potential negativity associated with counselling and psychotherapeutic systems. It is what the Lithuanian-born Frenchman and Jew Emmanuel Levinas (1906–95) referred to as the 'totalizing' impulse. He believed that throughout the history of Western philosophy, from Plato to Heidegger, the same serious mistake is repeated. That error is that philosophers fail to recognize the imperialist tendency in their systems. They are unaware of the way in which they colonize the 'other' with the themes and categories of their philosophical systems. Levinas describes totalization as a process involving the Other being taken over by the 'same' (the ego, the self, consciousness), and counsellors need to pay very careful attention to his insights and warning. Counsellees can be robbed of their autonomy, freedom and individuality by counsellors who insist on fitting counsellees' experiences of self, others and the world into the tightly prescribed categories dictated by the particular psychotherapeutic systems that counsellors are wedded to. In order to illustrate this pitfall and how it can be avoided, the illuminating and fascinating case of Anäis Nin is given here.

To help us gain a firm grasp of exactly what the tendency to totalizing is all about, a summary of Levinas's depiction of the relation between totality and infinity is outlined below. We will see that the central conviction that Levinas holds to is the ethical demand for affirmation of absolute alterity: Others need to be confirmed in their infinite otherness. To a theologian, the way Levinas frames the conversation sounds a lot like the general approach of Kierkegaard and Barth.[1] The early Barth was inspired by Kierkegaard's affirmation of the infinite qualitative distinction between time and eternity. Barth's critique of nineteenth-century liberal Protestant theology was that it had lost sight of this fact, and he set about re-establishing the deity of God as the One who is wholly other. Later he would revise this formulation by accenting the humanity of God. The human face of God is revealed in God's choice of togetherness with humankind in and through Christ. Therefore the question can be posed: If Barth finally recognized that it is wrong to view God and humankind as completely isolated from each other, is it reasonable to expect that a similar move would provide Levinas's extreme formulation of alterity in human relations with much needed nuancing? After all, the difference between God and humankind is massively larger than anything that might exist between two human beings. Though smoothing off the hard edge in Levinas's extreme language may seem a reasonable move, we will see that maintaining the absolute distinction between the I and the Other is essential to Levinasian ethics.

While there is this clear difference between the functioning of the God–human and the I–Other relations, there is also a strong point of connection. The partnership or covenant between God and humankind is grounded in reciprocity. That is, God has a moral claim on humankind, but humans for their part can legitimately make their claim on God. Similarly, Levinas contends that all humans both assume moral responsibility for others and lodge their own claims.

Having briefly introduced Levinas's notion of absolute alterity, we now turn to the task of developing it more fully. As indicated above, the terms 'totality' and 'infinity' play a central role in his discourse.

Levinas's conception of the totality–infinity relation

Emmanuel Levinas is a particularly difficult thinker. His philosophical reflections are unconventional and written in a dense and cryptic style. It is often not possible for even the experienced student of Levinas to be sure exactly what he is trying to communicate in a particular section of this work. It is only a slight exaggeration to say that the secondary literature is really a collection of variant readings of the various Levinasian texts. We are helped considerably in our descriptive work by the fact that we do not need to attempt a summary of his whole corpus. Rather, we can achieve our purposes through concentrating on just two sets of related concepts: (i) totality and infinity, and (ii) the Same and the Other.

A good place to begin any discussion of Levinas's thinking is with his central thesis. The proposition that shapes all of his philosophical work is that ethics is first philosophy, where ethics is understood as the claim that the Other makes on me to take infinite responsibility for his or her well-being. With reference to the second of his great books, *Otherwise than Being or Beyond Essence* (the first is *Totality and Infinity*), Levinas has this to say: 'In this book I speak of responsibility as the essential, primary and fundamental structure of subjectivity. For I describe subjectivity in ethical terms. Ethics, here, does not supplement a preceding existential base; the very node of the subjective is knotted in ethics understood as responsibility.'[2]

The central task that Levinas concerns himself with is describing a relation with the other person in terms other than *comprehension*. The phrase that captures this stance of total openness to the uniqueness and individuality of the other person, this refusal to understand or comprehend that individual through my categories, is *recognition of absolute alterity*. According to Levinas, it is in the face-to-face relation that the I encounters the infinite otherness of the Thou. Here we have just referred to two terms that need explication in order to fully appreciate what Levinas has in mind – namely, 'comprehension' and 'the face'. It is to this task of elucidation that we now turn.

Levinas's critique of the whole of Western philosophy from Plato to Heidegger is that the Other is reduced to that which can be expressed through thematization. The infinity of the Other is shrunk down to the ideas and categories assigned to it by the I (what Levinas also calls 'the Same', as we shall see below). The thought of Heidegger is a particular focus in the work of Levinas. He praises Heidegger for transcending intellectualism in the fundamental ontology that he developed so majestically in *Being and Time*, but he also criticizes him for his reduction of the Other through employment of his category of anonymous Being. That is to say, according to Levinas, Heidegger offers an advance beyond construing ontology as a contemplative theoretical activity (as Aristotle did), but his failing is that he nevertheless remains locked in the obsession of Western philosophy with colonizing the Other with this or that favoured theme. In his 1951 essay 'Is Ontology Fundamental?'[3] Levinas sets out to show that this is the case. In this essay, he outlines his task most succinctly: 'The pages that follow will attempt to characterize in a very general way this relation [to the Other] which is irreducible to comprehension, even to that comprehension beyond classical intellectualism described by Heidegger.'[4]

In *Being and Time*, Heidegger addresses a very fundamental question: What does 'to exist' mean? That is, he is interested in investigating the question of the meaning of Being. Most translators capitalize the word 'Being' (*Sein*) to mark a crucial distinction that Heidegger makes – namely, between Being and beings (i.e. entities such as rocks, trees, insects, animals and humans). Being is the being of this or that entity; it should not be interpreted as a kind of ultimate being. In order to help him answer the question of the meaning of Being, Heidegger introduces the idea of *Dasein* (*Da* = there and *Sein* = being, so the term literally means there-being). *Dasein* can be construed as the human being, as long as in using this term one does not think of it as 'the person' or as 'the biological human being'. *Dasein* is Heidegger's term for the particular type of entity that human beings as such are. What Heidegger is trying to achieve in *Being and Time* is the identification of the basic or *a priori* structures of *Dasein* (he calls them the 'existentials'), and in the pages of *Being and Time* we come across existentials such as understanding, state-of-mind, discourse and falling.

Although Levinas recognizes the greatness in Heidegger's achievement in providing such a penetrating analysis of the existence of *Dasein*, his critique is that in the end the great German thinker is unable to escape the totalizing tendency that features in all Western philosophy. The Other is viewed as that which is to be comprehended through a universal theme and concept, rather than as the one who faces me as this particular and unique being. In 'Is Ontology Fundamental?' he says this: '[C]omprehension, as construed by Heidegger, rejoins the great tradition of Western philosophy wherein to comprehend the particular being is already to place oneself beyond the particular. It is to relate to the particular, which alone exists, by knowledge which is always knowledge of the universal.'[5]

It is in the face-to-face relation that the I encounters the Other as a unique or particular being. To be faced by the Other is to be engaged in an ethical relation. If I look at the face of the Other and focus on that person's look – on the physical make-up of that particular face – I am operating in the realm of perception and knowledge. This is not what Levinas means by engaging face-to-face: 'The best way of encountering the Other is not even to notice the color of his eyes! When one observes the color of his eyes one is not in a social relationship with the Other.'[6]

The face is therefore not 'seen'; it is not that which is comprehended and interpreted. It is uncontainable; in this way it constitutes a relationship of transcendence: 'The epiphany of the Absolutely Other is a face ...'[7]

Levinas calls upon Descartes' notion of the idea of the infinite as developed in the Third Meditation to help him in developing his idea of the transcendence of the Other.[8] Descartes expresses the relationship between the finite thinking subject and the infinite in this way: 'While I may have the idea of substance in me by virtue of my being a substance, I who am finite would not have the idea of infinite substance in me unless it came from a substance that really was infinite.'[9] Levinas notes that in the Cartesian idea of the infinite the *ideatum* (i.e. the target of the thought) is infinitely greater than the act through which one thinks it. That is, there is a disproportionate relationship between the act of thought and that which it is aiming at. For Descartes, this constitutes a proof for the existence of God. The finite thinking mind is unable to produce something that exceeds its capacity; therefore this thought must have been put in us. The fact that we have an idea of the infinite can only be explained by positing an infinite being who lodged this idea in us. However, Levinas makes it clear that what interests him is not the use of the idea of the infinite as a proof for God's existence. Rather, it is the fact that the one who faces me expresses this idea in that individual's very being as Other. That is, Levinas substitutes the Other for God. There is a surplus of meaning in this Other; this particular person I am faced with exceeds every theme or concept that I may use to bring that individual under the control of my system of thought. In *Totality and Infinity*, Levinas expresses it this way:

> The distance that separates *ideatum* and idea here constitutes the content of the *ideatum* itself. Infinity is characteristic of a transcendent being as transcendent; the infinite is the absolutely other. The transcendent is the sole *ideatum* of which there can be only an idea in us: it is infinitely removed from its idea, that is exterior, because it is infinite.[10]

Note Levinas's use of the term 'exterior' in the last sentence of this statement. The subtitle of *Totality and Infinity* is 'An Essay on Exteriority'. The reference here is to his critique of the tendency in Western philosophers to interiorize that which is other. That is to say, the Other is assimilated to the Same (the ego, the self or consciousness).

In Levinas's approach, ethics consists of putting the ego into question. He constructs his approach over against Western philosophy which, for the most part, is an ontology. In this mode of doing philosophy, there is a reduction of the Other to the Same by a middle or third term (Being).[11] In seeking to represent the Other, the I assimilates the person to itself. The infinite distance separating the I and the Other has collapsed; that which is inherently exterior is interiorized. In Levinas's particular terminology, the Other is appropriated by the Same: 'We call it "the same" because in representation the I precisely loses its opposition to its object; the opposition fades, bringing out the identity of the I despite the multiplicity of its objects, that is, precisely the unalterable character of the I.'[12]

The resistance to this assimilatory tactic is achieved through the 'strangeness of the Other'.[13] The very character of absolute alterity means that the Other is irreducible to the I: there is an absolute demand made for the maintenance of the opposition between the Same and the Other. In this way, the stranger calls into question the Same; calls into question the I's spontaneity. This resistance of the Other to incorporation by the ego is ethics.

Levinas also employs the concept of absolute alterity in referring to God,[14] but he does so in a particular way: God can only truly be meant in reference to the self's total responsibility for the well-being of the Other. The place to start in (briefly) describing Levinas's thinking on God is with Heidegger's critique of traditional metaphysics as onto-theology. 'To on' in ancient Greek means 'being'; so 'onto-theology' is a theology that construes God as a being. According to Heidegger, the problem in this form of theologizing is the failure to take cognisance of the distinction between being and beings. As a result, God is wrongly conceived as the supreme being. God's supremacy in being is manifested in the fact that God is the uncaused cause of all that exists.

In the onto-theological perspective, thinking and being are aligned, with the result that even God is situated in the processes of being in the world. God is simply the being par excellence: the greatest possible being. Anselm defined God as 'that than which nothing greater can be conceived'.

Levinas also objected to onto-theology. For him, the way out of this faulty theology is via ethics. Only in the ethical relation do we encounter that which we are unable to assimilate to our subjectivity. In ethics we meet that which is wholly other, absolutely transcendent, 'otherwise than being'. Levinas expresses this perspective thus:

Ethics is not a moment of being; it is otherwise and better than being, the very possibility of the beyond. In this ethical reversal ... in this strange mission that orders the approach to the other, God is drawn out of objectivity, presence and being. He is neither an object nor an interlocutor. His absolute remoteness, his transcendence, turns into my responsibility ... for the other. And this analysis implies that God is not simply the 'first other', the 'other par excellence', or the 'absolutely other', but other than the other, other otherwise, other with an alterity of the other, prior to the ethical bond with another and different from every neighbour, transcendent to the point of absence ...[15]

Though he would strongly reject the contention that ethics is the primary means for an encounter with transcendence, Karl Barth also adopted the idea of the wholly Other as a central focus – especially in his early works. During World War One, Barth set to work on a commentary on the epistle to the Romans. *Der Römerbrief (The Epistle to the Romans)*, published in 1919, constituted an unrelenting and intensely sharp criticism of what Barth saw as the religionism, anthropocentrism and humanism of the nineteenth-century liberal Protestant theologians. He reacted against these theologians for turning the message of the Bible into a celebration of the greatness of humanity, rather than presenting it as a revelation through the Word of God of the free and sovereign God who is absolutely unique and utterly distinct from humankind. In a Levinasian perspective, Barth's issue was with the fact that the Other (God) was assimilated to the Same (humankind). The opposition between God and humankind was removed. In this new theological move, the wholly other God of the Bible is pulled into the orbit of religious piety and the glorified human.

Barth made a case for turning theological method on its head. The nineteenth-century human-centred theology from below needed to be replaced by a theology from above. Throughout *Der Römerbrief*, Barth accents time and again the absolute alterity of God, the gospel, eternity and salvation. Later he would write: '[T]here is in the Bible only *one* theological interest, namely, that in God; that only *one* way appears, namely, that from above downwards; that only *one* message can be heard, namely, that of an immediate forgiveness of sins ... [emphasis in the original].'[16]

The early Barth was influenced by the theological perspective of Søren Kierkegaard. For Kierkegaard, the fact of human sinfulness on the one hand, and the wholly other nature of God on the other hand, means that it is impossible for humankind to build a bridge to God through the use of reason. It is through a leap of faith that the paradoxical truths of God's self-revelation are appropriated. In his preface to the 1922 edition of *Der Römerbrief*, Barth acknowledges the debt he owes to Kierkegaard:

> if I have a system, it is limited to a recognition of what Kierkegaard called the 'infinite qualitative distinction' between time and eternity, and to my regarding this as possessing negative as well as positive significance: 'God is in heaven, and thou art on earth'. The relation between such a God and such a man, and the relation between such a man and such a God, is for me the theme of the Bible and the essence of philosophy.[17]

Barth always maintained this critique of the tendency in liberal theology to reduce the sovereign, free, independent and absolutely unique God to a pious symbol whose main purpose was to elevate the human to a place of greatness. However, he did later see a need to revise his formulation of the deity of God. After having emerged from the intense, emotionally charged atmosphere of the polemical period, he could see that the way in which he portrayed the wholly other God in an isolated and absolutized fashion standing over against a poor, feeble, miserable humanity was aligned more with the deity of the God of the philosophers than with the deity of the God of the Bible. What was missing in the early work was an emphasis on 'the humanity of God'.[18] Barth came to see very clearly that the message of the Bible is that the independent and mighty God does not stand aloof from humanity, but rather seeks togetherness and partnership with us. God's deity means that God is the superior partner and therefore takes the initiative. God's humanity is revealed in the fact that though God is independent and completely fulfilled in and through the triune relations, God nevertheless freely chooses to enter into a relation of togetherness with God's creatures.

Barth avers that when we look to Jesus Christ, we know immediately that God's deity does not exclude, but rather includes, his humanity. He puts it this way:

> In Jesus Christ there is no isolation of man from God or of God from man. Rather, in Him we encounter the history, the dialogue, in which God and man meet together and are together, the reality of the covenant *mutually* contracted, preserved, and fulfilled by them. Jesus Christ is in His one Person, as true God, *man's* loyal partner, and as true *man*, God's [emphasis in the original].[19]

If Barth could move from a one-sided, extreme formulation according to which the wholly other God stands over against the creature to acknowledge that God has a human face and is therefore in a certain sense like humanity, might not Levinas's philosophy of the ethical relation be improved by a similar revision? That is to say, rather than stating in such bald, absolute terms that the I and its interlocutor are wholly other, would his position be improved by softening the hard edge and acknowledging that the two are actually the same in certain regards? After all, they share a common humanity. They both feel pain if pricked with a needle or punched with a fist; they experience a range of basic emotions; their bodies insist that they eat, drink, defecate, urinate, sleep and have sex; death is a final horizon that confronts them both, to name just some of the commonalities. Others have also thought along these lines. A short time after the publication of *Totality and Infinity*, Levinas was invited to speak at the Société Française de Philosophie. Early in 1962, he presented 'Transcendance et hauteur' to the members of the society.[20] Two of the discussants challenged Levinas on his presentation by suggesting that human beings are in fact similar to one another. Jean Wahl quoted 'the beautiful words of Terence': 'I am human and nothing human is foreign to me'.[21] M. Minkowski picked up on this point and elaborated on it: 'I do not believe that we can say ... that men are absolutely different from one another ... because if that was the case, you would not have this audience in front of you, following you with interest. There is an element of understanding and similarity which occurs and which appears to me essential.'[22]

What Wahl and Minkowski say is of course true. Human beings *are* similar in many respects; it is this similarity that allows us to share thoughts, feelings and values. In his response, Levinas indicates that he concurs with the proposition. But in typical fashion, the way that he states his agreement has a cryptic element to it: '[I] agree with you: all men are alike, but they are not the same.'[23] What does he mean by his rider 'but they are not the same'? What he is alluding to is that the I and the Other occupy wholly other social locations. What defines these locations is that the one standing in the position of the Other makes an absolute claim on the I; the one standing in the position marked 'I' is thereby called to infinite responsibility. The Other stands there naked, destitute, exposed, and at the same time occupies the position of master. Levinas puts it this way: 'The nakedness of the face is destituteness. To recognize the Other is to recognize a hunger. To recognize the Other is to give. But it is to give to the master, to the lord, to him whom one approaches as "You" in a dimension of height.'[24] The 'master' commands a response of generosity. It is the claim of infinite responsibility asserted by the Other that constitutes the I qua I: 'The I is not simply conscious of this necessity to respond, as if it were a matter of an obligation or a duty about which a decision could be made; rather the I is, by its *very position*, responsibility through and through ... Hence, to be I signifies not being able to escape responsibility [emphasis in original].'[25] On the other hand, to be Other signifies facing the I in nakedness and destituteness, but at the same time acting as lord who commands a moral response.

Barth was right to revise the formulation of the absolute alterity of God to include an accent on togetherness between God and the human achieved in and through the mediation of Jesus Christ, true God and true human. Levinas, on the other hand, could not make a parallel move without completely undermining his whole philosophy. The social position that the I occupies is wholly other to the one that the Other stands in, and vice versa. Barth's move was necessary, given the fact that God chose to give himself a human face. Jesus Christ is the bridge between God and humanity. Levinas could not make a similar move, because there is an unbridgeable gulf between the spot in which the I stands and the spot in which the Other stands. From her/his particular social location, the 'Other' stretches her/his hand towards the I. The outstretched hand says, 'You have an infinite responsibility for me.'

Though there is a fundamental difference between the operation of the relationship between God and the human on the one hand, and between the I and the Other on the other, there is also a strong point of connection. The dynamics in the partnership between God and humankind that was established through a series of covenants culminating in the new covenant sealed in the blood of Christ correlate with those in the Levinasian construal of human relations. While there is certainly contractual theology operating in the Hebrew Scriptures that orbits around the blessing and curse dynamic, and construes calling to account as a one-way street (the traffic flow is always from God to Israel), there is also a lament theology found in Psalms, Job and Jeremiah that conceives of the covenantal relationship between God and humankind in terms of an I–Thou relation and reciprocity. According to the lament tradition, God makes God's claim on Israel, but equally Israel is free to make its claim on God. 'Complaint and lament subvert the thin claim of obedience by a practice that is genuinely dialogical so that Yahweh's primacy and preeminence in the relationship are provisionally overcome.'[26] Two very important aspects of the covenant relationship are alluded to in this statement. First, the covenant is a genuinely dialogical relationship. The God of the covenant is experienced by the people as a 'Thou' and this means that God can be addressed by them in a spirit of reciprocity.[27] That there is reciprocity in the covenant relationship means – and this is the second important aspect – that when Yahweh seems to have defaulted on his commitment, Israel has a right to reverse the roles and forcefully make its moral claim on him.

While not wanting to push it too far, we can see a parallel in the way Levinas constructs ethical responsibility. There is reciprocity in human relations when it comes to moral claims. According to Levinas, the most fundamental claim that the Other lodges with the I is this: 'Do not kill me'. One can easily think of a host of others: 'Do not refuse me bread and water; do not exploit me; do not seek to impose your values and ideology on me; do not exclude me; do not deny me justice.'

In discussing these moral claims, Levinas always constructs his discourse around the responsibility of the I for the Other. He does not employ tit-for-tat language, and there are at least two reasons for this. On the one hand, he construes the Other first and foremost as the one who is poor, hungry and powerless. The deprived or disadvantaged Other is my responsibility. The moral claim the Other makes on me is extremely pressing; I cannot evade it. On the other hand, Levinas speaks in this manner because he is aware that virtually all human beings have a selfish tendency to avoid their ethical responsibilities. One strategy commonly used to support our self-indulgence is to focus on our own rights, needs and moral claims on others. We become so preoccupied with this agenda that responding to the Other gets squeezed out. To counter this, Levinas relentlessly calls upon readers to take up their responsibilities for the Other. This needs to be their primary concern; there is little danger of them losing sight of their own rights and needs.

However, Levinas recognizes, of course, that in ethical relations there needs to be reciprocity. It would be bizarre to construe the lodging of moral claims as a one-way street. While Levinas shapes all his moral discourse around the I–Other relation, with the I having infinite responsibility for the Other, he clearly does not mean to imply that the I and the Other stand in a fixed place. If he did, the one locked into the I position would have no right to ever say 'Do not kill me'. All human beings simultaneously assume responsibility for others and lodge their own moral claims.

Learning from Levinas: on resisting the totalizing impulse in working with the counsellee

Grappling with the thought of Emmanuel Levinas is a challenging business. If readers have stuck with me thus far, they have a right to a pay-off. So what is the big lesson that we can learn from Levinas? Well, first I would want to say that there is quite a bit about being a faithful and effective counsellor that we can learn from Levinas. But if I were asked to identify the single most important lesson, it would be this: the counsellor needs to resist the urge to totalize – that is, to draw all the personal experience, thoughts, feelings, attitudes of the counsellee into the tight container constructed out of a particular set of psychotherapeutic categories. This is certainly not a novel approach to connecting Levinas and therapy. Edwin Gantt, for example, observes that well-established approaches to therapy such as Freudian psychoanalysis, Rogerian person-centred therapy, and certain existentialist therapies work with tightly prescribed theoretical categories and practices that ultimately rob the client of personal autonomy and freedom.[28] Drawing on Levinas's notion of the face-to-face relation, Gantt proposes an alternative model in which the therapist 'dwells-with' clients in the immediacy of their here-and-now experience of suffering. To give a second example, Fred Alford notes a general affinity between the approach of the British psychotherapist Donald Winnicott and Levinas: both resist the violence that is done to the Other when that person is subsumed under one's own categories. Alford puts it this way:

How can one relate to another without imposing oneself on the other, without doing violence to the other's awesome otherness? ... In turning to Winnicott, I am turning to a theorist who defines violence much as Levinas does – imposing oneself on another self, so as to make the other like me. Totalizing Levinas calls it, bringing everyone and everything under my categories.[29]

To illustrate both the destructiveness of the totalizing impulse in therapy, and the positivity of allowing space for clients to freely be and to express the selves that they truly are, we turn now to the report by Anaïs Nin on her experiences with first René Allendy (founder of the French Psychoanalytic Society) and then Otto Rank (one time special protégé of Freud). Anaïs Nin was born in Neuilly, a suburb of Paris. As a child she accompanied her father, the famous Spanish composer-pianist Joaquin Nin, on concert tours all over Europe. In her teens, long after her father had left the family, she broke out of the demoralizing confines of a poor existence with her Danish-born mother in New York to become an artists' model and later, a Spanish dancer. As a novice writer, she made her way back to Paris with its literary and cultural atmosphere. In 1929 she settled at Louveciennes and there, as after the outbreak of World War Two in her apartment in New York's Greenwich Village, she welcomed a host of little known, but destined to be famous, creative people.

Anaïs was the friend and confidante to important literary figures such as Henry Miller and Antonin Artaud. In the case of the former, she was more than a friend; she was also his lover. Her relationship with Miller was taut and volatile. Anaïs lived an intense and multi-dimensional life, moving with zest and vitality through the cosmopolitan world of art and society.

It is clear from her reflections in her journals that a sense of inferiority and shame-proneness plagued Anaïs. Consider, for example, this entry:

[With Dr Allendy] I talked about my work, and my life in general. I said I had always been very independent and had never leaned on anyone. Dr Allendy said, 'In spite of that, you seem to lack confidence'. He had touched a sensitive spot. Confidence![30]

She relates this lack of confidence to her figure. She feels inferior when she compares herself to women who are well-endowed. Men only love 'big, healthy women with enormous breasts', she laments.[31] She recalls the Spanish proverb quoted often by her mother: 'Bones are for the dogs'. To compensate for what she perceives as physical undesirability, she decided early to shape her persona around her artistic gifts. 'It was to forget this [a petite body] that I decided to be an artist, or writer, to be interesting, charming, accomplished. I was not sure of being beautiful enough …'[32]

Her father's hyper-critical and aloof manner made it very difficult for her to establish a healthy sense of pride:

My father did not want a girl. My father was over-critical. He was never satisfied, never pleased. I never remember a compliment or a caress from him. At home, only scenes, quarrels, beatings. And his hard blue eyes on us, looking for flaws. When I was ill with typhoid fever, almost dying, all he could say was: 'Now you are ugly, how ugly you are'.[33]

As writers on shame-proneness repeatedly observe, in reaction to these traumatic childhood narcissistic injuries, a person usually develops an intense craving for affirmation and approval.[34] This was certainly the case with Anaïs. She acknowledges her fear of being hurt and laments the associated need for constant confirmation of affection. 'I despise my own hypersensitiveness', she writes, 'which requires so much reassurance. It is certainly abnormal to crave so much to be loved and understood.'[35]

What is tragic in relation to Dr Allendy's therapy is the fact that he was so wedded to the categories of the Freudian system that he could not see what Anaïs really needed from him. She wanted to be accepted and affirmed as the unique person she was. She wanted her analyst to see her inner world of experience as she saw it. Instead, Dr Allendy, absolutely intent on probing her psyche to find the buried conflict, simply replicated the experience of the probing, judging eye of her father.

Anaïs remembers with pain the experience of her father's 'hard blue eyes on us, looking for flaws'. She felt oppressed and dominated by his critical eye. Admiration was only ever indirect. He could never look her straight in the face and speak gentle, affectionate words of affirmation. His communication of his appreciation of her was refracted through a camera lens. '[My father] liked', she writes, 'to take photos of me while I bathed. He always wanted me naked. All his admiration came by way of the camera. His eyes were partly concealed by heavy glasses (he was myopic) and then by the camera lens.'[36]

This partial and inadequate attempt at confirmation could never compensate for his repeated and devastating attacks on her. The 'eyes' would sometimes 'appear' when she was feeling exposed and vulnerable; she felt under attack even when he was not physically present:

[W]hen I gave a concert of Spanish dances in Paris, I imagined I saw his face in the audience. It seemed pale and stern. I stopped in the middle of my dance, frozen, and for an instant I thought I could not continue. The guitarist playing behind me thought I had stage fright and he began to encourage me with shouts and clapping. Later, when I saw my father again, I asked him if he had been at this concert.

He answered me, 'No, I was not there, but if I had been I would have disapproved absolutely. I disapprove of a lady being a dancer. Dancing is for prostitutes, professionals.'[37]

Sadly, Joaquin's gaze brought a sense of shame rather than fatherly support and encouragement. The lack of self-confidence combined with, and no doubt attributable in large part to, his judgmentalism meant, as we shall soon see, that Anaïs was extremely reluctant to share her secrets with others, including her analyst.

Anaïs had experienced the 'destructive persecution' of Joaquin Nin, and now she wonders whether Dr Allendy could really have 'freed me of the EYE of the father, of the eye of the camera which I have always feared and disliked as an *exposure*'.[38] Sadly, in therapy she has yet another experience of the look that shames: 'Enter this laboratory of the soul where every feeling will be *X-rayed* by Dr Allendy to *expose* the blocks, the twists, the deformations, the scars which interfere with the flow of life' [emphasis added].[39] Under Allendy's probing, she feels 'oppressed'; his questions are like 'thrusts'. It feels to her as though she is 'a criminal in court'.[40] Finally, she can take it no longer:

Anaïs:	'Today, I frankly hate you. I am against you'.
Dr Allendy:	'But why?'
Anaïs:	'I feel that you have taken away from me the little confidence I did have. I feel humiliated to have confessed to you. I have rarely confessed.'[41]

Allendy would only be happy if Anaïs submitted to his interpretations. He thought that he was providing helpful insights. In fact, he was actually doing violence to his client by imposing his Freudian-inspired formulas and categories in a rigid, authoritarian, and even defensive manner:

> Today I find flaws in Dr Allendy's formulas. I am irritated by his quick categorizing of my dreams and feelings. When he is silent I do my own analysis. If I do, he will say I am trying to find him defective, inadequate, to revenge his forcing me to confess my jealousy of his wife. At that moment he was much stronger than I.[42]

In Levinasian terms, Allendy seeks to subsume the Other under the Same. He robs Anaïs of her individuality and freedom through imposing Freudian theory on her. In contrast, the face-to-face relation is one in which otherness is confirmed. Martin Buber has a very similar idea: 'This person is other, essentially other than myself, and this otherness of his is what I mean, because I mean him; I confirm it; I wish his otherness to exist, because I wish his particular being to exist.'[43] The totalizing approach of Allendy in which there is a reduction of his client's feelings, thoughts and attitudes to fit his ready-made categories is a form of persecution. Tragically, Allendy intensified rather than healed Anaïs's feeling of inferiority. She felt misunderstood and devalued; it is as if she only existed in the terms defined by her analyst. To be understood in one's own terms is confirming; to have one's personhood compressed to fit another's mould is shaming.

There is a warning here for counsellors against sitting too closely to any particular personality theory. In those who have a doctrinaire approach to their chosen school of psychotherapeutic thought there is an almost irresistible temptation to view all counsellees through a theoretical grid. In this situation, one cannot see the person for the theory, so to speak. What is the root of this tunnel vision? It is to be found, I think, in the universal human tendency to use an ideology to establish a sense of security and control. All of the messiness of people and life is more manageable when one pulls it inside the boundaries of one's system.

Counsellors do well to remember that theories of personality and psychotherapeutic technique need to be applied within a person-centred orientation. When Anaïs finally gave up on Dr Allendy, she found in Otto Rank an analyst who valued her freedom and dignity as a person. In their first meeting, she shared with her new analyst her dissatisfaction over Allendy's categorization. Rank, in turn, communicated his valuing of particularity.

'I felt that Dr Allendy's formulas did not fit my life. I have read all your books. I felt that there is *more* in my relationship to my father than the desire of a victory over my mother.'

By his smile I knew he understood the *more* and my objection to oversimplification …

Immediately I knew that we talked the same language. He said, 'I go beyond the psychoanalytical. Psychoanalysis emphasizes the resemblance between people; I emphasize the differences between people. They try to bring everybody to a certain normal level. I try to adapt each person to his own kind of universe.'[44]

In counselling people we do need maps to guide us around the psychological territory. They are, however, *only* guides. Counsellees are more than the sum of the psychodynamic interpretations we can apply to their lives. Totalizing counsellors attempt to fit counsellees into a theory, rather than to locate them in their 'own kind of universe'. To have one's particularity recognized and validated is an experience of grace; to be categorized is to be reduced to the status of an object and to suffer dis-grace.

There is, of course, a place in counselling for theory-informed analysis. It is appropriate and helpful for the counsellor to work with the categories developed in the leading personality theories. In a counselling relationship, there will be moments of reflection and analysis. However, it is only when the counsellor is able to deeply respect the otherness of the counsellee that this individual feels confirmed at the deepest level. One hears notes of joy and pride sounded in Anaïs' recollection of her first impressions of Dr Rank: 'He was agile, quick, as if each word I uttered were a precious object he had excavated and was delighted to find. He acted as if I were unique, as if this were a unique adventure, not a phenomenon to be categorized.'[45] In stark contrast, Anaïs's lamentations concerning her experience with Dr Allendy have the tone of sorrow and shame. By way of introduction to these sad reflections, it needs to be noted that what Anaïs particularly appreciated about Rank was the way he viewed neurosis as a distortion in the creative spirit. Anaïs was not in his eyes a sick, disturbed person, but rather an artist whose creative energies had been wrongly directed. Allendy, on the other hand, had no appreciation of the value she attached to creativity and imagination; he could not fit these things into his ready-made categories. The tragic result was that far from facilitating healing and growth, Allendy's intervention provoked deep feelings of inadequacy, inferiority and discouragement. Anaïs tells the sad tale:

> The scientific rigidity acts very much like a trap, a trap of rationalization. The patient who is a hypersensitive person cannot help being influenced by what he is expected to say, by the quick classification baring the structure too obviously. The neurotic feels his next statement is expected to fit into a logical continuity whose pressure he finally succumbs to.
>
> The more this process becomes clear to him, the more he experiences *a kind of discouragement* with the banality of it. The 'naming' of his trouble, being in itself prosaic, links it to his physical diseases, and deprives him of that very illusion and creative halo which is necessary to the re-creation of a human being. Instead of discovering the poetic, imaginative, creative potentialities of his disease (since every neurotic fantasy is really a twisted, aborted work of art), he discovers the depoetization of it, which makes of him *a cripple* instead of a potential artist...
>
> To raise the drama instead of *diminishing it*, by linking it to the past, to collective history, to literature, achieves two things: one, to remove it from the too-near, personal realm where it causes pain; the other, to place the neurotic as a part of a collective drama, recurrent through the ages, so that he *may cease regarding himself as a cripple, as a degenerate type...*
>
> It is in this difference between individual expression that we find a new dimension, a new climate, a new vision. To reduce a fantasy is only a means of *dredging the neurotic imagination, of diminishing the stage* on which the neurotic must live out his drama with the maximum of intensity, for the sake of catharsis [emphasis added].[46]

Confirming counsellors have broad visions; they are able to see creative potential in people. In contrast, counsellors controlled by psychodynamic theory and its neat categories run the risk of shaming their counsellees. Note the shame cognates Anaïs uses in her reflections: 'discouragement', 'a cripple', 'a degenerative type', and 'diminishing the drama'. Counsellors with a big vision of life and of humanity will find a way to frame the stories they hear in a way that communicates admiration and approval (Rank focused on Anaïs's artistic gifts). Reductionist counsellors, on the other hand, allow themselves to be blinkered by their theoretical constructs. While they think they are providing insight, they succeed only in doing violence to their counsellees. The counsellee feels deeply discouraged and diminished. Technical prowess is important, but it is not nearly as important as a capacity to confirm individuality, uniqueness and freedom of the counsellee.

Summary

We began by acknowledging that it is a good thing for the counsellor to make judicious use of one or more of the available therapies for they offer a variety of interventions that in many cases prove efficacious in facilitating healing and growth. However, it is important for the counsellor to be aware of a potential problem associated with counselling and psychotherapeutic systems – namely, the totalizing impulse. Counsellors may fail to recognize the imperialist tendency in the systems they employ. When this is the case, they unwittingly colonize their counsellees with the themes and categories in that system. Sadly, counsellees then are robbed of their autonomy, freedom and individuality. In order to illustrate both the pitfall and how it can be avoided, we have looked at the illuminating and fascinating case of Anäis Nin. Anäis felt shamed and dominated by her first analyst, René Allendy. Her experiences and communications were only received by him after they had been passed through the filter of Freudian psychoanalysis. In stark contrast, Otto Rank was fascinated by Anäis's inner world of experience and, moreover, was ready to embrace it on its own terms and to confirm it for what it was. Under Rank, Anäis came to life and experienced genuine liberation and growth.

Our journey has begun with an absolutely fundamental attitude – namely, respect for the uniqueness and individuality of the counsellee. In the next chapter, we turn our attention to another very basic building block. We will discuss the nature and role of empathy in the therapeutic relationship, with a particular emphasis on the place of the body.

Notes

1 Others have also noted the connecting lines between the central insight of Levinas and that of Barth. See, for example, Steven G. Smith, *The Argument to the Other: Reason Beyond Reason in the Thought of Karl Barth and Emmanuel Levinas* (Chico, CA: Scholars Press, 1983). Smith points out that anyone reading both Barth and Levinas, especially the former's *Epistle to the Romans* and the latter's *Totality and Infinity*, cannot help but be struck by two things. First, the way in which both thinkers centre all their investigations on the concept of the wholly

other. Second, the fact that they insist that this concept must inform and shape all theological thinking (Barth) and all philosophical investigation (Levinas).

2 E. Levinas, *Ethics and Infinity: Conversations with Philippe Nemo,* trans. R. A. Cohen (Pittsburgh, PA: Duquesne University Press, 1985), p. 95.

3 See E. Levinas, 'Is Ontology Fundamental?', *Philosophy Today* 33, no. 2 (1989), pp. 121–9. First published in 1951.

4 Levinas, 'Is Ontology Fundamental?', p. 123.

5 Levinas, 'Is Ontology Fundamental?', p. 124.

6 Levinas, *Ethics and Infinity,* p. 85.

7 E. Levinas, 'Transcendence and Height', in A. T. Peperzak, S. Critchley and R. Bernasconi (eds), *Emmanuel Levinas: Basic Philosophical Writings* (Bloomington, IN: Indiana University Press, 1996), pp. 11–31, p. 17.

8 E. Levinas, *Totality and Infinity: An Essay on Exteriority,* trans. A. Lingis (Dordrecht: Kluwer Academic Publishers, 1991), pp. 48–9.

9 I have used Ronald Rubin's translation of the *Meditations.* See C. Biffle, *A Guided Tour of René Descartes'* Meditations on First Philosophy, 3rd edn (Mountain View, CA: Mayfield Publishing House, 2001), p. 51.

10 Levinas, *Totality,* p. 49.

11 Levinas, *Totality,* p. 43.

12 Levinas, *Totality,* p. 126.

13 Levinas, *Totality,* p. 43.

14 On this, see A. K. Min, 'Naming the Unnameable God: Levinas, Derrida, and Marion', *International Journal for Philosophy of Religion* 60 (2006), pp. 99–116; and G. J. Morrison, 'The (Im)possibilities of Levinas for Christian Theology: The Search for a Language of Alterity', in J. De Tavernier *et al.* (eds), *Responsibility, God and Society: Theological Ethics in Dialogue: Festschrift Roger Burggraeve* (Leuven: Peeters Publishing, 2008), pp. 103–22.

15 E. Levinas, *Collected Philosophical Papers,* trans. Alphonso Lingis (Pittsburgh, PA: Duquesne University Press, 1998), pp. 165–6.

16 K. Barth, *The Humanity of God* (Atlanta, GA: John Knox Press, 1982), p. 43.

17 K. Barth, *The Epistle to the Romans,* trans. Edwyn C. Hoskyns (London: Oxford University Press, 1933), p. 10.

18 See Barth, *The Humanity of God.*

19 Barth, *The Humanity of God,* p. 46.

20 See Levinas, 'Transcendence'.

21 Levinas, 'Transcendence', p. 28.

22 Levinas, 'Transcendence', p. 28.

23 Levinas, 'Transcendence', p. 28.

24 Levinas, *Totality,* p. 75.

25 Levinas, 'Transcendence', p. 17.

26 W. Brueggemann, 'Prerequisites for Genuine Obedience: Theses and Conclusions', *Calvin Theological Journal* 36 (2001), pp. 34–41, p. 36.

27 Cf. D. Blumenthal, *Facing the Abusing God: A Theology of Protest* (Louisville, KY: Westminster John Knox Press, 1993), p. 40.

28 See E. Gantt, 'Truth, Freedom, and Responsibility in the Dialogues of Psychotherapy', *Journal of Theoretical and Philosophical Psychology* 14, no. 2 (1994), pp. 146–58.

29 C. F. Alford, 'Levinas, Winnicott, and Therapy', *The Psychoanalytic Review* 94, no. 4 (2007), pp. 529–51, p. 530.

30 A. Nin, *The Journals of Anaïs Nin, 1931–1934*, ed. G. Stuhlmann (London: Peter Owen, 1966), pp. 75–6.

31 Nin, *The Journals*, p. 81.

32 Nin, *The Journals*, p. 81.

33 Nin, *The Journals*, p. 76.

34 See, for example, D. Capps, *The Depleted Self* (Minneapolis, MN: Fortress Press, 1993), pp. 14–15; H. Kohut, *The Analysis of the Self* (New York: International Universities Press, 1971), ch. 5, esp. pp. 114–16, and Kohut, *The Restoration of the Self* (New York: International Universities Press, 1977), ch. 4.

35 Nin, *The Journals*, p. 77.

36 Nin, *The Journals*, p. 87.

37 Nin, *The Journals*, p. 87.

38 Nin, *The Journals*, p. 88.

39 Nin, *The Journals*, p. 105.

40 Nin, *The Journals*, p. 82.

41 Nin, *The Journals*, p. 85.

42 Nin, *The Journals*, p. 108.

43 M. Buber, *Between Man and Man*, trans. R. G. Smith (London: Routledge & Kegan Paul, 1947), p. 61.

44 Nin, *The Journals*, p. 271.

45 Nin, *The Journals*, p. 272.

46 Nin, *The Journals*, pp. 298–9.

2

Empathy and the Body, or the Quest for Participatory Sense-Making

Empathic relating is right at the centre of the counselling process, and it is a topic that will come up at various points in the discussions in this book. Here, though, we give it focused attention.

I have learnt much about empathy through tuning into the philosophical conversation over social understanding. It is significant that some philosophers accent the role of embodiment in the interactive process of social cognition. In this chapter, we bring these two aspects of the philosophical discussion together. The main focus is on understanding as fully as possible the role of empathy in an effective counselling process. However, we also need to be reminded along the way that counselling in general and empathic relating in particular take place between two embodied persons.

Most philosophers who engage with the issue of social cognition frame it in terms of the problem of other minds. The assumption is that the mind of the other is inaccessible to us. And yet, we are able to grasp people's beliefs, desires and intentions. How is this possible? Two leading explanatory models are known as theory of mind theory, or theory-theory (TT), and simulation theory (ST). According to these theories, we need to utilize commonsense beliefs to infer what is going on in the mind of the other person (TT), or we need to use our own mind as a model (ST) in understanding another mind. Philosophers such as Fuchs, De Jaegher and Di Paolo contend that in relying on such high cognitive abilities, social cognition is located in a disembodied, Cartesian mind.[1] In their proposal, social understanding is interpreted as a process of embodied interaction through which common meaning is generated.

Psychotherapy has been commonly construed as a verbal/linguistic event. The following definition is typical: '... *the social unit we work with in therapy is a linguistic system distinguished by those who are "in language" about a problem*' [emphasis in the original].[2] Attending to the embodied approach of the philosophers of participatory sense-making (PSM) suggests that this view of the 'social unit' in psychotherapy/

counselling is too narrow. The same perspective emerges when one takes note of the prominent place assigned to the body in other areas of scholarly research. Here one thinks of the work on the embodied nature of perception[3] and cognition (discussed in Chapter 8), non-dualist approaches to the mind–body relation (humans construed as 'spirited bodies'),[4] and the Levinasian notion of the ethical subject as an embodied subject of flesh and blood in the field of philosophy, and the notion of 'felt sense' of a problem (Carl Rogers and Eugene Gendlin),[5] body empathy,[6] and the embodied nature of countertransference in the area of psychotherapy.[7] A review of all this literature suggests that counselling takes place between two embodied selves; it is not best construed as a linguistic event conducted between two Cartesian minds. This perspective will feature at certain decisive points in the ensuing discussion on the central role that empathy plays in the counselling relationship.

The philosophers of PSM also make the important point that the movement towards meaning-making is not one from non-synchronization to perfect synchronization.[8] The continuous fluctuation between synchronized and desynchronized states drives the process forward. The process of two people trying to understand each other is characterized as 'a participatory dynamic dance'.[9] This depiction of PSM as proceeding through alternation between attunement and alienation is highly relevant to the counselling process. Experiences of being closely attuned serve the all-important purpose of building strong rapport and establishing a warm and trusting counselling relationship. However, it is the movements out of alignment that are at least as significant in terms of promoting growth and healing. For example, Heinz Kohut observes that the capacity in a person suffering from narcissistic personality disorder for regulating self-esteem grows stronger as a result of the (inevitable) empathic failures on the part of the therapist.

In the exploration of the empathic 'dance' between the counsellor and the counsellee, the to-and-fro of attunement and alienation will feature in the following ways. First, there is recognition that a slight mismatch between the empathic formulation of the counsellor and the expression of the counsellee may lead to a fresh perspective. Or in the language of the dance metaphor, insight may be sparked as a result of counsellors being slightly out of step with counsellees in their empathic responses. Second, as I have already indicated with reference to Kohutian theory, empathic missteps, far from being destructive in certain therapeutic situations, actually lead to a stronger sense of self in the counsellee. Finally, a highly empathic counsellor is sometimes able to see something that is lying just outside the awareness of the client. This may be characterized as taking the lead in the empathic dance.

This chapter is structured as follows. We begin with a discussion of the three leading theories of social understanding alluded to above. Here the role that PSM plays in this process will be identified as especially significant. Second, we attempt to define empathy and discuss the role that the body plays in empathic relating. Finally, the various 'dance moves' in empathic relating are identified. These are characterized here as being slightly out of step, falling into missteps, and taking the lead.[10] Along the way, the important theological question of whether or not it is legitimate to speak of an empathic God will be raised. Although providing a full answer is clearly beyond the scope of the chapter, it is identified as one that pastoral counsellors need to give serious attention to. Having mapped the territory, we begin with a discussion of the various theories of social cognition.

Theories of social understanding: theory-theory, simulation theory and participatory sense-making

As indicated, the PSM approach has two main rivals in terms of theories of social understanding – namely, TT and ST. In order to appreciate and situate the critique that proponents of PSM mount against the traditional theories, it is necessary to provide a brief outline of each one. We begin with TT.

Theory-theory

Proponents of TT contend that humans make use of folk psychology in constructing their theory of the beliefs and desires of others. The first use of the term 'theory of mind' is found in a 1978 article by David Premack and Guy Woodruff entitled, 'Does the Chimpanzee Have a Theory of Mind?'[11] The term refers to our everyday ability to impute independent mental states to self and others in order to predict and explain behaviour. Theory of mind facilitates everyday social interaction. The claim is made that we need to be able to read the beliefs and desires in the minds of others in order to make sense of their behaviour. According to the TT approach, people make use of a belief-desire psychology in their mind-reading activity. To use a trivial example, we can explain the fact that Sarah is carrying a coat on her way out of the office by imputing to her a *belief* that it is cold outside and a *desire* to keep warm.

It is worth noting that there are two rival schools of thought in the TT cohort – namely, the child-scientist and the innate capacity (brain mechanism) approaches. The child-scientist advocates argue that a child's

37

acquisition of a belief-desire psychology is a matter of theory construction and revision, and that the process closely resembles the construction and revision of scientific theories in adult science.[12] The case is made through reference to the fact that whereas four-year-olds consistently exhibit an ability to attribute false beliefs, three-year-olds do not.[13] That is to say, three-year-olds most often base their explanation of an action on their own beliefs about a situation, rather than on false beliefs. In the classic false belief experiments, the child is presented with a hypothetical event (e.g., a story about another child who is deceived in some way). The hypothetical child is offered a sweets box that is really full of pencils; or a fake rock made of sponge material; or she sees her mother put chocolate in the blue cupboard, and then watches as the chocolate is surreptitiously switched to the red cupboard while her mother is out of the room. Let us take the last example to demonstrate the difference in cognitive capacity between a typical three-year-old and a typical four-year-old. If researchers ask (typical) three-year-olds the question 'When your mother comes back into the room, where do you think she will look for the chocolate?' researchers will get the answer, 'In the red cupboard.' By way of contrast, four-year-olds will typically respond with the correct answer: 'In the blue cupboard.' Proponents of the child-scientist perspective interpret this difference between three- and four-year-olds as a difference in the implicit theories of the world that children hold. Some go further and make a clear connection with scientific method by claiming that the advance from one theory to another is driven by the accumulation of evidence and counter-evidence.

Those in the modularity camp argue against the 'little scientist' approach by pointing out that pre-schoolers are exposed every day to the effects of many other abstract entities – such as laws of motion, electrons, the genetic code – but they never discover *them*.[14] There is therefore no compelling reason to believe that they discover belief-desire psychology through experimentation, observation and theory-building. Alan Leslie provided the first description of the computational infrastructure required for theory of mind.[15] This infrastructure he referred to as 'meta-representation'. Meta-representation explains the ability of children to engage in pretend play. Primary representations directly represent objects, states of affairs, and situations in the world: 'The cup is empty.' Meta-representations are 'representations of representations'. They allow us to pretend and to understand pretence in others: 'The empty cup is full of yummy juice.' In his later research, Leslie refers to a 'theory of mind mechanism' that is 'part of the core architecture of the human brain'.[16] This brain mechanism is specialized for learning about the beliefs and desires of others.

TT has been challenged by other philosophers of social cognition. Advocates of ST argue that it is our capacity to run simulation routines (i.e. to generate pretend desires and beliefs), rather than our use of folk psychological reasoning, that is the really significant factor in accounting for our mind-reading ability. It is to a consideration of the simulation heuristic that we now turn.

Simulation theory

Simulation in the general sense refers to representation or imitation of one thing by another. Hence, mental simulation is the representation or imitation of one mental process by another. It is a form of role-taking, or imaginatively putting oneself in the shoes of another person. Robert Gordon captures the fundamental concept well:

> The basic idea is that if the resources our own brain uses to guide our own behaviour can be modified to work as representations of other people, then we have no need to store general information about what makes people tick: We just do the ticking for them. Simulation is thus said to be process-driven rather than theory-driven.[17]

As we have seen, mind-reading is the process whereby an attributor (A) ascribes desires and beliefs to another person or 'target' (T), and on the basis of that ascription predicts T's behaviour. A common scenario in everyday life is as follows. T desires to attain a goal, g; T believes that employing a certain means, m, will lead to the attainment of g; T therefore decides to do m. ST accounts for the ability of an attributor, A, to read this desire and this belief out of T's mind, and to predict that person's action, in the following way.[18] In observing T's behaviour, A runs a mental simulation consisting of a pretend desire and a pretend belief. The pretend desire is what A imagines T wants to achieve. The pretend belief is that m is an effective means to achieve g. Through creating a pretend desire and belief, A is putting himself in T's (presumed) 'mental shoes'.

Proponents of ST argue that it is superior to TT as a theory of mind-reading for a number of reasons. Here we examine just two arguments; they have been chosen because they are especially relevant to our present concern. We are thinking of the claims that ST provides a better account than TT for empathy and for the function of mirror neurons. Ian Ravenscroft argues that empathy plays a much more significant role in philosophy of mind than is generally recognized.[19] He defines empathy as 'the capacity to bring about in ourselves another's affective states without actually placing ourselves in their situation'.[20] Ravenscroft uses the case of empathic connection with a rock-climber struggling on an overhang (an actual experience of his) to build his argument for the superiority of ST over TT. This unfortunate climber is trapped on the overhang. He is unable to repeat in reverse the difficult climbing manoeuvres that got him in this situation. The rope is positioned in such a way that it affords him no protection. A fall would be fatal. Becoming more and more exhausted, he desperately seeks a way out of his dilemma. In reflecting on the experience of observing the plight of the unfortunate climber, Ravenscroft has this to say: 'Looking on, I vividly experienced what it was like to be him, and not only because, as a climber, I had been in similar situations myself: any non-climber looking on could also experience what it was like to be that poor soul.'[21] He goes on to make the claim that our ability to have the experiences of another person raises serious problems for defenders of TT. Ravenscroft lays out the TT approach to this particular scenario, and points out what he sees as its obvious deficiencies. The TT take on empathic connection with the unfortunate climber would be as follows. Seeing the climber's situation and observing his behaviour, the observer employs folk psychology in reasoning about his mental states: he is afraid; he now regrets his decision to take on such a dangerous climb; he believes that if he can just find the next good hold there is a way out; and so on. The problem here, suggests Ravenscroft, is that there is a gap between this theorizing of the observer and what the climber is personally experiencing. In empathizing with the distressed climber, the observer is not simply generating via folk psychology a series of propositions about the climber's mental state, the observer is also experiencing a state very much like the climber's. The situation of the observer is not at all like the scientist who understands theoretically the process being investigated, but has no personal experience of it. Rather, such observers are putting themselves in the shoes of the distressed climber; they are experiencing what it is like to be him.[22]

The other argument that is commonly invoked – a related one – is that the matching facilitated by mirror neurons (MNs) is strongly associated with ST, but not at all with TT. MNs were discovered in macaque monkeys by a team of Italian researchers in the 1990s. These neurons respond both when a particular action is performed by the recorded monkey, and when the same action performed by another individual is observed. Thus, the neuron mirrors the behaviour of the other, as though the observer was carrying out the action. In humans, brain activity consistent with that of MNs has been found in the premotor cortex, the supplementary motor area, the primary somatosensory cortex and the inferior parietal cortex.

Vittorio Gallese and Alvin Goldman contend that our mind-reading abilities are grounded in our capacity to run a simulation routine.[23] The authors suggest that this capacity may have evolved from a system involving matching of observed behaviour, whose neural correlate is represented by MNs in monkeys. They further contend that MN activity is nature's way of allowing an observer to get into the 'mental shoes' of the target. Importantly, putting oneself in the place of the other is precisely what the simulation heuristic aims to do. Gallese and Goldman argue that these facts support ST and disconfirm TT: 'The point is that MN activity is not mere theoretical inference. It creates in the observer a state that matches that of the target. This is how it resembles the simulation heuristic. Nothing about TT leads us to expect this kind of matching.'[24]

Obviously there is some force to these and other arguments claiming superiority for ST over TT. Advocates of TT, as one would expect, provide compelling counter-arguments, but here is not the place to go into these. We can simply note that it is evident that what TT posits – namely, that we formulate propositions about the desires, beliefs and expected behaviour of the other using folk psychology – does in fact play a role in mind-reading. It cannot be legitimately argued that it plays no role. It is really the size or significance of its contribution that is debated. In fact, many philosophers argue not for either pure TT or pure ST, but rather for a hybrid theory.

While acknowledging that both TT and ST play a role in social cognition, some theorists contend that both theories have serious shortcomings. Most significantly, they suffer through a focus on the mental processes of an individual – that is, the observer; the really important factor is the nature of the social interaction. These theorists argue for a 'participatory sense-making' (PSM) paradigm. It will be immediately obvious that, in general terms at least, this attention to social interaction aligns with the interests of counsellors and psychotherapists. It is to a consideration of PSM that we now turn.

Participatory sense-making

In surveying the writings of social cognition theorists whose focus is on intersubjectivity, one finds three common objections to the traditional theories.[25] The first point of critique is the assumption held by proponents of both TT and ST of an opaque inner world. According to the traditional theories, in order to penetrate this hidden mental world the observer needs to employ either inference or imaginative projection. Shaun Gallagher claims, I think plausibly, to have exposed the flaw in this construal through demonstrating that we read off the mental state of another person through direct perception.[26] In order to understand the beliefs, desires and intentions of another, we do not need to engage in folk psychological reasoning or run a simulation; we are able to immediately perceive that person's mental state. Gallagher calls on the support of observations by both Scheler and Wittgenstein to bolster his argument:

> For we certainly believe ourselves to be directly acquainted with another person's joy in his laughter, with his sorrow and pain in his tears, with his shame in his blushing, with his entreaty in his outstretched hands … And with the tenor of this [sic] thoughts in the sound of his words. If anyone tells me that this is not 'perception', for it cannot be so, in view of the fact that a perception is simply a 'complex of physical sensations' … I would beg him to turn aside from such questionable theories and address himself to the phenomenological facts (Scheler).[27]

> Look into someone else's face, and see the consciousness in it, and a particular shade of consciousness. You see on it, in it, joy, indifference, interest, excitement, torpor, and so on … Do you look into yourself in order to recognize the fury in *his* face? (Wittgenstein).[28]

We will come back to Gallagher's approach below. For the moment, let us take up the second common objection to TT and ST – namely, that these theories fail to assign a proper role to embodiment in social understanding. It is claimed that social cognitive science 'largely assumes a disembodied sender-receiver relation between two Cartesian minds; the body usually functions only as a transmission device'.[29] The concept of an embodied mind, in contrast, is based in the assumption that minds are embedded in bodies, and bodies, in turn, are embedded in the surrounding environment. In arguing that the concept of an embodied mind is lacking in the popular theories, it is readily acknowledged, as we did above, that ST draws support from the research findings on the operation of motor neurons in social interaction. Here we do indeed find an emphasis on the body. The shortcoming, however, is that such theorizing fails to attend to reciprocity in the engagement between the embodied agents. It is not minds or brains that interact, but rather living bodies or persons. We need to locate cognitive processes in the whole body system, rather than in the brain alone.[30] In social interaction, we read off the beliefs, desires and intentions of others from their gaze, their facial expression, the tone of their voice, the movement of their heads, hand gestures, the comportment of their body, and more.

The third and final commonly stated objection to the traditional theories is that they assume that we primarily observe others from a third person stance. In TT, observers attempt to predict the behaviour of others based on theorizing about the meaning of the actions they see. The observer in the ST paradigm runs a simulation involving pretend beliefs and pretend desires. Proponents of PSM, in contrast, argue for a second person approach. On this view, meaning in a social context is generated through the interaction between the two agents. Further, the interaction itself shapes the meaning-making activity of the agents.

Proponents of PSM argue that in order to get to the heart of social cognition, it is necessary to develop a full description of the interactive process. They incorporate the thinking of Gallagher (and others with similar ideas) on the role of direct perception and the importance of taking a second person perspective. However, they contend that it is necessary to go further. In the end, so the argument goes, Gallagher leaves us stuck on the role of the individual mind. Hanne De Jaegher, for example, has this to say: 'Gallagher is arguing against TT and ST and this is needed indeed. But by staying on their turf, he risks facing problems very similar to the ones they face ... in traditional approaches to social cognition, and in Gallagher's too, the interaction process is all but neglected.'[31]

In analysing social interaction as a process, the concept of *coordination* is accorded a central role.[32] Coordination is defined as 'the non-accidental correlation between the behaviour of two or more systems that are in sustained coupling ...'[33] A correlation is 'a coherence in behaviour of two or more systems over and above what is expected, given what those systems are capable of doing.'[34] The authors, thankfully, put some flesh on the bare bones of these abstract definitions. Reference is made, for example, to the coordination between two skilled tennis players.[35] Let's call them A and B. A's direct perception of B's body position and move- ment, especially B's footwork and the way B is holding the racket, allows A to coordinate her/his position on the court to be in the right place to return the ball. However, at some point the coordination inevitably breaks down. For example, B feigns to hit a drive and instead produces a drop shot. Without such moments of uncoordination, the rally would go on for a very long time (skilled players don't make many mistakes when they don't have to cope with the unexpected), and it would be quite a boring game as a result. One also finds a reference to the way listeners coordinate their movements with the changes in speed and direction of the movement of the speaker and in the rapidity and tone of any utterances. The perception-action cycle consists of synchronization, resonance, rhythmic co-variation in gestures, and in facial and vocal expression. Sense-making in a social context may therefore be construed as 'a participatory dynamic dance'.[36] Through engaging in this 'dance', 'social agents are able to coordinate their sense-making in social encounters – that is: they can *participate in each other's sense-making* [emphasis in the original]'.[37]

Just as virtually all dance partners occasionally get out of step, there is sometimes a loss of coordination in social interaction. Rather than a process of constant attunement, we have one characterized by variable or even discontinuous interaction. This is not something to be lamented. Just as in life in general we learn very little from our successes but a great deal from our failures, so in social interaction a breakdown in coordination can lead to a significant gain in understanding.[38]

That completes our (overly brief) discussion of philosophical approaches to social understanding. It is evident that folk psychology and simulation do play a role in social cognition. Further, the work on mirror neurons and simulation clearly has important implications for our understanding of empathy in counselling and psychotherapy. However, as already indicated, it is PSM that particularly grabs my attention and there are a number of reasons for this. First, the emphasis on embodiment is significant, although some counselling theorists have virtually lost sight of this fact. Modalities such as language and thought are emphasized; the role of the body is all but overlooked. Obviously language and cognition play vital roles in the counselling process, but so does touch, smell, the gaze, blushing, dryness of mouth, shortness of breath, gesture, tears, tone of voice, body comportment, to name just some of the many important body modalities.

I am also convinced by the argument about the role of direct perception in social understanding. Counsellors do not have to look into themselves to know that counsellees are anxious or despairing. It is immediately evident in their bodies; we see it written all over their faces. We catch it in the way they hold their bodies. We hear it in the tone of their voices.

Finally, the concept of coordination is extraordinarily significant in understanding the counselling process. In fact, one very helpful way to characterize the counselling process is co-managing the communicative dance. Every counsellor knows that in the early stages of a counselling relationship, a primary focus is establishing rapport. Synchronizing with the counsellee's mood and bodily comportment, communicating acceptance, and engaging in empathic listening facilitate this coordination. But all counsellors also know that at some point they will need to temporally break the coordination – through confrontation, for example. Finally, and most importantly for our current discussion, the conceptualization in PSM of the to and fro movements between attunement and alienation is highly significant in understanding what takes place in empathic relating. First, it needs to be recognized that the aim in empathic communication is definitely not providing an exact copy of what the counsellee is communicating. A slight mismatch between the empathic formulation of the counsellor and the expression of the counsellee may lead to fresh insight. The nuance provided by counsellors in their empathic communication leads counsellees to see their experience and/or the way they are framing it in a slightly different light. Second, empathic missteps, far from being destructive in certain therapeutic situations, actually lead to a stronger sense of self in the counsellee. Finally, a highly empathic counsellor is sometimes able to see something that is lying just outside the awareness of the client. This may be characterized as taking the lead, and it is to a discussion of the empathic dance that we now turn. We begin by defining our term.

What is empathy?

Empathy is variously defined, and listed below is a sample of the definitions on offer. It is:

- the vicarious experiencing of an emotion that is congruent with, but not necessarily identical to, the emotion of another individual[39]
- the ability to experience and understand what others feel without confusion between oneself and others[40]
- an affective response that stems from the apprehension or comprehension of another's emotional state or condition, and that is similar to what the other person is feeling, or would be expected to feel, in the given situation[41]
- to perceive the internal frame of reference of another with accuracy, and with the emotional components and meanings that pertain thereto, as if one were the other person, but without ever losing the 'as if' condition.[42]

These definitions suggest that the essential elements in empathy are (i) the ability to think and feel oneself into the emotional experience of another, while (ii) maintaining self–other differentiation. Empathic capacity is clearly highly significant in terms of the aim of resonating with and attuning to the counsellee and that individual's experience of self, world and God. What is often overlooked in discussions of therapeutic empathy is the role played by the body. PSM theory reminds us that social understanding is an embodied process. With this in mind, we will now reflect briefly on body empathy.

Empathy and the body

Thought and language obviously play important roles in empathic relating. However, empathic listening is not an exclusively cognitive/verbal exercise. When I was taught the skill of empathy in my pastoral counselling class, the teacher, Charles Noller, would provide the group with a statement from a counsellee, and we were asked to write down the empathic response that we would offer. Charles would then ask us one by one to share what we had come up with, and he would provide his critique. I was recently reminded of Charles's approach when reading an article by Arthur Clark on the therapeutic distinctions between empathy and sympathy.[43] Clark provides a series of statements by a client, Stanley, and then offers both sympathetic and empathic responses. Comparing and contrasting the two sets of counsellor responses allows him to make certain distinctions between the two compassionate responses. Here our interest is not in that comparison, but rather in Clark's portrayal of empathic relating as primarily a cognitive and verbal event. Here is a typical example:[44]

> Stanley: I can't believe it. Because of my job, there is a possibility that I will have to move with my family to another part of the country. I'm so upset. I don't even want to talk about it.
> Counsellor (*Empathy*): This is hard for you to talk about, and it doesn't make any sense to you. The prospect of this change seems overwhelming to you at this point.

The approach that Charles Noller and Arthur Clark take to teaching empathy to trainee counsellors is a typical one. Indeed, I used it myself when I first started teaching pastoral counselling. It is certainly a useful approach, for it has an important place in developing the skill of resonating with the feelings, distress and confusion of a counsellee. However, what is missing is attention to the role that the body plays in empathic relating. By way of contrast consider the following therapeutic scenario:

> Nick was an unemployed chef who came to therapy to deal with depression brought on by losing his job. In session three, he described what his work was like for him at its best and what he missed about it. As the therapist listened, he let himself be carried away into the client's experience: he felt a tickling, tingling sensation in his stomach; he remembered the feeling of his own similar successes (rising sense of excitement, accompanied by a sense of feet planted firmly on the ground); he 'ran a movie in his head' of the client striding out of the kitchen, head held

high, accompanied by a sense of pride and happiness. He noted how his fantasy matched Nick's upright posture and firm position in the chair, and how he had shifted into a firmer position himself. During his description, Nick felt that his therapist was interested and – even though the therapist had not said anything – he experienced support and an invitation to dig deeper into his description.[45]

The body is very present and involved in an empathic engagement with the counsellee. The impact of Cartesian mind–body dualism remains strong in Western culture. We tend to elevate the role of mind and cognition, and downplay or ignore the part the body plays in human activity in general and empathic relating in particular. Research in social psychology, however, informs us that we are hard-wired for rapport-building and empathy. Unwittingly, we make changes to our posture, gestures, facial expression and tone of voice to match those of the person we are interacting with. It is called 'the chameleon effect'.[46] Chartrand and Bargh describe the effect this way:

> In the motion picture *Zelig*, Woody Allen plays a human chameleon who cannot help but take on the behavior, personality and values of whomever he is with. Like a chameleon changing its color to match its current surroundings, Zelig's behaviour changes to match the norms and values of the group with which he is currently involved. Although Allen's film took this phenomenon to laughable extremes, it is nevertheless a common experience to discover, after the fact, that one has taken on the accent, speech patterns, and even behavioural mannerisms of one's interaction partners.[47]

We non-consciously attune ourselves through our bodies to the personal style and mannerisms of the other person (the 'coordination' that proponents of PSM refer to). As one might expect, psychological research indicates that persons who are by nature empathic manifest the chameleon effect to a greater extent than do others.[48]

When counsellors and psychotherapists take the time to think about it, they realize that they are chameleons in the counselling office (as they are in everyday interactions also, of course). In talking to those suffering from depression, for example, therapists tend to speak in a calm and soothing manner. Though these therapists may usually speak rather loudly and in an animated way, they will instinctively dial it down to a gentle mode with the depressive client. In his article on empathy as an embodied practice, Michael Buchholz picks up on this natural tendency, and comments that this physical know-how is not something that one learns from a counselling manual:

You see your patient for the first time, you see her or his eyes and you 'know' how to respond. But this is not (static) 'knowledge' you have from a handbook, it cannot be written down in teachable and learnable sentences. It just happens, it is a process of 'knowing', less from 'knowledge'. You adopt [sic] yourself to something you sense and often it takes a long time to realize that you did.[49]

The body of the counsellor makes its presence felt in a forceful and uncomfortable manner in a therapeutic conversation when that individual is experiencing a high level of arousal in response to the story the counsellee is telling. This autonomic arousal works against the goal of empathic resonance.[50] This is because emotional resonance with another's suffering generates fear and an associated desire for self-protection. This leads in turn to avoidance and self-protective behaviour. It is also the case that the affective arousal the counsellor is experiencing consumes personal resources of attention and cognition that could otherwise be made available for empathic relating. A fundamental fact of counselling and of pastoral ministry more generally is that exposure to the pain and distress of others makes us vulnerable. Our bodies tell us just how vulnerable we are. The pastoral theologian Douglas Purnell captures this particularly well. He reports becoming acutely aware of his bodily experience of personal vulnerability through involvement in a Clinical Pastoral Education (CPE) seminar:

As I listened to those in the CPE program I became aware of important questions about the body – and how vulnerable I feel in my body when I stand beside someone whose body has been broken through accident or illness or decay. How vulnerable I feel when I try to be empathetic to the other ... how easy to imagine their body is my body. It is not just the broken body that makes me vulnerable; the sensual and the sexual body scares me too. My life is in this body.[51]

The fact that opening oneself up to the suffering of the other may result in a high level of arousal, which in turn mitigates attention and cognitive function, has not been lost on those who study empathy in a health-care context. These scholars make a distinction between cognitive and emotional empathy. A number of them maintain that medical empathy should be purely cognitive in its approach. Landau, for example, contends that 'deempathization' is required if the physician is to make sound, scientifically based clinical assessments.[52] In a similar vein, Hojat *et al.* contend that clinical empathy should be a purely cognitive activity.[53] While both empathy and sympathy involve sharing in the personal experience of the patient, the former is constituted through *understanding*, while the latter involves a *sharing of emotion*. The emotional factor associated with sympathy is viewed by these authors as a liability in a clinical setting. They contend that sympathy, if it is excessive, works against objective diagnosis and treatment. 'Affective distance' is advocated as a means of preventing 'bursts of emotion' interfering with clinical neutrality (Hojat *et al.*, 2002, p. 1563).

Others take the contrary view and argue that emotional resonance has an important part to play in clinical empathy. They argue that it is not possible for the doctor to gain a comprehensive understanding of the subjective experience of the patient without feeling some of the emotion that the individual feels.[54] On this view of clinical empathy, there needs to be an affective connection in which the empathizer '*experiences* the other's attitudes as presences, rather than as mere possibilities [emphasis in the original]'.[55] It is only when patients sense that the doctor has received their personal suffering as a real presence that they experience genuine care.

This discussion, I think, is suggestive in relation to what constitutes genuine empathy in the counselling context. Opening ourselves to the pain, anxiety and brokenness of another makes us highly vulnerable. The emotionally charged communication gets into our bodies. This is the experience of physical arousal that was discussed above. Sometimes the arousal is so strong that the counsellor loses a significant degree of personal control. The anxiety level rises to a point where it is almost overwhelming. Cognitive function is impaired; the counsellor cannot think straight. That person is unable to listen carefully and attentively. In recognizing personal vulnerability, the temptation is to transmute empathy into a purely – or at least largely – cognitive exercise. In this way, it is hoped that the discomfort and threat of bodily, emotional arousal will be warded off. The loss – and this is a big one – is that the counsellee will sense only relatively low levels of resonance and attunement. That is to say, a counsellee will have a weak experience of being cared for.

A personal experience testifies to this. Early on in my first pastorate I found that some of the new experiences I was encountering were stirring up personal issues and creating a significant degree of concern and distress. I knew a senior pastor who had extensive training in counselling and who was very experienced in that area of ministry. I therefore turned to her for help. As I began to tell my story, I found myself becoming disquieted by a sense of feeling out of tune with her. In essence, I didn't feel as if she was really connecting with me and my experience of distress. I found myself wondering about why this was so, and reflected on her empathic responses to my story of confusion and anxiety. They were all well-worded; they were mostly bang on target. So why did I feel that we were not in-step with each other in our conversation? I simply didn't feel a strong sense of connection and rapport, but what was causing that? It suddenly dawned on me that though she was clearly able to understand my situation intellectually, there was little emotional resonance. She was making 'textbook' empathic responses, but she was *feeling* very little of it. What gave it away? How did I know that she wasn't feeling with me? It was her body that said it all. In particular, I read it in her face and I heard it in her tone of voice. Her face and tone of voice told me that she was not feeling my pain in her guts. She understood perfectly well on an intellectual level what I was going through, but she didn't allow it to move her. I came away feeling as if she didn't really care. As a result, I didn't make a follow-up appointment.

An empathic God?

It is interesting to observe that theological debate over whether or not God feels with us in our suffering centres to some extent on this observation that emotional resonance may produce a high level of arousal which, in turn, militates against attention and therapeutic action. For most of the history of Christian theology, the idea of the impassable God was unquestioned. In recent times, however, an increasing number of theologians have advocated for the notion of an empathic God. J. Robbins captures the essence of this approach when he says that there is a 'religious truth that God shoulders the cross of the sufferer as well … God does not exempt the Godhead from the order of things, but identifies with the burdens and sorrows of humanity'.[56] The theologian who is most acutely aware of the debilitating effect of arousal that is overpowering and the implications for our image of God is Frances Young. But in order to understand what is at stake in some of the claims she makes, it is necessary to briefly survey both sides of the theological divide on this issue.

We can begin with a discussion of the approach of those theologians who resist the move to an empathic God. The line to those who argue against the notion of divine suffering starts with Plato and Aristotle and passes through Thomas Aquinas. In the cosmology of the Greek philosophers, the immutable substances are separated from the material ones. The realm of Being has no contact with the realm of 'becoming'. The Highest Substance, God, cannot enter into a relationship with the transient world. For God to make contact with the world of change, becoming would have to enter God's reality.

Aquinas works with this worldview. A fundamental starting point in his theology is that God does not change (God is 'immutable'). God is 'the unchanging first cause of change'.[57] All material substances are subject to the process of becoming, and they have a potential that is actualized in this transient process. God, however, is 'sheer actuality' (*actus purus*). 'In the first existent thing everything must be actual; there can be no potentiality whatsoever.'[58] This does not mean that in God something has been fully actualized; God is actuality pure and simple.

Now something is perfect when it has achieved actuality. It has moved from the state of potentiality to actuality and has thereby fulfilled itself. In this sense, it has reached perfection. God is pure actuality and therefore perfect.[59] Everything else requires an origin for its existence, but God is self-subsistent being itself (*ipsum esse*). Since God is the source of God's existence, there is within God the full perfection of being.

The *actus purus* tenet necessarily implies that there is no change in God.[60] God is sheerly actual; there is no potential in God. Any changing thing has potential. It follows that God cannot change.

It also follows that the unchanging God cannot have a 'real relation' with the transient world. To be open to the world of becoming involves introducing change into one's existence. God relates to the world through a 'mixed relation'.[61] The relation is real in one term (our relationship to God), but only logical in the other (God's relationship to us). The real term in the relationship is affected or changed, but the same is not true of the other term.

Depoortere sums it up well: 'For Thomas, it is more perfect not to move than to move, and it is more perfect not to have a relationship than it is to have one.'[62] But how can God express love if there is no real relation with God's creatures? God wills our good and acts for our good. But such an action affects only the beneficiary. God is unchanged. Divine love is expressed through the 'intelligent appetite', not through the 'sensitive appetite'. Indeed, there is no 'sensitive appetite' in God. The senses involve passion, and passion involves change. There is a movement from one emotional state to another. 'Loving, enjoying and delighting are emotions when they signify activities of the sensitive appetite; not so, however, when they signify activities of the intelligent appetite. It is in this last sense that they are attributed to God.'[63] God loves without passion.

In developing his argument that God does not suffer, the contemporary Roman Catholic theologian Thomas Weinandy builds on these insights of Aquinas and places them in a trinitarian framework.[64] The triune God loves us and acts fully and completely for our good, but does not – indeed, cannot – feel our pain.

Weinandy begins with the insight shared by both Augustine and Aquinas that what distinguishes the persons of the Trinity is the nature of the relationships they share. That is, they subsist as distinct persons in and through their relationships to one another. It is the actions of 'origination' and 'spiration' that define these relations. The Father is constituted as Father in and through the eternal acts of begetting the Son and 'breathing forth' the Holy Spirit. The Son subsists eternally as the Son through being begotten by the Father on the one hand, and through being conformed by the Spirit to be the Son of the Father on the other. Finally, nothing constitutes the Holy Spirit as Holy Spirit other than his proceeding from the Father and the Son and so shaping the Father–Son relationship in the Godhead. Thus, it is relationality that defines the Trinity. Each person is defined as who he (or she) singularly is, and so subsists as who he is, through the relationship he shares with the other two.

Now, if one takes on board Aquinas' doctrine that God is sheer actuality and therefore immune from change, the conclusion one reaches, according to Weinandy, is that Father, Son and Holy Spirit are subsistent relations fully in act and therefore immutable and impassible. He is aware that contemporary theologians frequently argue that such a view of God makes God look more like a stone than the dynamic, active, personal God of the Bible. Thus, Weinandy is quick to make the point that immutability in the Trinity does not imply inertness:

> [The persons of the Trinity] are immutable not because they are static or inert in their relationships, but precisely for the opposite reason. Because they are subsistent relations fully in act, because the terms 'Father', 'Son', and 'Holy Spirit' designate pure acts ... they do not have any relational potential which would need to be actualized in order to make them more relational – more who they are. As subsistent relations fully in act, the persons of the Trinity are utterly and completely dynamic and active in their integral and comprehensive self-giving to one another, and could not possibly become any more dynamic or active in their self-giving since they are constituted, and so subsist, as who they are only in their complete and utter self-giving to one another.[65]

So for Weinandy, Aquinas' view that God is immutable should not be taken to imply inertness. God is unchangeable not because God is static or inert like a stone, but for precisely the opposite reason. God is so active, so dynamic, that no change could make God more active. This dynamism is expressed in the life of the Trinity through relationship. The crux of Weinandy's argument is that God is *actus purus* and therefore has no potential to become more relational.

This absolutely dynamic relational life of the Trinity is extended to the world. God is at work in the world drawing human beings into this rich inner life: '[The] lack of any self-constituting relational potential, since they are subsistent relations fully in act, gives to the persons of the Trinity absolute positive relational potential, that is, they have the singular ability to establish relationships with others other than themselves whereby the persons of the Trinity can relate others to themselves as they are in themselves as a trinity of persons.'[66] Thus, on this view, the relationship offered to us by the Trinity is of the most intimate and dynamic kind possible.

Weinandy's main proposal is that an empathic God would actually be less compassionate than a non-empathic one. The chain of logic is as follows. The first step is to recognize that, on the classic view of the divine, the love and compassion with which the persons of the Trinity relate to one another and to the world is fully actualized. Since God is *actus purus*, it is not possible for the Trinity to give any more love in relations with others. Now an empathic God would feel the pain of the world. Divine sorrowing with the world would result in a change in God's internal state. Since God's love and compassion are perfectly realized, such a change would be a negative one: it could only lead to less of these qualities being offered.

Those theologians who refuse arguments such as these and contend for an empathic God attend to the biblical account, and especially to the story of the passion of Christ. They point out that throughout the Bible we find a picture of a suffering God. The first outlines of the picture, those found in the Old Testament, reveal a grieving and lamenting God.[67]

The story of God's grief begins with God's free choice to create a partner for Godself. In freedom and in love there is, as Barth puts it, an 'overflow' of the divine essence.[68] God does not will to be God alone, to be God for Godself, but God with us and for us. God chooses dialogue, and all dialogue involves risk. The risk is that one's overtures of love will be spurned. In the Hebrew Scriptures, we encounter a story of God reaching out to humankind, only to suffer the grief of rejection. The Flood story tells of a God who sorrows deeply over the human response to the offer of partnership. 'And the LORD was sorry that he had made humankind on the earth, and it grieved him to his heart. So the LORD said "I will blot out from the earth the human beings I have created – people together with animals and creeping things and birds of the air, for I am sorry that I have made them"' (Gen. 6.6–7). Wilfrid Harrington suggests that God feels sorrow and grief not because God has made a horrible mistake in choosing dialogue,[69] rather, the pain in the divine heart is the result of the wholesale rejection of God's love and grace. God *has* to respond to this situation. At first, the wrath of God rages and the earth is flooded, but then comes the abrogation of the decision to blot out humankind: 'I will never again curse the ground because of humankind, for the inclination of the human heart is evil from youth; nor will I again describe every living creature as I have done' (Gen. 8.21). God has decided to live with humankind's tendency to move towards evil.

The persistent rebellious streak in people is a dominant theme in the story of YHWH's covenantal relationship with Israel. God chose Israel to be God's own and lavishes blessings upon the people. But time and time again they wander from the straight path that YHWH has set before them. 'And I thought you would call me, My Father, and would not turn from following me. Instead, as a faithless wife leaves her husband so have you been faithless to me' (Jer. 3.19b–20). Israel is God's own and God is faithful in God's love for her. When God is faced with infidelity, the divine heart is grieved: 'My people are bent on turning away from me. To the Most High they call, but he does not raise them up at all ... My heart recoils within me; my compassion grows warm and tender' (Hos. 11.7, 8c).

The story of the suffering of God manifested in God's covenantal relationship with Israel reaches a climax in the passion and death of Jesus. The grieving God, the lamenting God, becomes the crucified God.

Traditional theology was happy to attach the suffering of the cross to the human nature of Jesus, but kept his divine nature immune from it. Jürgen Moltmann, however, has shown that the passion of Jesus is really a divine passion.[70] This divine passion is an event in the trinitarian life of God. The Father suffers the grief of giving over the Son, and the Son suffers the pain of 'godforsakenness'. It is here that we find the special element in the passion of Christ. Many other righteous and innocent people have suffered terribly. What sets Jesus' suffering apart is the ineffable pain of abandonment by the Father.[71]

Frances Young has one foot in both camps; she contends for a God who is at once both passionate and passionless. Young wrestles with the question of divine passibility in the context of the pain that she has lived with as a result of having a profoundly mentally disabled son, Arthur. Young seems to concur with the sentiments I have just expressed. For her, 'an uninvolved "do-gooder" will not do'.[72] She points to the Old Testament where we encounter a God who is distressed by the waywardness of God's people and who lovingly yearns for their return. She thinks, as I do, that a personal God must be intimately involved, and therefore must truly suffer in response to human suffering. The focal point of God's suffering with us and for us is found in the cross. 'For many sufferers the only answer is the Cross – the fact of God suffering, God entering into all the travail and pain, taking responsibility for it, overcoming it.'[73]

Despite reaching the point of embracing a suffering God, there are still some niggling worries for Young. She wonders if God's changelessness and impassibility remain important theological ideas. 'For how can a vulnerable God still be God, a God to worship and depend upon? If you are tempted to sigh "Poor old God", what kind of a God are you left with?'[74] To deal with her discomfort Young develops a notion of a God who is *both passionate and passionless at the same time*. She draws an analogy with human emotions. On the one hand, we value the capacity to feel deeply with another. This indicates that a person is truly human. But on the other hand, we value peace, serenity and calm in a person. We all know how the storms of passion play havoc with us. To be able to bring powerful emotions under control and to think and act calmly and peacefully is accorded a high value. Extending this thinking to the reality of God, God is the one who is involved in our suffering but who is at the same time an ocean of peace and serenity. A personal experience of Young's helped shape this view of God:

> Early in 1988, a couple close to me had a tragic experience in relation to the birth of a child – their daughter was still-born. To say the least I felt for them. But after a while I realised that my distress was not just for them. I was re-living my own pain, my own struggle to understand how things could go wrong, my own anguish and protest at the suffering of the world. I was too involved, and it was only when the self-involvement was purged that I could begin to be of use to those who were suffering.[75]

This experience led Young to reclaim the traditional insight that God is 'beyond suffering' in the sense that God is not emotionally involved. Rather, God 'is the ocean of love that can absorb all the suffering of the world and purge it without being polluted or changed by it'.[76] Clearly, those theologians who support the idea of an empathic God need to show how it is that God is able to share in our suffering, to feel with us in our pain, while suffering no diminution of the divine capacity for compassionate and loving action to relieve suffering.

I have not taken this detour into doctrinal theology simply because it is interesting for a pastoral theologian to contemplate the notion of an empathic God. When pastoral counsellors engage with people in deep suffering and distress, they are commonly confronted with questions like, 'Where is God in this?' and 'What does this mean for my relationship with God?' People of faith raise their hands in supplication, seeking God's grace and compassionate action in their lives. Beyond that, there are those who also want to know if God feels their pain. The notion of a God who is unmoved by their suffering doesn't sound very compassionate to them. It is a source of great comfort to such persons to hold the image of an empathic God. They resonate with Alfred North Whitehead's understanding of God as 'the great companion – the fellow-sufferer who understands'.[77] For others, it is perhaps enough to know that God's grace is sufficient for them and that God is acting compassionately in their lives. In any case, pastoral counsellors need to know how they will respond if and when the theological question is raised. Further, they need to know how they will pray with the counsellee. That is, do they plan to include references to divine empathy? If so, it is important for them to first discuss this with the counsellee. Such references may be deeply comforting, or they may jar and create a sense of alienation. Pastoral counsellors should not simply assume that their theology is shared by the counsellee and therefore will be well-received.

One of the main ideas structuring our discussion is the inevitable and necessary alternation in social interaction between attunement and alienation. It may help to briefly recap on this aspect of the conversation. We have just been discussing God's perfect attunement to our suffering. Whether one holds to an empathic (i.e. emotionally involved) or non-empathic view of God, it is the case that God has an infinitely full and accurate understanding of our suffering and acts in a perfectly compassionate way towards us. Counsellors are human beings; they cannot be perfectly attuned. Managing the movement between attunement and alienation is an important skill for the counsellor. That individual also needs to recognize the positive role that being out of step with the counsellee can play in empathic relating. The first topic is the therapeutic value in a slight misalignment between counsellee statement and counsellor empathic formulation.

Slightly out-of-step in the dance of empathy

Above we discussed the simulation theory of social understanding. Recall that a basis for this theory is the existence of a mirror neuron system. The neural circuits activated in a person executing actions, expressing emotion and experiencing sensations are activated at the same time in a person observing these actions, emotions and sensations. Heinz Kohut is well known for his use of empathic mirroring in working with clients suffering from narcissistic personality disorder.[78] Is it the case that what Kohut is talking about and the activity of the mirror neuron circuits amount to the same thing? The answer is 'no'. We all have a mirror neuron system and therefore when we observe another person experiencing or reporting a particular emotion it will fire, just as it is firing in the individual we are observing. But we know that this biological capacity does not necessarily translate into a high level of empathic capacity. It is simply the case that some of us are dispositionally more empathic than the rest. This suggests that there must be an extra step beyond the purely biological in the empathic process.[79] In this extra move, the observer's emotional expression is congruent with, and attuned to, the emotional expression of the other person.

Gallese, Eagle and Migone contend that the use of the term 'empathic mirroring' by Kohut and others is actually misleading. They put it this way: '[E]mpathic understanding of another is reflected not in imitation or duplication of the other's behaviour, but rather in congruent and attuned responses, including complementary or modulating responses.'[80] The authors make their point through reference to the reaction of a mother to her crying baby. If the mother was to literally act as a mirror, she would cry also. But of course this response would not be helpful in the slightest for the infant. Instead, an empathic mother says something like, 'Oh, poor baby!'

Though this all sounds entirely reasonable in terms of an argument, Gallese, Eagle and Migone actually misunderstand how Kohut uses the concept of positive mirroring. In order to appreciate what he means by it and how it works in therapy, it is necessary to connect it to his bipolar construction of the self.[81] According to Kohut, we each have a grandiose and an idealizing self. The poles correspond to two basic psychological functions – namely, 'healthy self-assertiveness vis-à-vis the mirroring self-object', and 'healthy admiration for the idealized self-object'. Healthy psychological functioning across both sectors is described through the use of the metaphor of a 'tension arc'.[82] The inner spark of the person suffering from narcissistic personality disorder is too weak to set up the tension arc. Such people are unable to employ their talents and pursue their goals, and in consequence find themselves beset by feelings of emptiness, inferiority, depression and shame.

Mirroring relates to the grandiose pole. A mother commonly has the experience of observing her young child glowing with pride over a particular achievement. The little one's face is lit up with pride. Mirroring as it is used by Kohut refers to the affirmation and admiration communicated through the mother's face similarly lighting up and reflecting back the feeling of pride that the child is experiencing. The use of the term 'mirroring' here is appropriate because the expression on the mother's face is a reflection of the one on the child's face. For the child, observing the facial expression of its mother is like looking in a mirror.

What Kohut discovered in his work with persons suffering from narcissistic personality disorder is that what they most need is affirmation, prizing and approval. Further, he found that empathy is the response that most powerfully communicates this stance. He theorized that those patients who suffered from feelings of emptiness, lack of zest for life and low self-esteem failed to receive adequate mirroring (bodily and verbal communication of affirmation and admiration) from their mothers. The restoration of the self that Kohut facilitated in therapy involved empathic mirroring that makes up for the severe maternal empathic failures experienced in childhood.

Kohut's central insight is that an effective therapeutic response to the grandiose behaviour of the narcissistic patient is not confrontation, but rather mirroring. His aim was to resonate with, approve and admire his patients' grandiose expressions. He was replicating the maternal response of lighting up with admiration and pride when the child 'shows off' for her. If one relates the term 'mirroring' to the grandiose pole of the self, it is evident that it is not actually a misleading one but, to the contrary, quite an accurate descriptor.

While I think that Gallese, Eagle and Migone are mistaken in their critique of Kohut's terminology, I do think that they say something very significant in suggesting that the empathic response of the therapist should not be an exact (or even exact but for an odd word here or there) replica of what the client has expressed, but rather a slightly different formulation. They note that the fact that the response by the therapist is slightly out-of-step with the expression of the current feeling of the client is transforming. It is important that this difference is only a small one, otherwise it will have a destabilizing effect: '[T]herapeutic change is made possible only when the "quantitative" difference between the two feeling states (i.e. the patient's state and the one that has been internalized from the therapist) is small enough that it does not destabilize the patient's identity.'[83] If what the client internalizes is simply a 'representational replica' of the patient's own thinking and feeling, there is little or no scope for healing and growth. To make their point, Gallese, Eagle and Migone refer to the caricature of so-called Rogerian non-directive counselling in which the counsellor woodenly and almost verbatim reflects back the counsellee's expression of his or her suicidal feelings. The caricature ends with the counsellee jumping out of the window and the counsellor offering one final exact reflection of experience: 'Plop'!

To make it clear what is being said here, we need to distinguish between two cases of a slight difference between the counsellor's empathic response and the counsellee's expression of distress. First, every experienced counsellor is aware that in reflecting back a feeling state it is important to capture it in one's own words. Apart from sounding wooden and artificial, a response that is an (almost) word-for-word recitation of the counsellee's own statement cannot communicate empathy and understanding. Just as teachers know that students have really understood a concept when they are able to capture it in their own words, counsellees know that they have been truly understood when their feeling states are accurately captured in the counsellor's own expression. While this is an important principle, it is not what Gallese, Eagle and Migone are referring to. What they are identifying is an intention by the therapist/counsellor to spark insight or a fuller exploration of feelings through an empathic response that is slightly misaligned with the expression of the client/counsellee. Here is an example. Tom is a 35-year-old administrative officer. He has been raised in a family and church culture of niceness. He is not very comfortable either with feeling angry or with giving it expression. Tom is talking with his pastor, Sarah, about a bad experience he had recently during a work meeting. He had just finished putting forward his idea for a new data management system, and it hurt him when a co-worker responded with a curt and cynical put-down:

Tom: He was so rude. His snide dismissal of what I thought was a pretty good idea hurt me. I have to say that I was a bit steamed up afterwards.
Sarah: That's really unpleasant and hurtful. Your co-worker's cynical put-down really stung you. You were infuriated with him.
Tom (now much more animated and with flushed face): Yes ... Yes, that's right! I was as mad as hell with him. How dare he? I mean to do something about it. I'm going to tell him that his cynical and dismissive manner really hurts people, and that he needs to change it.
Sarah: Good for you, Tom!

There is a mis-match between Tom's expression 'a bit steamed up' and Sarah's empathic response, 'You were infuriated ...' This is intentional on her part. Sarah knows that her congregant likes to be 'nice', to be emotionally contained, and is uncomfortable with feeling angry. She makes the judgement that Tom is probably feeling angrier than he is prepared to admit. The empathic connection is with what Sarah thinks is Tom's true feeling state, rather than with his expression of it. As she was on target, Sarah's response produced a positive shift in Tom.

We have begun the discussion of how small failures in synchronization between the communication of the counsellor and that of the counsellee may be efficacious. The next topic is the therapeutic value in empathic failure.

The therapeutic value of empathic missteps

We have just seen how empathic mirroring is at the core of Kohut's therapeutic approach. However, he recognizes that therapists are only human; they cannot be flawless in their empathic relating. This is not something that Kohut sees as necessarily inhibiting the therapeutic process. On the contrary, provided the empathic failure is acknowledged and appropriately worked through, it can lead to a more robust and coherent self in the client.

Kohut contends that the root cause of the very weak sense of self in clients diagnosed with narcissistic personality disorder can be found in childhood experiences of extreme empathic failures on the part of self-objects (the term refers to the fact that the object – a parent – is experienced as part of the self). It is not the case, however, that the emerging self needs perfect empathic attunement from parents in order to become strong and vital. Indeed, 'optimal frustration' serves the purpose of the laying down of self-esteem regulating psychological structure. When there is small-scale empathic failure (e.g. Mum is having a bad day, bad week, or even a bad month, and reacts with little or no excitement to the grandiose displays of the child), the child borrows the self-esteem regulating function of the parent. This process Kohut refers to as 'transmuting internalization'.[84] The developing self needs to internalize the self-soothing function in order to be strong enough to cope with the empathic failures that are an inevitable part of interpersonal relationships in later life.

Kohut uses the term 'a cohesive self' to describe the person who is able to engage robustly and joyfully with the tasks and challenges of life. Cohesion in the self exists when there is relative harmony between talents and ambitions on the one hand (the grandiose self), and ideals and goals on the other (the idealizing self).

Shame – the feeling that one is inferior, flawed, defective – is a prominent feature in the symptomology of the patient diagnosed with narcissistic personality disorder. Andrew Morrison argues that it is, in fact, the *primary* affect associated with narcissism.[85]

Kohut suggests that the admiring, affirming and approving stance of the therapist over time facilitates increased self-acceptance and a higher level of self-esteem. Such mirroring is expressed through empathic attunement. Therapists must be able to consistently think and feel themselves into the inner world of experience of their clients in order to communicate understanding and acceptance. However, the therapist is not perfect. There will be empathic failures. These missteps in the empathic dance, far from being destructive, are actually therapeutic (provided they are acknowledged and appropriately worked through). Kohut provides this outline of the healing process:[86] (i) optimal frustration in the mirror transference resulting from inevitable small-scale empathic failures leads to (ii) transmuting internalization, which results in (iii) the laying down of the missing psychological structure. When the mental structure is built up the self becomes more cohesive, and a more cohesive self allows for self-esteem regulation in the face of one's own failures and the assaults of others. A stronger, more integrated self also means that there is relative harmony between its grandiose and idealizing sectors.

Empathy, countertransference, and taking the lead in the empathic dance

I want now to explore a different aspect of the relationship between empathy and therapeutic change. Empathy has a link to countertransference, though the two concepts need to be carefully distinguished. Countertransference is a phenomenon that is recognized and utilized in both psychodynamic and humanistic approaches to psychotherapy. It is a reaction that is stimulated by the client's transference. In classical psychoanalysis, transference is the unconscious transferral of certain dynamics from a conflictual childhood relationship to the current relationship with the analyst.

The meaning of the term 'countertransference' has changed in the years since Freud first introduced it.[87] He construed it as the analyst's unconscious affective responses to the analysand in general and to her transference in particular. That is to say, this transference reaction of the analyst was viewed by Freud as neurotic. Thus, he saw it as a hindrance to effective therapy. In the middle of the twentieth century psychoanalytic thinkers began to re-think both the conceptual understanding and therapeutic role of countertransference. Theorists such as Heimann,[88] Little[89] and Winnicott[90] construed the concept as including *all* the feelings and reactions that the analyst experiences in the interaction with the patient. This all-encompassing approach to countertransference is captured well in Kernberg's summary: '[Countertransference is] the total emotional reaction of the psychoanalyst to the patient in the treatment situation. [It is considered] that the analyst's conscious and unconscious reactions to the patient in the treatment situation are reactions to the patient's reality as well as to his transference, and also to the analyst's own reality needs as well as to his neurotic needs.'[91] Along with this shift in conceptualization of the notion came a new, more positive understanding of its place in therapy. It was no longer seen as an impediment to therapeutic goals, but rather as a consequence of its ability to reveal important data about the inner life of the patient, as a route to therapeutic change.[92]

Siegfried Zepf and Sebastian Hartmann,[93] and David Aitken,[94] along with a number of other authors, note that countertransference and empathy are related terms. The former authors suggest 'reserving the term "countertransference" for the analyst's preconscious object relations as activated in the present by the patient's transferences ...'[95] Empathic understanding, on the other hand, develops as a result of 'the analyst's capacity to use his countertransference reactions as a means of acquiring knowledge about another person's psychic life – not only to feel together with his patient ... but also to understand the patient's feelings in terms of the patient's internal frame of reference, which might still be unknown to the patient himself'.[96] Clearly, Zepf and Hartmann subscribe to the current thinking on countertransference – namely, that it is diagnostically and clinically useful.

Zepf provides a case study showing the close link between countertransference and empathy.[97] What is interesting in terms of our metaphor of the dance of empathy is that the case demonstrates the therapeutic value in not simply empathically resonating with clients' expressions of their inner worlds, but in also occasionally taking the lead to capture something that is currently just beyond their awareness. Writers on empathy sitting outside the psychoanalytic school make a similar observation. For example, Carl Rogers suggests that when the empathic therapist is on-song, that individual is 'so much inside the private world of the other that he or she can clarify not only the meanings of which the client is aware but even those just below the level of awareness'.[98] In his book *The Empathic Healer*, Michael Bennett is sceptical of approaches that posit empathy as capable of grasping unconscious material. However, he considers that while empathy is associated primarily with what is conscious, he recognizes that it can capture the unexpressed: '[T]he empathic therapist may give voice at times to ideas or feelings that the patient has failed to see as relevant or even present.'[99]

The case study in question involves a depressive patient who was raised mainly by her nanny, while her older sister was the primary focus of their mother's attention and affection. In the therapy session, the woman first told Zepf about a social gathering she had attended at which a matronly waitress had given her a big piece of Black Forest cake. She then recounted a story about a visit to her sister whom, as she emphasized time and again in the therapy sessions, she liked very much and also admired because she was talented, a woman of style and taste, and had made a success of her life.

As he listened, Zepf thought first of the matronly waitress who had given his patient a piece of cake. This in turn brought two things to his mind. The first thought concerned his dead aunt and his longing for her, and how, when he was little, the aunt had taken him from his home town because of the war in order to live with his grandparents. Second, he reflected on his patient's nanny, and her off-hand negative comments about this woman. The patient spoke about the many 'boring' games she had played with her nanny, about their 'tiring' walks together, about the 'stupid' folk songs that were part of the bedtime ritual, and about her parents dismissing the nanny because they thought she was guilty of theft. Zepf reports that he connected his longing for his aunt to the patient's longing for her lost nanny.

Zepf also informs us that in attempting to put himself in his patient's shoes, he remembered his cousin, whom he had spent time with at his grandparents' home during the war. He greatly admired this cousin for his sporting ability. It is also reported that the young Zepf and his cousin were both very fond of their grandfather. The cousin's father died young, and for this reason he was treated preferentially by the grandfather. Zepf called to mind his feeling of being 'hard done by' when one Christmas the other boy received a toy train, while he was only given a comb and mirror. The inequitable gift-giving was accompanied by this justification: 'After all, you get enough from your father.' Zepf's next reflection constitutes an empathic stepping beyond the current level of awareness of his patient:

> As I recalled this scene, it also occurred to me that at the time I had greatly envied my cousin for his present. I identified transitively the scene in which I was envious with the scenes described by my patient, seeing both as cases of envy. I considered this envy and the longing from the perspective of my understanding so far of the object-relations structure of my patient's life history – *an understanding that extended beyond her own self-understanding* – and felt that it was consistent with my ideas about her ... [emphasis added][100]

The communication of this insight concerning envy that was sitting outside the awareness of the patient, and was grasped empathically through countertransference, constituted a significant therapeutic moment.

Summary

We began with the suggestion that a useful way to think about empathy is provided by the philosophical conversation on social understanding. It was significant for us that some philosophers accent the role of embodiment in the interactive process of social cognition.

After surveying the three leading approaches to social cognition, we were grasped by the emphasis that theorists of PSM place on the body, direct perception, the interactional process and coordination. These elements are clearly very significant for a conversation about the counselling process in general and about empathic relating in particular.

In reflecting on empathic relating, we found it useful to work with the observation by PSM theorists that social cognition revolves around the moments of attunement and alienation. Drawing also on the dance metaphor that these theorists employ, we discussed the therapeutic value in being slightly out-of-step (that is, subtly altering counsellees' expressions of their inner states may lead to new insights), falling into missteps (in certain therapeutic contexts empathic failures are positive), and taking the lead (a highly empathic counsellor can grasp something that is outside the counsellee's awareness).

Our theological reflection centred on the question of whether or not there is a biblical and systematic theological justification for the notion of an empathic God. While developing a full answer to this important question was clearly beyond the scope of the chapter, we noted that it is very important for pastoral counsellors to give it serious attention. When the question 'Where is God in my suffering?' is raised in a pastoral conversation, pastors need to know how they will respond.

In the next chapter, our attention turns to deep listening. We will be guided in our thinking by the insights of Simone Weil on attention and of Thomas Merton on the true self.

Notes

1 See H. De Jaegher and E. Di Paolo, 'Participatory Sense-Making: An Enactive Approach to Social Cognition', *Phenomenology and the Cognitive Sciences* 6 (2007), pp. 485–507; H. De Jaegher, 'Social Understanding Through Direct Perception? Yes, by Interacting', *Consciousness and Cognition* 18 (2009), pp. 535–42; T. Fuchs and H. De Jaegher, 'Enactive Intersubjectivity: Participatory Sense-making and Mutual Incorporation', *Phenomenology and the Cognitive Sciences* 8 (2009), pp. 465–86; and L. Galbusera and T. Fuchs, 'Embodied Understanding: Discovering the Body from Cognitive Science to Psychotherapy', *In-Mind Italia* V, n.d., pp. 1–6, p. 1. Accessed from http://it.in-mind.org, 7/10/15.

2 H. Anderson and H. Goolishian, 'Human Systems as Linguistic Systems: Preliminary and Evolving Ideas about the Implications for Clinical Theory', *Family Process* 27 (1988), pp. 371–93, p. 371.

3 See M. Merleau-Ponty, *Phenomenology of Perception*, trans. Colin Smith (London: Routledge & Kegan Paul, 1965).

4 N. Murphy, *Bodies and Souls, or Spirited Bodies* (Cambridge: Cambridge University Press, 2006).

5 E. Gendlin, 'Thinking Beyond Patterns: Body, Language, and Situations', in B. den Ouden and M. Moen (eds), *The Presence of Feeling in Thought* (New York: Peter Lang, 1991), pp. 22–152; A. Ikemi, 'Carl Rogers and Eugene Gendlin on the Bodily Felt Sense: What They Share and Where They Differ', *Person-Centered and Experiential Psychotherapies* 4, no. 1 (2005), pp. 31–42.

6 M. Dekeyser, R. Elliott and M. Leijssen, 'Empathy in Psychotherapy: Dialogue and Embodied Understanding', in J. Decety and W. Ickes (eds), *The Social Neuroscience of Empathy* (Cambridge, MA: The MIT Press, 2009), pp. 125–38; J. C. Watson and L. S. Greenberg, 'Empathic Resonance: A Neuroscience Perspective', in Decety and Ickes, *The Social Neuroscience of Empathy*, pp. 125–38; M. Buchholz, 'Patterns of Empathy as Embodied Practice in Clinical Conversation: A Musical Dimension', *Frontiers in Psychology* 5 (2004), pp. 1–20.

7 M. Ross, 'Body Talk: Somatic Countertransference', *Psychodynamic Counseling* 6, no. 4 (2000), pp. 451–67; K. Gubb, 'Craving Interpretation: A Case of Somatic Countertransference', *British Journal of Psychotherapy* 30, no. 1 (2014), pp. 51-67.

8 Fuchs and De Jaegher, 'Enactive Intersubjectivity', p. 471.

9 Galbusera and Fuchs, 'Embodied Understanding', p. 1.

10 Every metaphor limps a little. We will be discussing skilled empathic moves, but our metaphorical dancer sometimes seems more like a beginner.

11 See D. Premack and G. Woodruff, 'Does the Chimpanzee Have a Theory of Mind?', *The Behavioral and Brain Sciences* 4 (1978), pp. 515–26.

12 See A. Gopnik and H. M. Wellman, 'Why the Child's Theory of Mind Really *Is* a Theory', *Mind and Language* 7, nos 1–2 (1992), pp. 145–71; A. Gopnik, 'The Scientist as Child', *Philosophy of Science* 63, no. 4 (1996), pp. 485–514; A. I. Goldman, *Simulating Minds: The Philosophy, Psychology, and Neuroscience of Mindreading* (Oxford: Oxford University Press, 2006), ch. 4.

13 See, for example, H. Wimmer and J. Perner, 'Beliefs about Beliefs: Representation and Constraining Function of Wrong Beliefs in Young Children's Understanding of Deception', *Cognition* 13 (1983), pp. 103–8; A. Gopnik and J. W. Astington, 'Children's Understanding of Representational Change and its Relation to the Understanding of False Belief and the Appearance–Reality Distinction', *Child Development* 59 (1988), pp. 26–37.

14 Cf. A. M. Leslie, O. Friedman and T. P. German, 'Core Mechanisms in "Theory of Mind"', *Trends in Cognitive Science* 8, no. 12 (2004), pp. 528–33, p. 528.

15 A. M. Leslie, 'Pretense and Representation: The Origins of "Theory of Mind"', *Psychological Review* 94, no. 1 (1987), pp. 412–26.

16 Leslie, Friedman and German, 'Core Mechanisms', p. 528.

17 R. Gordon, 'Folk Psychology as Mental Simulation', in *Stanford Encyclopedia of Philosophy*. Available at http://plato.stanford.edu/entries/folkpsych-simulation/.

18 See V. Gallese and A. Goldman, 'Mirror Neurons and the Simulation Theory of Mind-Reading', *Trends in Cognitive Sciences* 2, no. 12 (1998), pp. 493–501; Goldman, *Simulating Minds*, pp. 28–9.

19 See I. Ravenscroft, 'What Is It Like To Be Someone Else? Simulation and Empathy', *Ratio* XI (1998), pp. 170–85.

20 Ravenscroft, 'What Is It Like …?, p. 171.

21 Ravenscroft, 'What Is It Like …?, p. 171.

22 Frederick Adams argues quite persuasively against Ravenscroft that TT can in fact provide a plausible account of the empathic experience of an observer (he calls this person 'Al'). (See his article 'Empathy, Neural Imaging and the Theory versus Simulation Debate', *Mind and Language* 16, no. 4 (2001), pp. 368–92.) Adams contends that Al would scan his memory banks for experiences similar to the ones the distressed climber is experiencing. Adams gives a number of examples such as the following one: 'Al would … note that the climber is in a situation likely to produce exhaustion. Thus to know what it is like for the climber, Al would have to consult a sentence of TT of the form 'Extreme physical exhaustion feels similar to this _____ (Al consults episodic memories from Al's past about extreme exertion)' (p. 378). Adams concludes: 'Al will know what it is like to be a climber not because he has exactly the feelings the climber has, but because Al has enough experiences with enough similarity to those of the climber that Al and the climber share the same quality spaces' (p. 378).

23 Gallese and Goldman, 'Mirror Neurons'.

24 Gallese and Goldman, 'Mirror Neurons', p. 478.

25 For a helpful summary of these objections, see Fuchs and De Jaegher, 'Enactive Intersubjectivity', pp. 467–8.

26 See S. Gallagher, 'The Practice of Mind: Theory, Simulation, or Primary Interaction?' *Journal of Consciousness Studies* 8 (2001), pp. 83–108; and S. Gallagher, 'Direct Perception in the Intersubjective Context', *Consciousness and Cognition* 17 (2008), pp. 535–43.

27 M. Scheler, *The Nature of Sympathy* (London: Routledge, Kegan Paul, 1954), pp. 260–1; cited in Gallagher, 'Direct Perception', p. 538.

28 L. Wittgenstein, in G. E. M. Anscombe and G. H. von Wright (eds), *Zettel* (London: Blackwell, 1967) section 229; cited in Gallagher, 'Direct Perception', p. 538.

29 See Fuchs and De Jaegher, 'Enactive Intersubjectivity', p. 468.

30 Cf. Galbusera and Fuchs, 'Embodied Understanding', p. 5.

31 De Jaegher, 'Social Understanding', p. 537.

32 See De Jaegher and Di Paolo, 'Participatory Sense-Making'; De Jaegher, 'Social Understanding'; Fuchs and De Jaegher, 'Enactive Intersubjectivity'.

33 De Jaegher and Di Paolo, 'Participatory Sense-Making', p. 490.

34 De Jaegher and Di Paolo, 'Participatory Sense-Making', p. 490.

35 See Fuchs and De Jaegher, 'Enactive Intersubjectivity', p. 474.

36 Galbusera and Fuchs, 'Embodied Understanding', p. 1.

37 Fuchs and De Jaegher, 'Enactive Intersubjectivity', p. 470.

38 Cf. De Jaegher, 'Social Understanding', p. 540.

39 M. Barnett, 'Empathy and Related Responses in Children', in N. Eisenberg and J. Strayer (eds), *Empathy and Its Development* (Cambridge: Cambridge University Press, 1990), pp. 146–62.

40 J. Decety and C. Lamm, 'Human Empathy through the Lens of Neuroscience', *The Scientific World Journal* 6 (2006), pp. 1146–63, p. 1146.

41 N. Eisenberg, 'Emotion, Regulation, and Moral Development', *Annual Review of Psychology* 51 (2000), pp. 665–97, p. 671.

42 C. Rogers, 'A Theory of Therapy, Personality, and Interpersonal Relationships as Developed in the Client-centered Framework', in S. Koch (ed.), *Psychology: A Study of Science: Vol. 3. Formulation of the Person and the Social Context* (New York: McGraw-Hill, 1959), pp. 184–256, p. 210.

43 A. J. Clark, 'Empathy and Sympathy: Therapeutic Distinctions in Counselling', *Journal of Mental Health Counselling* 32, no. 2 (2010), pp. 95-101.

44 Clark, 'Empathy and Sympathy', pp. 96–7.

45 Dekeyser, Elliott and Leijessen, 'Empathy in Psychotherapy', pp. 113–14.

46 T. L. Chartrand and J. A. Bargh, 'The Chameleon Effect: The Perception–Behaviour Link and Social Interaction', *Journal of Personality and Social Psychology* 76 (1999), no. 6, pp. 893–910; J. L. Lakin and T. L. Chartrand, 'Using Nonconscious Behavioral Mimicry to Create Affiliation and Rapport', *Psychological Science* 14, no. 4 (2003), pp. 334–9.

47 Chartrand and Bargh, 'The Chameleon Effect', p. 893.

48 Chartrand and Bargh, 'The Chameleon Effect', p. 905.

49 Buchholz, 'Patterns of Empathy', p. 1.

50 J. Coutinho, P. Silva and J. Decety, 'Neurosciences, Empathy, and Healthy Interpersonal Relationships: Recent Findings and Implications for Counseling Psychology', *Journal of Counseling Psychology* 61, no. 4 (2014), pp. 541–8, p. 545.

51 D. Purnell, 'Pastoral Ministry and the Fleshly Body', *Pastoral Psychology* 53, no. 1 (2004), pp. 81–5, p. 81.

52 R. L. Landau, 'And the Least of These is Empathy', in H. M. Spiro *et al.* (eds), *Empathy and the Practice of Medicine: Beyond Pills and the Scalpel* (New Haven, IN: Yale University Press, 1993), pp. 103–9.

53 See M. Hojat *et al.*, 'Physician Empathy: Definitions, Components, Measurement, and Relationships to Gender and Speciality', *The American Journal of Psychiatry* 159, no. 9 (2000), pp. 1563–9.

54 See J. Halpern, 'Empathy: Using Resonance Emotions in the Service of Curiosity', in H. M. Spiro *et al.* (eds), *Empathy and the Practice of Medicine* (New Haven, CT: Yale University Press, 1993), pp. 160–73; Halpern, 'What is Clinical Empathy?', *Journal of General Internal Medicine* 18 (2003), pp. 670–4; J. L. Coulehan, 'Tenderness and Steadiness: Emotions in Medical Practice', *Literature and Medicine* 14, no. 2 (1995), pp. 222–36.

55 Halpern, 'Empathy: Using Resonance Emotions', p. 167.

56 J. Robbins, 'Theological Table-Talk: A Pastoral Approach to Evil', *Theology Today* 44 (January 1988), pp. 488–95, p. 491.

57 Aquinas, *Summa Theologiae*, 1a.3.1.

58 Aquinas, *Summa Theologiae*, 1a.3.1.

59 Aquinas, *Summa Theologiae*, 1a.4.2.

60 Aquinas, *Summa Theologiae*, 1a.9.1.

61 See T. Weinandy, *Does God Suffer?* (Edinburgh: T&T Clark, 2000), p. 130.

62 K. Depoortere, *A Different God* (Leuven: Peeters Publishers; and Grand Rapids: Eerdmans, 1995), p. 91.

63 Aquinas, *Summa Theologia*, 1a.20.1.

64 See Weinandy, *Does God Suffer?*, pp. 115–71.

65 Weinandy, *Does God Suffer?*, p. 119.

66 Weinandy, *Does God Suffer?*, p. 128.

67 In tracking the suffering of God through the Hebrew Scriptures, I use Wilfred Harrington's helpful outline. See his *The Tears of God* (Collegeville, MN: The Liturgical Press, 1992), chs 1 and 2.

68 K. Barth, *Church Dogmatics* II/1 (Edinburgh: T&T Clark, 1957), p. 273.

69 See Harrington, *The Tears of God*, p. 20.

70 See J. Moltmann, *The Crucified God* (London: SCM Press, 1974), pp. 241–9; and J. Moltmann, *The Trinity and the Kingdom of God* (London: SCM Press, 1981), pp. 75–82.

71 See Moltmann, *The Crucified God*, pp. 241–3; and Moltmann, *The Trinity and the Kingdom*, p. 75.

72 F. Young, *Face to Face* (Edinburgh: T&T Clark, 1990), p. 238.

73 Young, *Face to Face*, p. 238.

74 Young, *Face to Face*, p. 237.

75 Young, *Face to Face*, pp. 238–9.

76 Young, *Face to Face*, p. 239.

77 A. N. Whitehead, *Process and Reality* (New York: Harper & Row, 1960), p. 532.

78 See H. Kohut, *The Restoration of the Self* (New York: International Universities Press, 1977); and H. Kohut, *How Does Analysis Cure?* (Chicago, IL: University of Chicago Press, 1984).

79 Cf. V. Gallese, M. N. Eagle and P. Migone, 'Intentional Attunement: Mirror Neurons and the Neural Underpinnings of Interpersonal Relations', *Journal of the American Psychoanalytic Association* 55, no. 1 (2007), pp. 131–76, p. 151.

80 Gallese, Eagle, Migone, 'Intentional Attunement', p. 151.

81 Kohut, *Restoration of the Self*, p. 177.

82 Kohut, *Restoration of the Self*, p. 178.

83 Gallese, Eagle and Migone, 'Intentional Attunement', pp. 161–2.

84 See H. Kohut, *The Analysis of the Self* (New York: International Universities Press, 1971), p. 49.

85 See A. P. Morrison, 'Shame, Ideal Self, and Narcissism', in A. P. Morrison (ed.), *Essential Papers on Narcissism* (New York: New York University Press, 1986), pp. 348–71.

86 See Kohut, *How Does Analysis Cure?*, pp. 98–9.

87 S. Freud, 'The Future Prospect of Psychoanalytic Therapy', in *Standard Edition of the Complete Psychological Works of Sigmund Freud,* Volume XI (1910) (London: Hogarth Press, 1971), pp. 141–51.

88 P. Heimann, 'On Countertransference', *International Journal of Psychoanalysis* 31 (1950), pp. 81–4.

89 M. I. Little, 'Countertransference and the Patient's Response to It', *International Journal of Psychoanalysis* 32 (1951), pp. 32–40.

90 D. Winnicott, 'Hate in the Countertransference', in *Collected Papers through Paediatrics to Psychoanalysis* (New York: Basic Books, 1958), pp. 194–203.

91 O. Kernberg, 'Notes on Countertransferences', *Journal of the American Psychoanalytic Association*, 13, no. 1 (1965), pp. 38–56, p. 38.

92 See S. A. Peabody and C. J. Gelso, 'Countertransference and Empathy: The Complex Relationship between Two Divergent Concepts in Counseling', *Journal of Counseling Psychology* 29, no. 3 (1982), pp. 240–5; Gubb, 'Craving Interpretation'.

93 S. Zepf and S. Hartmann, 'Some Thoughts on Empathy and Counter-transference', *Journal of the American Psychoanalytic Association* 56, no. 3 (2008), pp. 741–68.

94 D. E. Aitken, 'The Experiences of Countertransference as Empathy, Attunement, and Mutual Regression in Individual Psychotherapy: An Intersubjective, Psychoanalytic Study', unpublished doctoral thesis, Chicago School of Professional Psychology, 2014.

95 Zepf and Hartmann, 'Some Thoughts on Empathy', p. 757.

96 Zepf and Hartmann, 'Some Thoughts on Empathy', p. 757.

97 Zepf and Hartmann, 'Some Thoughts on Empathy', pp. 758–9.

98 C. Rogers, *A Way of Being* (Boston, IL: Houghton Mifflin, 1980), p. 116.

99 M. Bennett, *The Empathic Healer* (Waltham, MA: Academic Press, 2001), p. 10.

100 Zepf and Hartmann, 'Some Thoughts on Empathy', p. 759.

3

Deep Listening, or Being Formed in the Discipline of Attention

It is patently obvious that a primary task for the pastoral counsellor is attentive listening. However, those who have never done any counselling usually underestimate how difficult and demanding listening is. Jeanne Ellin has it just right when she says this: 'This is a simple-sounding task – many of us like to think we are good listeners. Just sitting and listening sounds like one of those dream jobs like mattress tester or taster in a brewery.'[1] It is true that listening comes more naturally to some than to others, but the view that it is a simple task is very far wide of the mark.

Attentive listening involves 'hearing the counselees' stories in all their experiential richness and complexity'.[2] The question that immediately arises is this: How does one become attuned in this deep way to counselees and their personal stories? The thinker who has helped me the most in this regard is Simone Weil (1909–43). In order to give you a sense of why I have chosen her to guide us in unpacking attentive listening, I submit this quote: 'Those who are unhappy have no need for anything in the world but people capable of giving them their attention. The capacity to give one's attention to a sufferer is a very rare and difficult thing; it is almost a miracle; it *is* a miracle. Nearly all those who think they have this capacity do not possess it.'[3] Already we have learnt something that is vitally important: do not underestimate how difficult it is to attend to a person who is in pain and distress.

Weil has been described as 'a mystic without a church, a political activist without a party, a wandering Jew with a Christian faith'.[4] For the majority of her short life, Simone adopted an agnostic stance. She took the view that there simply is not enough information available to make an informed decision one way or the other concerning God's existence. However, in her late twenties she had a beautiful and intense experience of the love of God. She describes it thus: 'In my arguments about the insolubility of the problem of God I had never foreseen the possibility of that, of a real contact, person to person, here below, between a human being and God ... [I]n this sudden possession of me by Christ, neither my senses nor my imagination had any part; I only felt in the midst of my suffering the presence of love, like that which one can read in the smile on a beloved face' (*WG*, p. 20). We find in her later reflections an intense interest in the Gospels, and especially in the passion of Christ.

Weil is a challenging and unconventional thinker. The ideas she generates are unsettling, provocative, and most often cryptically expressed. Many readers of Weil's work report that they find it difficult to pin her conceptualizations down; the meaning is not immediately clear. But the wrestling is thoroughly worth it. She produces insights that are sparkling lights and deeply transformative of one's consciousness.

Her work on attention[5] is no exception. Attention involves fully opening yourself to that which is before you. In order to attend in this way, it is necessary to exert negative effort (to be passively active), to wait and be receptive, and to empty out the 'I' (to be 'decreated').

Though I clearly have a deep appreciation for Weil's thought, I do not embrace it fully. Some of her theological ideas I reject completely. I have in mind such things as her positing of Necessity rather than Providence, and her categorical rejection of miracles. When it comes to ideas that relate directly to the current topic, I take issue with the way in which she formulates decreation. I fully accept the need for self-emptying in order to advance in the spiritual life. However, I believe that when it comes to this evacuative process a distinction such as Thomas Merton makes between the false and true selves, or that Paul draws between the inmost self that is oriented to the divine will and the slave-self that is in bondage to sin, needs to be employed. Weil's language is extreme; it gives the impression that she intends the literal destruction of the 'I'. It is not the decreation of the self *in toto* that is required, but rather of the sinful tendencies in the false self.

Having offered this caveat, we will move on to a presentation of the plan for applying Weil's notion of attention in the counselling context. In what follows, the three facets of attention are outlined – negative effort, waiting and self-emptying – and it is shown how they help us in understanding the nature of attentive listening. An important part of this process will be drawing out and commenting on the theological dimension in Weil's ideas, but first port of call is reflection on attention as negative effort.

Attention as negative effort

My first degree was in engineering, and when I came to the study of theology and the humanities I was very aware of my deficits. I had devoted most of my secondary education to the study of maths, physics, chemistry and biology. At university I progressed to algebra, calculus, computer science, materials science, and soil and water engineering (I trained in agricultural engineering). There was virtually no place in my education for the great historical works, the literary masterpieces, and the brilliant works of philosophy. (I say 'virtually no place' rather than 'no place' because engineering students at my institution were required to take two elective courses in the humanities.)

At the beginning of my new direction in tertiary education I had a strong sense of needing to fill in the gaps. I remember buying a copy of Tolstoy's *Anna Karenina*. I was motivated not so much by the thought that I would have the wonderful privilege and joy of engaging with a masterfully told story. In fact, I didn't really expect to become absorbed in the plot, to get caught up in the sexual tension, or gain fresh insight into human frailty or Russian cultural mores in the latter part of the nineteenth century. At the time of making the purchase I didn't actually know what the book was about. But I decided to buy and read the book because it had the reputation of being a great work of literature. It presented as the sort of book that a young man embarking on the study of theology and the humanities really should read. Almost from the start, it was clear to me that this was not my kind of novel; it simply wasn't engaging me. But I manfully ploughed on, determined that I would read this novel that was considered essential reading for any truly cultured person. I almost made it to the end. After many months of going to it on and off, I had about 80 pages to go and I stopped. I just couldn't bring myself to read one more page. My wife, intrigued that I was reading *Anna Karenina*, asked me about the story. Though I had read most of it, I could barely remember anything.

What would Simone Weil say about my failed foray into the world of great literature? She would no doubt remark that I had confused attention with 'muscular effort' (*WG*, p. 54). In her essay on attention in school studies, she has this to say:

> If one says to one's pupils: 'Now you must pay attention', one sees them contracting their brows, holding their breath, stiffening their muscles. If after two minutes they are asked what they have been paying attention to, they cannot reply. They have been concentrating on nothing. They have not been paying attention. They have been contracting their muscles (*WG*, p. 54).

She goes on to say that this kind of muscular effort is 'entirely barren' (WG, p. 55). When we muscle up on a task, so to speak, the result is that we get tired. This creates the false impression of actually having done some work. But '[t]iredness has nothing to do with work' (WG, p. 55).

According to Simone, will power helps the person doing intellectual work only a little. The learning process is led by desire, and by pleasure and joy in the work. 'The joy of learning is as indispensable in study as breathing is in running. Where it is lacking there are no real students, but only poor caricatures of apprentices who, at the end of their apprenticeship, will not even have a trade' (WG, p. 55).

It may seem that Simone is arguing here for something that experience tells us simply is not true. Students by the tens of thousands muscle their way through courses and programmes. Desire for learning is not what drives them; they get almost no pleasure and joy out of their studies. Simone is of course aware of this. She distinguishes between learning and passing examinations: 'Studies conducted in such a way [through muscular effort] can sometimes succeed academically from the point of view of gaining marks and passing examinations, but that is in spite of the effort and thanks to natural gifts; moreover such studies are never of any use' (WG, p. 55).

I find a direct correlation between Weil's concept of attention led by desire and really hearing the counsellee. Counsellors who engage in highly attentive listening, generally speaking, love doing what they do. Though inevitably there are times when intense listening is a struggle, most often they find deep satisfaction in hearing and responding to the stories others tell them. For them, engaging with the subtleties and complexity of another's life-world and making sense of it is an interesting challenge.

Listening intently to another person is demanding, challenging and draining. Sometimes the stories are dull and boring and the task unrewarding. The job is difficult; that goes without saying. It is also true that there are days when virtually all counsellors feel they are not up for the task. But the salient fact is that, for the most part, the act of listening carefully to a person at a point of crisis is something that an effective counsellor wants to do. Counsellors count it as a privilege that vulnerable, distressed people trust them enough to share their stories and their lives. Being led by desire and experiencing joy in one's counselling work are the necessary conditions of attentive listening. Attention in counselling is counterfeit if it is driven by muscular effort.

I do not mean to create the impression that a pastoral counsellor must float at every moment on a cloud of joy and passion. Counsellors are flesh and blood beings; they are not divine spirits who never fall from the perfection of love and attention. In speaking about his love of engaging in the therapeutic process, Rollo May once commented that he looked forward to being with his clients, but added the rider, 'depending on how much sleep I have had the night before'. The well-known British psychotherapist Robert Hobson was honest enough to admit that sometimes the intensity of the therapeutic conversation is so great that it all becomes too much for him. At that point, he tunes out for a moment and 'thinks about the cricket'.

What these personal revelations from May and Hobson tell us is that counselling requires effort. One human being aims to be fully present to another; it is a process that needs to be energized in some way. While Simone is insistent that muscular effort helps not a bit in paying attention, she also says that '[a]ttention is an effort, the greatest of all efforts' (WG, p. 55). However, the exertion of which she speaks is a negative one. For a long time I struggled to understand what Weil could possibly mean by the term 'negative effort'. Some of the authors writing on it failed to help me because they simply paraphrased or quoted what Weil herself says. Her only elaboration on the term is that 'it does not involve tiredness' (WG, p. 55). This tells us something – namely, that attending through negative effort is energizing in some way. But we are still none the wiser about the exact nature of negative effort. I am helped in this regard by the way in which Angelo Caranfa associates the term with 'passive activity'.[6] Caranfa does not elaborate on his offering. In my mind, there is a connection with the Taoist concept of wu wei or 'effortless effort'. It expresses the idea that sometimes the most effective action is non-action. It is effortless effort, acting spontaneously, and in tune with nature.[7] While wu wei can certainly be translated as non-action (wu means 'not' or 'no', while wei means 'to do' or 'to act'), the Eastern religions expert Ray Billington points out that '[a] more accurate translation of wu wei would be … "spontaneous action", not far removed from Zen's idea of hitting the target without taking aim. It means behaving intuitively, even unintentionally …'[8] There is clearly not a complete match between wu wei and Weil's concept of negative effort, but there are definitely similarities and points of connection. Attention is a spontaneous and instinctive action; it cannot be forced. In attending to an object or to a person, we need to be active through passivity. We cannot force meaning out of that which is in front of us; we must wait for the meaning to emerge. The object needs to show itself, so to speak. Mary Dietz captures this aspect nicely when she comments: 'For Weil, attention is a quality of openness to the world, a quiescent readiness toward the "out there", without any solid expectation of what one will find.'[9] Attention requires us to wait upon the other to reveal herself to us.

Attention as waiting

Prayer is first and foremost about waiting on God. According to Simone, '[i]t is the orientation of all the attention of which the soul is capable towards God' (*WG*, p. 51). The most important question is not what I must say to God but, rather, what does God want to say to me?

Attention is like prayer; it is a contemplative act. In contemplation, one maintains a state of suspension. The French words *attente* (wait) and *attention* (attention) have the same etymology. They both refer to being in a state of tension in relation to an object that has yet to show itself.[10] Weil puts it this way: 'Attention consists of suspending our thought, leaving it detached, empty and ready to be penetrated by the object, it means holding in our minds ...' (*WG*, p. 56).

Weil's insight that if we really want to know an object, a phenomenon, or a person we need to be open and receptive to it is an insight shared by other important thinkers. For example, Jay McDaniel champions an 'acoustic' mode of knowing over the 'seeing' model of reductionist science.[11] In the form of deep listening that McDaniel has in mind, there is no sharp separation between the observer and that which is observed. Listening to the world around us can be compared to the experience of shutting one's eyes and listening to a piece of music. The music is 'out there'; it is being broadcast from an external source of some kind. But it is also 'in here'. When people really listen to music, the sounds are inside them at the same time as they sit outside them.

The kind of deep listening that McDaniel has in mind requires a receptive stance. The person needs to wait to be spoken to. There is a crucial distinction between listening to music being played and really hearing it in the depths of one's being. If the piece is really to speak to the soul one needs a 'quiescent readiness'.

Another notion that is quite close to Weil's idea of attention that is empty and ready is Bernard Meland's 'appreciative awareness'. In order to understand the phenomenon of lived religion as fully and deeply as possible, Meland contends that one must wait upon it in an attitude of expectancy. 'In an act of reflection', he writes, 'there is not simply a direct act of observation, but, as it were, a waiting and an expectancy that what is so envisaged will disclose its fuller pattern of meaning.'[12] If one is to glean 'a sense of the *More*' in the reports of religious experience that one is attending to, it is important not to let preconceived ideas or categories 'impose their image' on the realities under observation.[13]

In order to be a pastoral counsellor who really hears the other, it is essential that one works out of a waiting stance. It takes time for the patterns in the life-world of the counsellee to manifest; this process cannot be rushed. It is uncomfortable living with confusion and messiness. There is a natural urge to bring order out of the chaos. What is crucial here is to take a receptive rather than an active stance in the listening process. The deep meaning in what counsellees are saying about themselves, their view of the world and of God, their pain, their confusion, their struggles and fears, their hopes and joys, needs to be allowed to unfold. The patterns need to show themselves; they cannot be forced through the grid of one's own particular way of seeing the world.

In making this last comment, it is not intended to give the impression that I think it is possible to throw off our unique experience of life, our preconceptions, biases and personal values in order to receive in some pure, 'objective' way what the other is communicating. We have, after all, learnt something from Gadamer.[14] Our horizon, consisting of personal and cultural experience, knowledge and values plays an essential role in interpreting what is in front of us. Malcolm Evans seems to have this insight of Gadamer's in mind when he notes that being anchored in one's personal view of reality is foundational in appreciative awareness as depicted by Meland.[15] Evans refers to his own experience in making the point. In connection with the writing of his article, he read for a second time J. D. Salinger's novel *The Catcher in the Rye*. When he first read Salinger's novel, he was a junior high principal. Holden Caulfield seemed to him to capture the experience of the many confused and troubled young adolescents that he felt affection for and spent quite a bit of time worrying about. The close experience with the 12–15-year-olds he interacted with day in and day out was the basis for his emotionally engaged reading of *The Catcher in the Rye*. In coming to the book for a second time decades later, other experiences influenced his reception. This time he was thinking more analytically and his sensitivity was dulled. There would be no repeat of the moving experience and personal connection at a deep level that he had when serving as a junior high principal.

In attending to the other, what pastoral counsellors hear will be shaped to a significant extent by their personal horizon; there is no pure, objective access to the experience and perspectives of another person. What is vitally important is to engage in a self-reflexive way, to bring as much awareness as possible to the pastoral conversation of how our personal frame of reference impacts on what we hear. With full awareness that we come to the conversation anchored in our personal view of the world, we endeavour to be as open, receptive and expectant as possible.

This attitude of openness and receptivity is grounded in a capacity for self-emptying. If the ego fills the interpersonal space, there is no room left for the other to be heard. The third element in Weil's notion of attention is decreation.

Attention and self-emptying

Renunciation is a major theme in Weil's writings. The spiritual person is the humble one who consents to be nothing. Such people contract their ego in order to make maximum space available for others and for God. The renunciation that a human being engages in is an imitation of the divine renunciation in creation.[16] In the creative act, God made space for the universe and thereby renounced being everything. Thus, reasons Weil, the 'I' needs to withdraw from the position it has assumed at the centre of the universe.

Here Weil presents something that is very similar to the Kabbalistic notion of *zimsum* that is associated with Isaac Luria. *Zimsum* refers to the contraction within God that is required for the creation of the world to take place. Before the world was, God was the fullness of existence. The original state was therefore not one of *nihil*. In primordial time, all is God; there is no empty space. Luria posits the notion that God, in order to produce the space that is required for the creative act, releases a portion of God's being. This idea has found its way into Weil's thought. 'For God, the Creation consisted not in extending himself but in withdrawing. He refrained "from commanding wherever he had power".'[17] The creation, then, represents an abdication. What God requires of us, according to Weil, is a similar kind of abdication. The 'I' needs to give up its position at the centre of the world.

The destruction of the 'I' Weil refers to as 'decreation'. For Weil, the ultimate spiritual act is 'to make something created pass into the uncreated' (*GG*, p. 28). The 'uncreated' Weil construes as reality – being in its pure mode. It is God's way of being. Uncreated love is God's love for God's self; it is our privilege to share in it. Weil puts it this way: 'At each moment of our existence is God's love for us. But God can only love himself. His love for us is love for himself through us' (*GG*, p. 32). Since God is greater without us, God asks of us 'our acceptance not to exist' (*GG*, p. 32). God created each person in order that the individual might decreate.

Uncreated love – the love between the Father and the Son – passes through creation. A truly spiritual existence requires that a person assume a proper role in relation to this wondrous event. Weil uses the metaphors of 'consent', a 'screen' and 'the eye' to convey what is required. They all point to the same reality: genuinely spiritual people become as nothing to ensure that they in no way interfere with the great event of love that defines the existence of every created thing. Such people view themselves as simply the medium through which God loves God's self. The divine love passes through creation. 'All we are asked to do is consent to its

77

passing through. We are nothing else but this consent' (*FLN*, p. 102). We consent to be the eye that receives the light of divine love. 'God as an object of love is the light', says Weil, 'and the human soul is the eye, the organ of vision; it is the organ of the individual "I". But when the individual "I" has become effaced, without the organ having lost its virtue, the soul then becomes an organ of God's vision.'[18] We must consent to withdraw lest we impede the divine love. The human person is like a screen that needs to be removed so that God is able to see through (*NB*, p. 364).

Simone Weil traces the source of our spiritual malaise to the fact that we were born 'wrong side upward' (*GG*, p. 34). We came into the world with a tendency to elevate that which is lowest. Base tendencies such as a desire for social prestige, pride and self-sufficiency are promoted to the top. The result is that the 'I' is puffed up and there is no room for God. The direction of redemption, according to Weil, is downwards. 'We must become nothing,' she avers, 'we must go down to the vegetative level; it is there that God is bread' (*GG*, p. 36). Simone makes a distinction between 'vegetative' and 'supplementary' energy. Supplementary energy is connected with a giving of self that is controlled, kept within the bounds of comfort. The person who gives at this level has not sacrificed anything essential.[19] That is, such people are still able to rely on their resources for emotional, physical and spiritual survival; the 'I' is not seriously challenged. To go down to the vegetative level, on the other hand, is to be totally spent. At this point, one becomes acutely aware of one's reliance on God. Weil puts it this way:

> It is the supplementary energy that places the soul in the sphere of the conditional. One says 'I'm prepared to go two kilometres if I can get an egg'. So one has the strength for two kilometres in spite of feeling tired. But total exhaustion is the feeling: 'I couldn't go ten meters, even to save my life'. This corresponds to a state in which the vegetative energy is all that is left ...
>
> It is then that the soul cries 'I must ...!'
>
> I must see so-and-so! I must rest! I must drink! This pain must abate for just a moment! (*FLN*, p. 233).

For Weil, the movement downwards should only stop when one has reached the bottom. That is, the 'I' needs to shrink until it becomes nothing. As long as a person keeps something in reserve, the reaching out for God will be weak, half-hearted. The one who has gone down to the vegetative level cries out, 'I must have the bread of life; I cannot take another step without it.'

Decreation has a central place in attention. Weil makes the link in this way:

> We liberate energy in ourselves, but it constantly reattaches itself. How are we to liberate it entirely? We have to desire that it should be done in us – to desire it truly – simply to desire it, not to try to accomplish it. For every attempt in that direction is vain and has to be dearly paid for. In such a work all that I call 'I' has to be passive. Attention alone – that attention which is so full that the 'I' disappears – is required of me. I have to deprive all that I call 'I' of the light of my attention and turn it on to that which cannot be conceived (*GG* p. 118).

Attention 'consists of suspending our thought, leaving it detached, empty, and ready to be penetrated by the object' (*WG*, p. 56). This mode of engaging with the world necessarily involves shifting the gaze away from the 'I'. A genuine encounter with an object takes a people out of themselves. It requires the emptying out of all desires (except the desire to engage with the object on its own terms) and imaginative projections. A person must create a vacant space to receive the other. Attention is thus an act of receptivity. The condition of the possibility of receptivity is psychic emptying out: 'Only when one has suspended a way of seeing that has the values of the personal self or ego as its interpretative principle can one approach reality instead of illusion.'[20]

I certainly take Weil's point that in order to fully attend to an object or a person it is necessary to engage in a process of self-emptying to make space for the communication of the other. But is it true that such self-emptying must be a total decreation? Let's be clear about what decreation is. I have discussed it above, but some of Weil's aphorisms bring the concept into sharper relief. She says, for instance, that '[t]here is absolutely no other free act which is given to us to accomplish – only the destruction of the "I"' (*GG*, p. 26). In another place, she writes: 'If only I knew how to disappear there would be a perfect union of love between God and the earth I tread, the sea I hear ...' (*GG*, p. 42). Is she really saying that the world would be a better place if she simply disappeared? Does she actually believe that her presence in the world is an impediment to the love relationship God has with the world? I do not think that Weil intends us to draw these conclusions. It is certainly true that her language suggests nihilism. But I think it is more appropriate to view her pronouncements in a metaphorical way rather than a literal one.

Simone's extreme formulation of the concept of decreation consti- tutes an impediment to understanding. For this reason, I prefer Thomas

Merton's reflections on self-emptying. Merton discusses the way in which the attributes in the false self need to pass into nothingness. The false self is the one that is imprinted with sin. Its essential characteristics are ego, pride, hard-heartedness and selfishness. It is these tendencies that block attentive listening. I will postpone the discussion of exactly how they do this. For now, I want to reflect more on Merton's notions of the true and false selves.

As just indicated, Merton recognized very clearly that the central spiritual task is to empty out the destructive elements in the self. Pride and egoism expand the self to proportions it was never meant to have; the result is that there is little or no space for God. The path to spiritual fullness involves radical self-emptying. 'For I know I will possess all things', writes Merton, 'if I am empty of all things, and only You can at once empty me of all things and fill me with Yourself; the Life of all that lives and the Being in Whom everything exists.'[21] When Merton says that he desires to be 'empty of all things', he clearly means all things that bend him away from love of God and neighbour. He does not want to be emptied of faith, hope and love. What needs to be emptied out is the false self. This task, of course, can never be finalized. The aim is to so open oneself to God in love and obedience that the true self that lies deep within will become more expansive and shape one's way of being in the world in conformity to Christ.

In drawing close to God, the Christian both comes to know the divine will and is empowered to live it out. To refuse the divine life and purpose is to contradict one's self. This self-contradiction that characterizes the false self is the result of sin: 'To say I was born in sin is to say I came into the world with a false self. I came into existence under a sign of contradiction, being someone that I was never intended to be and therefore a denial of what I am supposed to be.'[22] Every one of us, observes Merton, is 'shadowed' by an illusory person. It is an illusion to believe that one can live outside God's will. An attempt to do so puts a person outside reality, outside life.

The motive forces behind the illusion are pride, egoism and self-assertion. People think of themselves as a 'completely free autonomous self, with unlimited possibilities'.[23] Such individuals act as if they are gods, with everything within their reach. They think that they are truly free, but the truth, says Merton, is that they are gripped by a 'psychic and spiritual cramp'.[24]

Every person, to a greater or lesser extent, has a tendency towards pride, lovelessness and self-assertion. Everyone suffers from an inner cramp. It is through prayer and contemplation, observes Merton, that we are able to free it up. In coming before God in a spirit of poverty, honesty and openness, a person comes to see the ego and the trickery of the false self: '[T]he dimensions of prayer in solitude are those of man's ordinary anguish, his self-searching, his moments of nausea at his own vanity, falsity and capacity for betrayal. Far from establishing one in an unassailable narcissistic security, the way of prayer brings us face to face with the sham and indignity of the false self …'[25]

We have just seen that Merton connects the false self to a tendency to see oneself as a god. In *The New Man* (1961), a new image appears. The picture shifts from striving to be like God to attempting to steal from God. Echoing Prometheus, the false self tries to steal life and meaning from God. In a perverse manner, those with a 'Promethean self' think that their spiritual perfection is something that God wants to stop them from attaining. Such people resort to stealing their fire from heaven. They should be focused on God's glory; instead they are preoccupied with their own perfection. Merton finds here the image of humanity's psychological situation. We are 'guilty, rebellious, frustrated, unsure of [ourselves], of [our] gifts and of [our] own strength, alienated, yet seeking to assert [ourselves]'.[26]

The twin problems are pride and self-centredness, and like a dog chasing its tail they draw us into a circle of emptiness and futility. '[P]ride is simply a form of supreme and absolute subjectivity. It sees all things from the viewpoint of a limited, individual self that is constituted as the centre of the universe.'[27] Pride and selfishness, when they go unchecked, suck a person into a world of ever-decreasing proportions. In the end, this world is empty and meaningless. Life and meaning are found only when one is hidden in Christ. In drawing near to Christ we find ourselves, and all that we need to be fully alive is given freely to us. Pride stops us from opening ourselves to this grace.

In order to lose ourselves, we need to embrace spiritual poverty. Humility, Merton stresses time and again, is the condition of the possibility of coming to the true self. In humbling ourselves we experience true freedom.[28] It is the freedom of finally finding ourselves in God. This is our first and last task: '[T]here is only one problem on which all my existence, my peace and my happiness depend: to discover myself in discovering God. If I find Him, I will find myself; and if I find my true self, I will find Him.'[29]

The true self is animated by the love and grace of Christ. Merton was very fond of Paul's affirmation in Galatians: '[I]t is no longer I who live, but it is Christ who lives in me' (2.20a). In order to fully attend to the other, one needs to be compassionate, open, humble, patient and other-centred. These are some of the qualities of the true self. Christ alive in the soul of the pastoral counsellor infuses that person with these all-important attributes. Clearly, the true self needs to be nurtured; it most certainly does not need to be emptied out.

One wonders why Weil failed to recognize the bipolar nature of the self. In her writings, she barely acknowledges that part of the human being that Merton refers to as the true self. The most likely explanation in my view is that her propensity for self-loathing[30] created a blind-spot in her vision of herself and of humankind in general. When one reads her scathing and dismissive self-appraisals in her letters, it comes as no surprise to find that she has such a pessimistic view of people. In one letter, for example, she says, 'I am really nothing in it at all. If one could imagine any possibility of error in God, I should think that it has all happened to me by mistake. But perhaps God likes to use cast-away objects, waste, rejects' (WG, p. 24). Later in the same letter she talks of feeling 'hatred and repulsion' towards herself (WG, p. 26). To give one last example, in another letter she denigrates herself in these terms: 'I am such a poor unsatisfactory creature', a person with 'miserable weaknesses' (WG, pp. 38–9).

Merton's understanding of the nature of the self reflects the view of the New Testament. To give just one example, in Romans 7.14–25 Paul clearly identifies the two poles in human selfhood. The first is the one oriented to God; he calls this 'the inmost self'. The other is that part of him that is bending him away from God and God's law. This pole he denotes as 'the law of sin'.

Ernst Käsemann[31] suggests that the key to understanding this inherent opposition within the self that is depicted by Paul is to be found in verse 14c: 'I am a creature of flesh and blood sold as a slave to sin.' This functions as a heading for the passage. Possessed by sin, it is inevitable that at every turn there will be a forced exchange of the good that is desired with the evil that is unwanted. It is not just that evil has an influence; Paul sees himself as 'demonically enslaved'.

In describing the bondage he is in, Paul casts his 'inmost self' against the 'law of sin'. That he regularly experiences defeat in his intention to live according to the divine will is the result of being a prisoner to this law: 'In my inmost self I dearly love God's law, but I see that acting on my body there is a different law which battles against the law in my mind. So I am brought to be prisoner of that law of sin which lives inside my body' (vv. 22–23). Here, then, Paul recognizes very clearly that he is caught in the battle between his inner opposites. The inmost self represents the self that is oriented to God's will. It expresses itself through a commitment to total love of God and neighbour. Over against this self is the law of sin. 'Law' here is meant in the sense of a principle or rule of action.[32] Or it can also be understood as a 'squatter'.[33] He is not legitimately in residence, but he is very difficult to evict. He is also a very powerful squatter, because he takes Paul prisoner and directs him against his better intentions.

To continue with the metaphor, the squatter residing in the souls of counsellors weakens their capacity to fully attend to the other. We saw above that Merton identifies the primary destructive tendencies in the false self as pride, hard-heartedness and self-centredness. These negative attributes can be aligned with failures in attention to the other. Pride, first, results in over-confidently believing that one knows exactly what the other is trying to communicate. The counsellor suffering from pride underestimates how difficult it is to get into the internal frame of reference of another person and make sense of it on its own terms. There is richness, depth and complexity in the personhood and life experiences of an individual that are exceedingly difficult to catch hold of. The prideful self needs to be decreased if a person is to pay attention to the other. Mary Dietz captures this aspect of Weil's thought nicely when she comments that attention is '... a humility in the face of the incompleteness of one's own knowledge ... a real effort to take in a reality beyond the self'.[34]

If counsellors are to fully attend to others they need also to empty out any hardness of heart. Good listeners show mercy. There is a close connection between compassion and patience. A compassionate person takes the time to listen carefully and fully to the story of distress and confusion that the other brings. Such a person is aware that patient listening is required in order to really hear another individual. To begin, an extended series of questions need to be asked. It is not a matter of flooding the counsellee with queries; the pastoral conversation should not degenerate into an interrogation. But it is necessary to ward off impatience in listening. What is to be avoided is the 'speed-counselling approach' in which only a small number of questions are asked and counsellors fall into the illusion that they actually know the life-world of the counsellee.

It is also the case that perceptions need to be checked out. Counsellors need to take the time to get the feedback that confirms for them that they are really hearing the counsellee. The business of attending to the other is not for people in a rush. The world has sped up over time. We want everything from food, to information, to dating in the fast mode. Compassion is an old-world animal; it likes to take its time.

Lastly, really hearing the other requires emptying out egocentrism. The ego has a natural tendency to inflate; its ardent desire is to fill the whole space in relations with others. An empty area is needed to accommodate the thoughts and feelings, fears and hopes of the other. Weil puts it this way: 'The soul empties itself of all its own contents in order to receive into itself the being it is looking at, just as he is, in all his truth' (*WG*, p. 59). So what are some of the 'contents of the soul' that need to be evacuated? First, there is intention. Henri Nouwen talks about the need for attending without intention.[35] The intentions of the counsellor militate against the goal of really hearing the counsellee. Counsellors may have the intention of proving to themselves and to the counsellee that they are wise, knowledgeable and generally capable. Or their intention may be to try out the latest therapeutic technique they have picked up. Or it might be to satisfy their own curiosity, thus indulging themselves by asking useless questions. We could go on listing unhelpful intentions almost *ad infinitum*. The false self has a strong tendency to satisfy its own desires and interests and to set aside those of the other. It is this false tendency that needs to be evacuated.

The second content to be emptied out is extraneous thought. It is inevitable that personal thoughts that are not related to the story the counsellee is telling will come into our minds. They need to be acknowledged and then quickly dispatched. The glazed eyes look is the sign that distracting thoughts have been accommodated and attention lost. That look, if it is a feature of the conversation, is demoralizing for the counsellee. There is a meditative technique that is useful in handling diversions. The meditator, like the counsellor, is prone to distraction by extraneous thoughts. Meditation teachers instruct their pupils to view such thoughts as like a bird that has flown into the window of one's house. It is to be noticed, but then it must be immediately allowed to fly out the opposite window.

A third content to be expelled, the last we will deal with, is self-indulgence. We all have propensities and desires that are unhelpful in the counselling process. Some of us, for example, feel a need to inject humour at regular intervals into any conversation that we have. Please do not misunderstand me; humour can be a powerful tool in a pastoral conversation. But it needs to be used sparingly, and always in the service of healing and growth. What is being referred to here is the overuse of humorous interjections that stem from a personal inclination rather than from a therapeutic aim. We can also indulge our intellectual side. Some of the people we work with are not particularly interesting or engaging people. Self-indulgence can manifest itself through making connections that we find personally interesting and mentally stimulating, but that contribute little if anything to the therapeutic process. It is not necessary to give multiple examples; the point has been made.

We cannot pretend we have covered the complete contents of the false self that can interfere with attending to the counsellee. The aim has been to be illustrative rather than exhaustive. The central point is that there is in all of us a false self that demands to be indulged. It needs to be emptied out if we are to be truly attentive in our listening.

Summary

The attempt here has been to show how Simone Weil's notion of attention informs our understanding of what it means to really hear the counsellee. The first insight that we gained from Weil is that attention flows from desire and an experience of joy in being with another. Muscular effort is no substitute for being led by desire. Attending to the other does, however, require a certain type of effort. Weil refers to the need for negative effort or passive activity. It is counterproductive to force oneself to be attentive. Genuine attention is spontaneous and instinctive; it emanates from a deep desire to know, to understand, and to support the other. It is both dispositional and a free gift of grace. We cannot make ourselves good listeners simply by an exercise of will.

The second connection that was made is that attention requires the stance of waiting. Pastoral counsellors need to listen with openness and expectancy. They should be aware that they must not attempt to wrestle meaning from what the counsellee is saying. The patterns in the story that is being told must be allowed to unfold, and an attempt to force the process will derail it.

The final insight to emerge was that attention is founded on self-emptying. If the ego fills the interpersonal space, there is no room for the communications of the other. Weil's notion of decreation is helpful in this context, but the way she articulates it is less so. The language she uses sounds nihilistic, and it was for this reason that we turned to the thought of Thomas Merton on the true and false selves. It is clearly not the self *in toto* that needs to pass into nothingness, but rather the sinful tendencies in the false self. Pride, hard-heartedness and selfishness all militate against attention. It is these, along with other similarly sinful traits, that need to be emptied out.

In the next chapter, we continue our journey into fundamental attitudes, values and skills. Taking a lead from the thought of Martin Buber, we will reflect on the nature and role of authenticity, inclusion and confirmation.

Notes

1 J. Ellin, *Listening Helpfully: How to Develop Your Counselling Skills* (London: Condor, 1994), p. 40.

2 D. Capps, *Living Stories: Pastoral Counseling in Congregational Context* (Minneapolis, MN: Fortress Press, 1998), p. 14.

3 S. Weil, *Waiting on God* (London: Routledge & Kegan Paul, 1951), p. 58. Referred to hereafter in the text as *WG*.

4 J. Delaruelle, 'Attention as Prayer: Simone Weil', *Literature and Aesthetics* 13, no. 2 (2003), pp. 19–27, p. 19.

5 Weil's thoughts on attention can be found in *Waiting on God* and in *Grace and Gravity* (London: Routledge, 2002); and scattered throughout her various notebooks.

6 See A. Caranfa, 'The Aesthetic and the Spiritual Attitude in Learning: Lessons from Simone Weil', *Journal of Aesthetic Education* 44, no. 2 (2010), pp. 63–82, p. 67.

7 See S. Sorajjakool, '*Wu Wei* (Non-doing) and the Negativity of Depression', *Journal of Religion and Health* 39, no. 2 (Summer 2000), pp. 159–66, p. 160.

8 R. Billington, *Understanding Eastern Philosophy* (London: Routledge, 1997), p. 92.

9 M. G. Dietz, *Between the Human and the Divine: The Political Thought of Simone Weil* (Totowa, NJ: Rowman & Littlefield, 1988), p. 97.

10 I am indebted to Jacques Delaruelle for this insight. See his 'Attention as Prayer', p. 20.

11 Leslie Murray comments on McDaniel's idea of the acoustic mode of knowing in his article, '"Poet in the Scientist": The Mystical Naturalism of Bernard E. Meland', *Encounter* 68, no. 2 (2007), pp. 19–31, p. 26.

12 B. E. Meland, 'Can Empirical Theology Learn Something from Phenomenology?', in B. E. Meland (ed.), *The Future of Empirical Theology* (Chicago, IL: The University of Chicago Press, 1969), pp. 283–306, p. 301.

13 Meland, 'Can Empirical Theology Learn Something from Phenomenology?', p. 302.

14 See H. G. Gadamer, *Truth and Method* (London: Sheed & Ward, 1979).

15 See M. D. Evans, 'Appreciative Consciousness: Learning to Go Beyond', *English Quarterly* 36, no. 1 (2004), pp. 10–15.

16 See Weil, *Grace and Gravity*, p. 33. Hereafter referred to in the text as *GG*.

17 S. Weil, *First and Last Notebooks*, trans. R. Rees (London: Oxford University Press, 1970), p. 79. Hereafter referred to in the text as *FLN*.

18 S. Weil, *The Notebooks of Simone Weil*, trans. A. Willis, vol. 2 (London: Routledge & Kegan Paul, 1976), p. 344. Hereafter referred to in the text as *NB*.

19 Cf. S. Cameron, 'The Practice of Attention: Simon Weil's Performance of Impersonality', *Critical Inquiry* 29 (2003), pp. 216–52, p. 237.

20 A. Pirruccello, 'Interpreting Simone Weil: Presence and Absence in Attention', *Philosophy East and West* 45, no. 1 (1995), pp. 61–72, pp. 61–2.

21 T. Merton, *Entering the Silence: Becoming a Monk and a Writer – The Journals*, vol. 2 (San Francisco, CA: HarperSanFrancisco, 1995), p. 49.

22 T. Merton, *Seeds of Contemplation* (London: Burns and Oates, 1949, 1957), p. 11.

23 T. Merton, *Conjectures of a Guilty Bystander* (New York: Image Books, 1968, 1989), p. 224.

24 Merton, *Conjectures*, p. 224.

25 Merton, *Contemplative Prayer* (New York: Image Books, 1971, 1996), p. 24.

26 Merton, *The New Man* (New York: Farrar, Straus and Giroux, 1961, 2000), p. 23.

27 Merton, *The New Man*, p. 102.

28 See *New Seeds of Contemplation* (London: Burns and Oates, 1961), p. 45.

29 Merton, *Seeds*, p. 13.

30 Peter Roberts makes this comment: 'At times Weil's words seem to be almost an act of self-loathing. She speaks of herself as unworthy and ignorant' (P. Roberts, 'Attention, Asceticism, and Grace: Simone Weil and Higher Education', *Arts and Humanities in Higher Education* 10, no. 3 (2011), pp. 315–28, p. 325). Two of her closest friends, Father Perrin and Gustave Thibon, have this to say about her personality in their book *Simone Weil as We Knew Her*: 'Simone Weil had the greatest contempt for herself as an empirical personality ... her humility in this realm bordered on an inferiority complex' (J. M. Perrin and G. Thibon, *Simone Weil as We Knew Her* (London: Routledge, 2003), p. 128).

31 See E. Käsemann, *Commentary on Romans* (Grand Rapids, MI: Eerdmans, 1980), p. 204.

32 See L. Morris, *The Epistle to the Romans* (Grand Rapids, MI: Eerdmans, 1988), p. 295.

33 See Morris, *The Epistle*, p. 293.

34 Dietz, *Between the Human and the Divine: The Political Thought of Simone Weil* (Totowa, NJ: Rowman & Littlefield, 1988), p. 133.

35 See H. Nouwen, *The Wounded Healer* (New York: Image Books, 1979), p. 88.

4

Conditions for Genuine Dialogue, or It's the Relationship that Heals

There is a school of counselling and psychotherapy that has as its central tenet the notion that the work of healing and growth is promoted primarily by the quality of the therapeutic relationship that is established. It is variously referred to, but the most common names used are dialogical therapy and relational therapy/psychotherapy. It is recognized that psychotherapeutic psychology and the related techniques are important; however, when it comes to the efficacy of the therapy the contention is that the really decisive factor is the relationship. This approach immediately gains the interest of the pastoral counsellor. After all, while many pastoral counsellors do employ techniques of one kind or another (e.g. cognitive-behavioural therapy (CBT) strategies; externalization, letter writing, and assembling an audience, taken from narrative therapy; the empty chair technique from Gestalt therapy; 'becoming' the client to sharpen empathy, to name just a few), it is generally the case that they lack extensive training in the theory and practice associated with these interventions. On the other hand, a capacity to enter into a genuine, honest and compassionate relationship with others is, or certainly should be, central in the personal spirituality of a pastoral counsellor.

A number of those who align with this general philosophy of counselling and psychotherapy acknowledge the pivotal role that the philosophy of Martin Buber (1878–1965) has played in the development of their approach. Buber was primarily a philosopher and religious thinker; however, he had a keen interest in psychotherapy. In his body of work we find a number of insightful reflections on the topic, and he engaged through letter correspondence with a number of leading psychoanalysts and psychiatrists of his time, such as Hans Trüb, Ludwig Binswanger and Leslie Farber. He issued a call to these and to all psychotherapists to step out of their 'confidently functioning security of action' – a security established through professional training and faith in one's chosen theoretical frame and therapeutic method – into the abyss.[1] In the abyss, the selfhood of the therapist stands naked before the selfhood of the client. Therapists cannot hide behind training and theory. The therapist must answer the call of the client through a full and genuine personal involvement.

Buber is famous for his articulation of intersubjectivity or a genuine meeting between two persons as an I–Thou encounter. I–Thou is a translation of the German *Ich-Du*. German employs both formal and informal pronouns. *Du* is the informal form and is used between family members, lovers and close friends. There is no English equivalent, hence the resort to an old English form. What Buber communicates through his use of *Ich und Du* is a meeting between two subjects. This is to be distinguished from the subject–object relation of the I–It world. For Buber, the central fact about human existence is not the thinking, feeling, hoping and acting of the individual ego, but rather the relationship between persons. By extension, personal growth is not first and foremost a function of internal processes, but rather a process that is supported via confirmation by the other. He has this to say: '[T]he inmost growth of the self is not accomplished ... in [a person's] relation to himself, but in the relation between the one and the other, between [persons], that is, pre-eminently in the mutuality of the making present – in the making present of another self and in the knowledge that one is made present in his own self by another – together with the mutuality of acceptance, of affirmation, and confirmation.'[2]

In the previous three chapters, we identified essential elements in healing through authentic relationship – namely, respect for uniqueness, empathy and attention. Here we take a lead from a thinker who has inspired many psychotherapeutic theorists and practitioners – namely, Martin Buber – as we posit three more (one of which is similar to empathy). The first is *offering a genuine presence*. To be authentically present to the other involves a willingness to drop image and pretence (what Buber refers to as choosing 'being' over 'seeming'). We also discuss an element that is quite close to empathy, but that nevertheless has its own distinctive quality. I refer to *inclusion in the life experience and view of life of the counsellee*. For Buber, including oneself in the world of another involves an imaginative engagement with that person's thoughts, feelings, fears, hopes, strengths, weaknesses and values. The final element is *confirmation of counsellees as who they are at present and as who they have the potential to become*. According to Buber, confirmation begins with acceptance of people as they are, but goes further and points to the people they could be were they to grow into their God-given potential.

The chapter is structured as follows. First, the scene is set for a Buber-inspired approach to healing through meeting by outlining a number of prominent approaches within the school of dialogical therapy. Next there is an overview of Buber's dialogical philosophy. Finally, the three essential elements are discussed. We begin with a survey of approaches to healing through meeting.

Representative approaches to healing through meeting

The aims of therapy are variously described. If asked, clinicians would refer to one or more of the following: a lowering in levels of anxiety, mood elevation, enhanced ego strength, establishing a more coherent self, authoring a new and more positive life-narrative, a greater level of personal autonomy, enhanced capacity for rational engagement with life, and the emergence of the real or organismic self. Along with pluralism in terms of the main aims of therapeutic work, there is also great variety in theories of personality and in therapeutic strategies. Together with all these theoretical splits, there is a fundamental dividing line that can be drawn. On one side of this line are those therapists who elevate the importance of the therapeutic relationship over theory and technique, and on the other side we find those who hold the reverse position. Those influenced by Buber's dialogical philosophy (and by other similar philosophies) clearly locate themselves in the former camp. The mantra of those in the dialogical school is this: 'It's the relationship that heals'. This summary line is potentially misleading. It should not be taken to mean that advocates of dialogical therapy place little stock on techniques. They certainly acknowledge the efficacy of skilled and well-timed technical interventions, but for them the primary factor is the quality of the therapeutic relationship. In the following brief survey of various approaches in this 'broad church', it will be evident that many of the leading psychotherapeutic techniques feature.

In classical psychoanalysis we perhaps find the approach to therapy in which the relational dimension is accorded the least value. In Freud's view, the analyst takes on the role of a detached, analytical observer. This individual operates in a state of 'evenly hovering attention', attempting all the while to identify the history and dynamics associated with the intrapsychic conflict in the patient. In probing the unconscious, the analyst must deal with the thwarting capability of resistances. Free association provides a means of bypassing these defence mechanisms. As the material from the unconscious becomes available, analysts need to clear their presuppositions in order to accurately formulate the intrapsychic dynamics. They are present in the role of detached, quasi-scientific observers. Their primary aim is to reach that point of objective understanding (as if this could ever be fully possible) of the intrapsychic conflict that indicates how they should intervene to bring the patient to insight and cure. We must be careful, however, not to underestimate the role of the relational in psychoanalytic therapy. A central place in the treatment of neurosis is accorded to transference. Transference refers to a phenomenon in which clients unconsciously repeat certain feelings and reactions from conflictual and distressing relationships in their past in their current relationship with their analyst. It is when the neurosis is mobilized through an activation of early conflicts and traumas within the therapeutic relationship that healing really begins. What is important in the context of our present discussion is that transference is a relational phenomenon.

Even though in all approaches to therapy there is an acknowledgement that the relationship between the therapist and the client is important, there is a school in which being fully present and available is identified as the critical factor in achieving therapeutic goals. The existentialist therapist Irvin Yalom tells a story that illustrates well the convictions of the members of this school.[3] As a student, he went with a group of his friends to visit an old Armenian lady to learn the art of producing fine cuisine. Yalom would assiduously follow her recipes, but he could never reproduce the wonderful taste sensations he experienced at the home of his tutor. One evening, while waiting at her table to receive his meal, he noticed that as the young female servant brought the food to the table, she quickly and as inconspicuously as possible threw in a range of condiments. There was the answer to the puzzle! The extra touch he was missing out on came from what the servant girl added in between the kitchen and the table. He offers this experience as a psychotherapeutic parable. While, he observes, the psychotherapeutic profession likes to attribute its successes to highly technical factors such as strategic interventions, the development and resolution of transference, and the analysis of object relations, 'when no one is looking, the therapist throws in the "real thing"'.[4] It is easy to list but difficult to define the 'extras' that contribute so substantially to client improvement. Included in this collection of therapeutic qualities are the following: 'compassion, "presence", caring, extending oneself, touching the patient at a profound level ... [and] wisdom'.[5]

What Yalom presents here is a conviction that unites a group of theorists and clinicians with various psychotherapeutic pedigrees into a loose school of thought that I would term 'dialogical therapy' or 'relational therapy'. Carl Rogers was a pioneer in this school. He argued that the way the therapist is present to the client is the really critical factor in therapy. In his understanding of what constitutes genuine presence in the therapeutic relationship, he was significantly influenced by Martin Buber, referring to him as one of his favourite thinkers.[6] Rogers described the experience in therapy of a 'deep realness in one [meeting] a deep realness in the other' as an I–Thou moment.[7] He identified three key attitudes in the project of establishing a healing relationship – namely, acceptance, genuineness (or congruence) and empathy.[8] It is absolutely essential, he contended, that the therapist communicates acceptance or unconditional positive regard to the client. Clients, must know that everything they are feeling – aggression, anger, guilt and lust along with more positive affects – is accepted by the therapist. This accepting, 'prizing' attitude provides clients with a unique opportunity to really understand themselves.

Acceptance, however, must not be confused with 'phoniness'. In order for therapists to establish themselves as trustworthy, they must be 'dependably real'. 'Genuineness means that the therapist is openly being the feelings and attitudes flowing within at the moment.'[9] There must, in other words, be congruence between what therapists are presently feeling at 'gut level' and what they express to the client.

Empathy, lastly, is the capacity to think and feel oneself into the inner world of the client. Imaginatively, the therapist is able to begin, at least, to see the feelings and personal meanings as the client does. Rogers held that the therapist who is sensitive and attuned could even grasp meanings just outside the client's awareness.

Existentialist therapists have an orientation to helping persons engage honestly with their potentialities and to experience their existence as fully as possible. It is not possible to genuinely promote these ideals without modelling them in the therapeutic relationship. Among those in this camp who have contributed significantly to thinking on relational therapy we find Irvin Yalom[10] (whom we have already encountered), Rollo May,[11] James Bugental,[12] and Jim Lantz.[13] In order to get the flavour of this approach, key features in the approaches of May and Bugental will be highlighted here.

Rollo May, first, characterizes therapy in terms of an encounter between therapist and client aimed at helping the latter 'experience his existence as real [his emphasis]'.[14] For their part, therapists need to be fully 'present'. That is, they need to facilitate a 'total relationship', one that operates on a number of levels.[15] The levels include 'realness', friendship, *agape* and *eros*.

Bugental also identifies the 'presence' of both therapist and client as the heart of therapy. 'Looking back now,' he writes, 'it is surprising to me how long I overlooked the fundamental importance of presence to therapeutic work. It is even more surprising to me how many therapists and therapeutic systems also overlook it. All too often, therapists seem to be so attentive to the content of what is being said and to their prior conceptions about client dynamics and needs that they don't notice the distance that exists between themselves and their partners.'[16] The art of therapy consists of reducing that distance to the point where there is a real meeting, a sharing in presence. 'Accessibility' and 'expressiveness' in clients are indicators that they are really present in the therapeutic relationship.[17] The former term refers to openness to the 'press' for change and growth coming from the therapist; whereas the latter identifies a genuine, honest sharing of subjective experience.

Another important figure in this school is the British psychotherapist Robert Hobson. He takes an eclectic approach to therapy; however, his background is Jungian. The stress he places on relationship in therapy is evident in the name he gives to his approach – namely, 'the conversational model'. Therapist and client, alone and together, develop a 'feeling-language':

> *Dialogue* entails the recognition of the other person as an experiencing subject. In a simultaneous acting and being acted upon, knowing and being known, there is a mutual creation of a personal feeling-language. 'I and you' becomes 'I–Thou'. Empathy, a one-way apprehension of what Joe Bloggs is experiencing, moves towards a mutual understanding in which Joe and I are at once alone and together.[18]

According to Hobson, healing begins when the client is able to share those images of pain, anxiety and alienation that arise in the heart. It is the therapist's dialogic presence, creating with the client a mutuality that encompasses both individuality and communion (aloneness-togetherness), which facilitates this movement into 'feeling-images'.

John Gunzburg uses Buber's central categories to inform and shape his understanding of, and approach to, psychotherapy. Gunzburg notes that in establishing a genuine meeting with the client, the therapist establishes a 'holding environment' (he employs Donald Winnicott's term).[19] What is critical here is that it is not the psychotherapeutic dogma or expert techniques of the therapist that establish this environment. Rather, it is the capacity of the therapist to be present in such a way that an atmosphere of trust, security, genuineness, empathy and unconditional positive regard is created.

I have already referred to the psychoanalytic tradition. It is also worth noting Heinz Kohut's self psychology[20] (a theory we discussed in Chapter 2) and the research into the place of empathic presence in psychoanalysis by Stolorow, Brandchaft and Atwood.[21] In the 1960s and 1970s Kohut established himself as a leading theorist and practitioner in the treatment of narcissistic personality disorder. The narcissistic personality, according to Kohut, suffers from feelings of emptiness and depression, of inferiority and rejection, and of not being fully real. Based on his clinical experience, Kohut contends that what these depleted selves need most is to admire (to 'idealize') and to be admired (or 'mirrored'). Mirroring is expressed through empathic responses.

Stolorow, Brandchaft and Atwood build on the insights of Kohut. Indeed, they contend that the empathic presence of the analyst is the critical factor in effective analysis. They reject the view of classical psychoanalysis in which the analyst is seen as a detached, objective observer engaged in the 'archaeological' work of excavating archaic repressed material. Instead, they construe the analytic encounter as a dialogue between two subjectivities. Rather than interpreting analysis through a reference to the intrapsychic world of the analysand on the one hand and the interpretive skill of the analyst on the other, Stolorow and his colleagues think in terms of an 'intersubjective field' set up between the two partners in the therapeutic project.

They reject the old 'rule of abstinence' (according to this rule, the analyst must refrain from providing any gratification of the patient's instinctual urges as this militates against the attempt to bring the repressed material into consciousness). In its place, they put 'sustained empathic inquiry'.[22] Such a stance, they suggest, establishes the analyst as 'an understanding presence with whom early unmet needs can be revived and aborted developmental thrusts reinstated'.[23]

The last figure to be discussed in the psychoanalytic group is Carl Goldberg.[24] Goldberg endorses Buber's view that the major flaw in classic psychoanalytic theory is its attempt to understand the human person as a monad. It is not so much unconscious conflict as it is destructive interpersonal relationships that contribute to unhealthy development of the personality. The relational sphere is the most significant site for damage to the psyche; it is also the most important zone for healing of the psyche. Goldberg, following Buber's lead, contends that what is required for a patient to experience greater wholeness is *radical discovery* [his italics].[25] The healing surprise is that in the therapeutic relationship patients are granted the freedom to be the person they intend to be, rather than the person others have demanded them to be in the past. The discovery element needs to also feature in the experience of analysts. They need to be surprised by an increase in their creative capacities as they experience themselves in the dialogue with the patient. 'In fact', writes Goldberg, 'the depth of healing is a product of the healer's capacity to sustain the unexpected in relation to the sufferer.'[26]

Maurice Friedman[27] and Richard Hycner[28] have developed what they call a 'dialogical' approach to therapy. They are also inspired by Buber's notion of 'healing through meeting'. Buber characterizes the dialogue between therapist and patient in this way:

> In a decisive hour, together with the patient entrusted to and trusting in him, [the psychotherapist] has left the closed room of psychological treatment in which the analyst rules by means of his systematic and methodological superiority and has stepped forth with him into the air of the world where self is exposed to self. There, in the closed room where one probed and treated the isolated psyche according to the inclination of the self-encapsulated patient, the patient was referred to ever-deeper levels of his inwardness as to his proper world; here outside, in the immediacy of one human confronting another, the encapsulation must and can be broken through, and a transformed, healed relationship must and can be opened to the person who is sick in his relations to otherness – to the world of the other which he cannot remove into his soul.[29]

Informed by this vision, Friedman describes 'dialogical psychotherapy' as 'a therapy that is centred on the *meeting* between the therapist and his or her client ... as the central healing mode, whatever analysis, role playing, or other therapeutic techniques or activities may also enter'.[30]

Hycner is a Gestalt therapist who declares an interest in the relationship between the intrapsychic and the interpersonal. He argues, following the Jungian therapist Hans Trüb, that intrapsychic conflict or neurosis is really a 'flight from meeting'.[31] In dialogical work, the therapist aims to be both a real person and a 'proxy' for the world. That is, such therapists use the therapeutic relation to repair the dialogical bridge between clients and the community.

Lastly, Alexandra Adame and Larry Leitner have observed the affinity between Buber's dialogical philosophy and the therapeutic approach Leitner has developed called Experiential Personal Construct Psychology (EPCP).[32] The authors put it this way: 'Buber's core writings ... have many similarities with EPCP's focus on relationality and the primacy of dialogue as the locus of meaning and healing in the therapeutic context. EPCP and Buber's approaches both place their focus on the realm of "the between" that exists in the dialogue between self and other.'[33]

The primary orientation of EPCP is on mutually intimate relationships in which both therapist and client come to an understanding of the fundamental ways in which each one views self and world. It is not a matter of both persons completely independently formulating their construal of reality, communicating it to the other, and then having it received. Rather, meaning is co-constructed in the dialogical relationship. With this in mind, the deep, intimate relationship established in therapy is called a ROLE relationship (capitalized to avoid confusion with the sociological term). This way of naming the relationship constitutes an acknowledgement of the fact that each person plays a role in the way others construe their views of self and world.

Underpinning the understanding of the ROLE relationship is the notion that we can never fully know the other. While there is acknowledgement of the communion that is established through the experience of sharing deep thoughts, feelings and values, there is also recognition of the 'separateness and unique mystery' of each person.[34] Given the inevitable limitations in awareness and insight, on the one hand, and the capacity to fully communicate on the other, the goal is to endeavour to understand the other as comprehensively as possible. And in coming to understand, there is also a move to confirm other people's core sense of who they are.

That concludes our survey. It is evident that the therapists we have discussed above cover a wide spectrum of psychotherapeutic theory. They indicate, moreover, that they happily use the techniques in which they were trained. What indicates their dialogical orientation is the conviction that *the therapeutic relationship is primary*. While they all recognize the benefits in using technical interventions as required, they are convinced that the most potent factor in promoting improvement is the capacity of the therapist to facilitate a genuine relationship with the client.

Having introduced the idea of healing through meeting, I now want to turn to a discussion of Buber's dialogical philosophy. The central ideas in the philosophy will then be used to launch an approach to pastoral counselling built around three essential components.

Buber's dialogical philosophy

What should one know before engaging with Buber's dialogical philosophy in order to ensure the correct point of entry? Well, there is quite a bit that one should know, but the response of Maurice Friedman – who spent a lifetime studying, interpreting and translating Buber's works – to this question at a religious studies seminar at San José University captures the really essential element: 'It must be understood first that *Thou* is not an object but a *relationship*.'[35]

A philosophical analysis of authentic human existence can start either with subjectivity or with relationality. While existentialist thinkers such as Sartre and Heidegger locate authentic existence in self-being, in communication with the self, Buber orients his thinking around the sphere of the 'between'. It is out of the I–You relation that real life emerges. A person's deepest identity is to be found in the need, the urge, for dialogue. The innate 'You' reaches out for its realization in the meeting with the other.

In endeavouring to understand Buber's description of meeting in *I and Thou*, I find myself captivated by the power and depth of the vision, on the one hand, and confused and frustrated by the abstract nature of the language, on the other. Where, I ask, is the concrete guidance for the person wishing to learn the way of genuine presence? During the 1920s and 1930s Buber began, in fact, to flesh out the bare bones of his philosophy of the interhuman. It was during this period that he developed his thought on the nature of genuine dialogue. He identified confirmation as one of the key elements in dialogue. Confirmation is grounded in an acknowledgement of otherness. As I enter into dialogue with others, I accept their uniqueness and particularity, and struggle with them in the release of their potential as individuals.

Confirmation depends on a capacity for *inclusion*. Inclusion is the attempt to grasp the thoughts, feelings, values and wishes of the other while maintaining your own concreteness and particularity. Through inclusion an individual is able to catch hold of otherness. This grasp of the particularity of the other is the first step in confirmation.

Anyone familiar with person-centred therapy will see immediately in Buber's formulations of inclusion and confirmation close connections with Carl Rogers's concepts of empathy and acceptance (or unconditional positive regard), respectively. In fact, the two entered into a dialogue over their respective theories during an American Midwest conference on Buber in April of 1957.[36] Below we will attempt to fix points of convergence and divergence in the thought of Buber and Rogers in order to identify the unique contribution the former makes to psychological thought and therapeutic practice.

The I–Thou relation

A person sits in quiet, contemplative mood gazing at a lake surrounded by snow-capped mountains. Two strangers seated beside each other on a busy commuter train exchange glances in a moment of mutual confirmation. A person shares with a friend thoughts and feelings that are deep and intimate. It is in moments such as these that the I–You world is constituted. In these 'peak' experiences there has been a genuine meeting. Surrounding these fleeting moments of communion is a sea of ordinary, mundane, everyday reality. It may seem, as one interpreter suggests,[37] that Buber establishes a contrast between the extraordinary, 'spiritual' world of the I–You and the ordinary, routine, drab world of the I–It. The polarity, though, that Buber is really interested in is, on the one hand, the actualizing power of immediacy and, on the other, the depersonalizing effect of an instrumentalist ethos. A direct relation is humanizing; objectification produces a soul-destroying sense of alienation.[38]

Tönnies had already located the fundamental problem of modern life in the shift from organic, voluntary communities (*Gemeinschaft* or community) to depersonalized, contract-oriented social structures (*Gesellschaft* or association).[39] The modern capitalist and industrial society is founded on the canons of efficiency, production and goal-setting. Not only material goods become objectified, but also persons; they become things that can be used to achieve a purpose. This instrumentalist ethos and its alienating effects must be countered, Buber believes, through the actualizing power of communion. In *Daniel*, Buber contrasts *orientation* with *realization*.[40] The former describes the rational, technocratic, goal-oriented mode of consciousness rampant in the modern industrialized society. Realization refers to the pure life experience in which two persons come to each other with their whole being. In genuine community it is 'immediacy which ... makes it possible to live the realizing as real'.[41] Buber is under no illusions about the extent of the problem facing his society. In an early essay entitled 'Productivity and Existence'[42] (1914), he laments the fact that the technological, production-oriented ethos has permeated even the sphere of human creativity. There is no longer any immediacy between authors and readers. The sense that authors are holding back their essential being is disturbing for readers. The former seem only intent on producing more and more books. 'The overvaluation of productivity that is afflicting our age has so thrived and its par-technical glance has set up a senseless exclusiveness of its own that even genuinely creative men allow their organic skills to degenerate into an autonomous growth to satisfy the demands of the day.'[43] Buber's teaching on the intersubjective world in *Ich und Du* needs to be set in the context of his deep concern over the alienating effect of an instrumentalist mentality.

Ich und Du

In the utilitarian ethos of modern society, life with others is construed in terms of a subject–object split. The other is viewed as an object, a thing, to be used and manipulated. In this cultural context, Buber pleads for humanization of human life through intersubjectivity. In a genuine meeting between two persons, the *I* encounters the *You*. It is important to realize that Buber does not envisage here an experience on the psychological or emotional level. As Gerhard Wehr has observed, there is no attempt to develop an I–Thou psychology.[44]

Buber imagines new 'forms of speech' in an attempt to reshape modern consciousness. In place of the language of atomization – I, You, It, She, He – he offers the word-pairs I–You and I–It.[45] A word-pair is immediately suggestive of communion. The one who speaks the word 'You' appears as a *person*, a person-in-relation.[46] Such individuals are aware of their subjectivity, but they do not think of themselves as subjects over against an object. Only *egos* construct themselves in terms of the over-against. Setting apart, possession, experience and use – these are the categories the ego uses to shape the person's life in the world. The individual lives in the sphere of goal-directed activity.[47] Such people want, perceive, feel or use something. On the other hand they are conscious of themselves as being-with, as participating in being. Being-with is unmediated.[48] In the relation nothing is allowed to get in the way. Preconceptions, purposes and goals prevent communion; they have no place in the world of the 'You'.

There are persons and there are egos. Indeed, we all partake to a greater or lesser extent in both poles of existence. In virtually every encounter with another person, there is a mix of immediacy and distance, of personalism and objectification. While the intention may be to simply 'be there' with the other, one finds it almost imposssible to cast aside any thought of how the other can be useful, or any thought of what one can get out of the encounter.

The I of humanity is twofold. The I of the I–You is different from the I of the I–It.[49] Apart from the relation, the I does not exist: 'There is no I as such but only the I of the basic word I–You and the I of the basic word I–It.'[50] It is my attitude to the other which establishes that person as either a You or an It. Anyone or anything can become an object. There is nothing that cannot become a You. My comportment to the other is in the form of either presence or object-ification. It is my attitude that constitutes either a You-world or an It-world.

Intending something, having a purpose in mind, analysing and evaluating – the mindset characteristic of the It-world – objectifies the other. You-saying, on the other hand, creates a relation. 'Whoever says You does not have something for his object. For wherever there is something there is also another something ... Whoever says You does not have something; he has nothing. But he stands in relation.'[51] In the relation no thing, no object, is intended or constituted. No purposes, perceptions, imaginings are allowed to come between the I and the You. There is simply the immediacy of presence. As soon as a person contemplates utilizing the other in some way, however, the immediacy of the moment has been lost and now all the individual has are representations. The person with whom we shared a moment of presence and wholeness is now split apart in analysis and judgement, and regarded as a bundle of predicates.[52] The other has become the man with the lively face, with a liking for stylish clothes, and someone with a quick wit. The person we were speaking *to* a moment ago we are now speaking *about*.

The reader may at this point be put off by this tendency to construct human relations in an either-or fashion. *Either* we live in the personalism of the I–You world, *or* we fall into the objectifications of the I–It world. Surely human relations in fact range over a continuum between the two poles? This concern is certainly valid. Indeed, it is one that Buber responds to in his later writings. There he incorporates various gradations into his thinking on the interhuman realm.[53] Reflexion, the tendency to view the other only as an extension of oneself, appears in a variety of guises: self-concern, self-pity, enjoyment of the self, and even self-worship.[54] Further, when speaking about the various forms of perception in the interhuman sphere, Buber presents three possibilities.[55] One can approach the other as a collection of traits (as would a scientist), or as a communicative existence (as an artist), or as a word calling for a response (as a partner in dialogue).

The way humans use language, unsurprisingly, plays a central role in Buber's dialogical philosophy. We address others directly on the one hand, and we talk about them on the other. Language establishes the interpersonal sphere. This becomes clear when we contrast relations with other persons with relations in two other spheres. Buber refers, first, to a relation with *nature*, but this operates on the 'threshold of language'.[56] When I talk to a dog, for example, I may receive a response but never a reply. Second, in the relation with '*spiritual beings*' (the immaterial entities of art and knowledge, for example) there is a 'demanding silence'.[57] The form 'calls out' demandingly to the artist – to use that example – to be actualized. It is through the relation between the form and the artistic mind that a work is generated. Relations in the interhuman sphere, in contrast, are distinguished by the capacity of language to create address and response. In the interpersonal domain 'language is perfected as a sequence and becomes speech and reply. Only here does the word, formed in language, encounter its reply. Only here does the basic word go back and forth in the same shape; that of the address and that of the reply are alive in the same tongue ...'[58] Language enables reciprocity. In the human relation there is an essential similarity between asking and answering, assertion and counter-assertion, loving and being loved. 'My You acts on me as I act on it.'[59]

While Buber uses language to set the interhuman apart from the other two spheres, he also stresses the power of silence in the I–You relation. He refers, for example, to the glance silently exchanged between strangers. 'Speech can renounce all the media of sense, and it is still speech.'[60] In fact, Buber is somewhat ambivalent about the role of language. It is possible, he observes, to say You with your lips while treating the other as an It.[61] The spoken word can so easily be distorted and misused. Almost without realizing it, a person utters the word that objectifies the other. It is difficult to address the other in such a way that the person's freedom is absolutely guaranteed. Gabriel Marcel expresses the matter well: 'Only silence ... leaves the Thou its freedom, and subsists with it in unobtrusiveness; then, spirit no longer announces itself, but *is*.'[62]

The moment in which the spirit simply 'is' never lasts long. Speaking-to inevitably passes over into speaking-about. There is always and necessarily a swing between presence and objectivity. 'The human being who but now was unique and devoid of qualities, not at hand but only present, not experiencable, only touchable, has again become a He or She, an aggregate of qualities, a quantum without shape.'[63] Buber recognizes that a movement into the It-world is necessary; we cannot live totally in the You-world. The swing from actuality to latency is inevitable, as it should be. The world of the It is an ordered one. It is reliable; it has 'density and duration'; one can turn again and again to that which has been analysed, catalogued and stored away.[64] It is only when the sphere of objectivity is allowed to assume mastery, and in this way pushing immediacy and communion to the margins of human coexistence, that it becomes a destructive force.

Buber characterizes this movement from presence to objectivity as a swing from the present to the past. '[I]nsofar as a human being makes do with the things that he experiences and uses, he lives in the past, and his moment has no presence. He has nothing but objects; but objects consist in having been.'[65] In the directness of the encounter with the other the partners are caught up in a moment of actuality of being. It is not a point in time that is experienced but the 'actual and fulfilled present'.[66] In order to describe, analyse or use something I must be able to 'look back on it', so to speak. I need some temporal distance in order to be able to formulate descriptive terms and categories.

The I of the I–You relation is not only released from temporality in the immediacy of presence, but also from the system of spatial coordinates we use to locate the elements in the physical world. It is only the world of the It that is set in a spatio-temporal-causal context.[67] A You measured, analysed, described and catalogued is transformed into an It. It becomes a thing that can be integrated into a space-time grid. The You also appears in space, but only in the context of a direct encounter in which

everything else becomes a background rather than a means of measurement. The You appears in time, but only as a fulfilled, actualized
presence, not as part of an organized sequence.

It is important to recognize that Buber's commitment to humanizing
life in an instrumentalist world has deep religious roots. His engagement
with the Jewish mystical movement known as Hasidism conditions his
way of thinking. In a genuine meeting with the other, there is also a
meeting with God. Wehr observes that in Buber's perspective it is in and
through the I–You relation that the God–human relation is actualized.[68]
Put differently, in every encounter with a You there is an orientation
to the absolute You. Extended, the lines of all relationships intersect in
eternity. 'Every single You is a glimpse of [God]. Through every single
You the basic word addresses the eternal You.'[69]

Every genuine encounter, those in which God is an explicit theme and
those in which it is not, orients a person to God. Though people may
repudiate the idea of God, when they address with the whole of their
beings the You given to them, they address God.[70] In the relation to God,
there is both an unconditional exclusiveness and an unconditional inclu-
siveness.[71] On the one hand, nothing in heaven or on earth, no particular
thing or being, retains any importance in the context of this relation.
And yet, on the other, everything is included in it. Entering into a relationship with God does not involve cutting oneself off from the things of
this world, but rather locating them in the context of the absolute You.
'Looking away from the world is no help toward God; staring at the
world is no help either; but whoever beholds the world in him stands in
his presence.'[72] A 'worldly' life cannot separate us from God. Only life in
the It-world, in the world of experience and use, is alienating. Whenever
we live in the world in truth we live in God.

Buber's vision is the actualization of God in the world through the
community of persons who actualize being through the I–You relation.
It is not appropriate or even possible to banish the It-relation from the
world. Rather, we are to sound the 'holy basic word' in order to human-
ize the world of the It. In this vision, all I–You encounters are the radii
that lead from all I-points to the centre of a circle.[73] It is this common
relation to the centre, to God, that assures genuine community and
actualization of the real in the world.

Clearly, Buber's language for the I–You relation is abstract and difficult. It may be helpful at this point to present some concrete examples of
intersubjectivity. Indeed, Buber himself offered some. Responding to the
criticism that his thoughts do not connect with everyday experience, he
referred to the confirming glance shared between two strangers on a bus
or a train. We have all had the experience of being 'looked up and down'

by a fellow commuter. That this individual is making some observation or judgement is evident. The person could be thinking, 'I don't think much of his dress sense.' Or, 'He's really tall; I wonder if he plays basketball.' Perhaps the person is trying to decide what line of work the other happens to be in. We are for that person no more than an object of passing interest. On other occasions, though, we experience a look that is warm and encouraging. Through the smile or the nod of the other there is a sense of being recognized as a person. Buber also refers this experience of confirmation to the factory floor. As two workers labour at their machines, battling with monotony and boredom, they validate and encourage each other through a warm glance.

Think, too, of the experience of shopping for a gift for loved ones. Shop assistants who engage fully with you in the project of finding just the right present establish an I–You relation. Their warmth and genuine interest *person*alizes the experience. They could have constructed it in terms of a 'customer' making a 'sale', thereby entering the world of the I–It. Instead, they choose to focus on you as a person, as a caring partner, who wants to find a nice gift for his or her beloved.

Distance and relation

More than 30 years after the publication of *Ich und Du*, Buber investigated a new problem in the idea of relation. In an important essay entitled 'Distance and Relation',[74] he inquired into the condition of the possibility of the encounter between the I and the You. In other words, he was searching for the anthropic foundation of meeting.

Buber refers to the twofold nature of the principle of human life.[75] Human existence involves a twofold movement such that one movement is the presupposition of the other. The 'primal setting at a distance' is the presupposition for entering into relation. That is to say, it is only possible to establish a relation with a being that has been set at a distance, has become 'an independent opposite'.

That this is in fact the case becomes clear when human life is contrasted with life in the animal world. Animals exist in an environment (understood in the sense used in biology). Only those things that immediately concern them, with which they are directly engaged through their drives and needs, constitute their environment. Out of the elements they utilize to meet their requirements, animals construct their realm or 'world'. An animal is totally immersed in its realm of existence. Only the human can imagine a unity that exists in and for itself. The total experience of an animal is a segment of the world. This experienced environment lacks a horizon. Humans, on the other hand, adopt a perspective that allows them to 'grasp a totality'.[76] 'An animal in the realm of its perceptions is like a fruit in its skin; man is, or can be, in the world as a dweller in an enormous building which is always being added to, and to whose limits he can never penetrate, but which he can nevertheless know as one does know a house in which one lives – for he is capable of grasping the wholeness of the building as such.'[77] Humans are able to detach 'what is', the other beings in the world, from themselves and so establish them as independent realities. This setting at a distance establishes a world.

In the second movement, the human turns to 'the withdrawn structure of being'[78] and enters into a relation with it. It is only possible to relate to that which is set apart from oneself, existing in and of itself. This view of reality is not obtained simply from the action of 'setting at a distance'. Establishing the independence of the world simply means that objectivity is constituted. It is only when I am fully present in the world, relating to it with my whole being, that I experience the world as whole and one. Buber is quick to point out, however, that the idea of establishing other entities as independent opposites is not the same as the idealist conception of the I who establishes the world[79] (as in Husserl's philosophy of transcendental subjects who project their world). Rather, he means to say only that the humans can cut the world away from themselves and make it an independent whole; animals, on the other hand, live immersed in a realm constituted by things they need and use. It is the act of establishing the other as an independent opposite that is the condition of the possibility of entering into relationship. The fact of distance grounds the possibility of human existence. The realization of a human person is founded in the movement of relation. 'Distance provides the human situation, relation provides man's becoming in that situation.'[80] The movement that creates distance is the fundamental act that makes us human – beings who are able to enter into relation. An essential element in genuine human relating is confirmation of otherness. It is to a discussion of this central Buberian concept that we now turn.

Confirming the other

For Buber, an essential element in dialogue is the confirmation of otherness. Maurice Friedman rightly points out that this affirmation of the uniqueness of another person rests on the human capacity to both establish distance and enter into relation.[81] Buber's notion of confirmation is indissolubly linked to his understanding of the two ontological movements that make us human in distinction from other animals. We can only confirm the uniqueness of others through first establishing them in their concrete, particular existence. Setting at a distance necessarily precedes entering into a relationship and, as a central dynamic in it, affirming uniqueness.

Particularity implies *difference*. To acknowledge the particularity of others we must be able to grasp the breath of potential difference. We become aware 'that this one or that one does not have merely a different mind, or way of thinking or feeling, or a different conviction or attitude, but has also a different perception of the world, a different recognition and order of meaning, a different touch from the regions of existence, a different faith, a different soil ...'[82] The challenge is to live in genuine openness to alternative opinions and perspectives without losing the seriousness of the struggle for truth and justice. A debate can go in one of two ways.[83] If we fail to acknowledge the independence and individuality of the other, we engage in propaganda and self-promotion rather than dialogue. The desire to influence is expressed through an injection of what we take to be right and true. Our aim, whether or not we are fully conscious of it, is to deceive the other into thinking that this view we inject is really something coming from within that person, and needing only our assistance to allow it to rise into full awareness.[84] The other, rather than being allowed the freedom and dignity of otherness, is constituted simply as an extension of our existence. This Buber terms *reflexion*, and it happens

> when a man withdraws from accepting with his essential being another person in his particularity – a particularity which is by no means to be circumscribed by the circle of his own self, and though it substantially touches and moves his soul is in no way immanent in it – and lets the other exist only as his own experience, only as a 'part of myself'.[85]

Opposed to this imposition of self, there is what Buber calls *unfolding*.[86] If we confirm others in their uniqueness we naturally seek for that truth that lies within them as potentiality. Through our sharing of ourselves and our views we hope for an opening out of this latent truth.

Inclusion

In order to confirm others in their uniqueness, we need to gain as full an understanding of who they are as is possible. Buber contends that this involves a 'swing over' into the internal frame of reference of the other. This process of *inclusion* involves 'imagining the real'.[87] A person attempts to imagine what at this moment the other is thinking, feeling, wishing and perceiving. This can only be achieved through a 'bold swinging, demanding the most intensive stirring of one's being, into the life of the other'.[88]

Inclusion can also be thought of as 'experiencing the other side'.[89] This can be illustrated through somatic references. A man caresses a woman. He feels the touch from two sides – with the palm of his hand and with her skin.[90] Or maybe we attempt to experience the pain of the other. As we try to imagine that person's pain – the individual's particular pain and not simply physical discomfort in general – the two of us are embraced by a common existential situation.[91]

Through imagining the real, people endeavour to move over into the inner world of others – their physical experiences, their emotional states, their personal struggles, and their hopes and fears. It is a cornerstone of all genuine dialogue.

Three essential elements in the pastoral counselling process

Having discussed the main aspects in both the general approach of dialogical therapy and in Buber's dialogical philosophy, we are in a position to use this thinking to develop a way of thinking about pastoral counselling that is centred on the contention that the really decisive factor in facilitating healing and growth is a genuine meeting between counsellor and counsellee. I suggest that there are three central elements in such an approach:

- offering a genuine presence
- inclusion in the life experience and view of life of the counsellee, and
- confirmation of counsellees as the individuals they are at present and as the people they have the potential to become.

We begin with a reflection on what it means to be authentically present in the counselling relationship.

Offering a genuine presence

We discussed above Buber's understanding of how distance and relation function in authentic interpersonal life. It is the act of setting others at a distance that allows them to be who they genuinely are. The act of coming too close to others constitutes a smothering of them. They are not given the space that they need to truly be themselves. This leads to unhealthy, enmeshed relationships, where others meet with approval only to the extent that they think, feel and act according to the template that they have been handed. That template is stamped with the personal preferences of the one who is doing the dominating.

At the opposite end of the relational spectrum we find a distant relationship. In this case, there is too much space between the two persons, and there is little intimacy. Neither partner feels that any claim on the other can be made, and there is virtually no meaningful communication of cherished ideals, precious hopes, dark fears, and intense feelings.

It is important to recognize that space is a key category in an anthropology grounded in trinitarian theology. Colin Gunton uses this category in shaping a relational ontology based in the trinitarian dynamic.[92] This space needs to be correctly defined. Here Gunton makes observations that are very similar to the ones we outlined above. If there is too much space in the relational sphere there is a fall into individualism. Mutual participation in relationships implies nearness. Too little space, on the other hand, is also a problem. When others sit on top of us, so to speak, we lose our freedom. They fail to make room for us and so show a lack of respect for our otherness.

In developing his theological anthropology, Gunton picks up on the notion of the Greek theologians that God is a communion of persons. Each person is distinct and yet the Three indwell each other and so share in an essential unity. There is both nearness and space to be. Gunton contends that a positive anthropology needs to be developed along these spatial lines.

Counsellors need to appropriately manage the interpersonal space. They make themselves authentically present in the counselling relationship by resisting any move counsellees may make to refuse counsellors the space to be the people they truly are. Counsellees may come with an image of their ideal counsellor, and will have a range of expectations of what they think their counsellor should offer them. In their mind there is a picture of how counsellors should conduct therselves in the sessions, and counsellees may exert pressure on the counsellor to conform to a preconceived model. Such attempts to coerce the counsellor to be a certain type of person, to think and speak in certain approved ways, constitutes a shutting down of the interpersonal space. According to Buber, the first movement in the establishment of a genuine relationship is setting at a distance. This allows both persons to engage from the position of independent personhood, and it is through an independent presence that a counsellor is able to really help a counsellee.

There are, on the other hand, counsellees who do not seek to gain control of the interpersonal space, and do not exert any real pressure on the counsellor to conform to their template for how things should go in the counselling relationship. Consequently, the counsellor does not feel a strong weight of expectation. To be sure, there is some push coming from the counsellee; that is entirely to be expected, since we all have our preferences as to how a relationship is to be enacted. But it is a gentle push. It is one thing to be granted the freedom to be oneself; it is another to exercise that freedom. Counsellors can easily fall into engaging the other through false presences. That is, they relate to the other as if they are wearing a mask, creating an image, pretending to be someone they are not.

Buber was acutely aware of this problem. He refers to two fundamental human modalities – namely *being* and *seeming*.[93] Being is grounded in 'what one really is' whereas seeming is oriented to image, impressions and appearances. The 'lie' associated with seeming, Buber suggests, is not so much a distortion of facts as a falling away from spontaneity and authenticity. He offers a telling illustration of the confusion and deceit flooding a meeting between two persons – he calls them Peter and Paul – intent on projecting an image:

> Let us list the different configurations which are involved. First, there is Peter as he wishes to appear to Paul, and Paul as he wishes to appear to Peter. Then there is Peter as he really appears to Paul – that is, Paul's image of Peter, which in general does not in the least coincide with what Peter wishes Paul to see; and similarly there is the reverse situation. Further, there is Peter as he appears to himself, and Paul as he appears to himself. Lastly, there are the bodily Peter and the bodily Paul. Two living beings and six ghostly appearances, which mingle in many ways in the conversation between the two. Where is there room for any genuine interhuman life?[94]

How can there be communion when all there is are 'ghostly appearances'? Buber suggests that a real meeting between two people requires courage: 'To yield to seeming is man's essential cowardice, to resist it is his essential courage.'[95] It takes courage for counsellors to make themselves present as the people they truly are in the counselling relationship.

The move from the mode of seeming to being present in a genuine way is beautifully illustrated in a vignette offered by Carl Goldberg.[96] At the time of the event, Dr Goldberg was on the teaching faculty of a medical school. He was asked by several senior psychiatric residents (house officers) to be the faculty discussant at a clinical case conference. He recounts that he 'was flattered by the request and determined to perform more wisely and compassionately than the discussants in the clinical conferences during [his] own training'.[97]

The patient, Mrs Franz, was an intelligent, middle-aged, upper-middle-class mother of two daughters. She had received a good education in a convent school in Europe, and was the co-owner of an esteemed art gallery in the city. Her partner in the business, Dr Danton, was a family friend and an influential faculty member of the medical school. He attended the conference. Mrs Franz's husband, apparently a strikingly handsome and urbane man, was a history professor at the local university.

Mrs Franz was subjected to a strict and punitive upbringing. Her parents used the method of humiliation and ridicule in the exercise of discipline. A dominant theme in her upbringing was the directive from her parents that she should only associate with people of good moral character and high intellect. She was inculcated with the idea that people not in this class tend to be derisive about what they cannot understand or appreciate. The message had clearly sunk in. Mrs Franz conducted her life and the gallery business accordingly. She was unwilling to sell, or even to show, her paintings to anyone she judged to be uncultured.

Mrs Franz had been hospitalized for a little over a week prior to the conference. During this hospitalization, she had become increasingly secretive and aggressive. Despite the best efforts of her family, Dr Danton and the medical staff, Mrs Franz flatly refused to communicate about what was troubling her.

At the conference, Dr Levy, a mild-mannered resident, began the interview. Mrs Franz had had a number of previous conversations with him, but the fact that he was not a stranger helped not one bit in terms of her responding to his questions about her guarded, non-communicative behaviour. Dr Goldberg makes this comment, '… I heard hushed whispers of annoyance and disapproval around me. Recalcitrant patients do not make stimulating conferences!'[98]

Dr Levy was almost beside himself with frustration. Initially he was at a loss as to what to do. Finally, he turned to Dr Goldberg and asked him if he would take over. In looking for an opening, Dr Goldberg latched on to Mrs Franz's slender figure. He sensed that she was proud of her ability to stay thin, and decided that asking her about her diet was a non-threatening way to lead into questioning her about more significant aspects of her life. Despite the trivial nature of the inquiry, there was no response from the patient. Dr Goldberg then asked her how she found conditions in the hospital. Even in a well-administered hospital, the patients in a psychiatric ward are usually happy to offer their criticisms. Dr Goldberg reports that he 'had previously found that this sort of question is effective in getting angry and withholding patients to speak freely'.[99]

Unfortunately for Dr Goldberg and the other psychiatrists participating in the conference, Mrs Franz refused to respond to this or any of his other questions. She simply reacted with 'contemptuous expressions and gestures'.[100] Further, the few words she did utter made it very clear that she did not think she belonged in a psychiatric ward and, furthermore, even if she did in fact need help, Dr Goldberg was not the person she would turn to.

The fact that he could not get Mrs Franz to engage with him was making Dr Goldberg increasingly self-conscious. He was embarrassed in front of his peers and began to doubt himself: '[M]y idealized imago of myself as a competent clinician was quickly dissipating under the critical scrutiny of my colleagues.'[101]

The turning point in Dr Goldberg's engagement with Mrs Franz came when he realized that he was keeping her at a distance through relating to her out of his professional persona. So instead of presenting himself as a 'professionally aloof being', he determined to relate to Mrs Franz as 'a fellow sojourner'. In reflecting on this moment of insight, he recalls a saying of Buber: 'The origins of all conflicts between me and my fellow-men is that I do not say what I mean, and that I don't mean what I say.'[102] Dr Goldberg chose the difficult and brave path of truly being himself in the interview. It was, of course, extremely threatening having to reveal his personal vulnerabilities in front of his colleagues, who, he feared, were critically judging everything he said and did.

Dr Goldberg decided to simply say what he was thinking and feeling. He indicated to Mrs Franz that he had been asked to interview her because others thought he was particularly well equipped for the task. He added that he had no idea where that 'absurd notion' came from. He then smiled and pointed to the audience, while saying to her that she must be aware, along with everyone else in the room, how woefully he was doing. Dr Goldberg recounts what happened next in this way:

For a moment Mrs Franz appeared not to know what to make of my statement. Then, for the first time in the interview, a slow smile crept across her face. Her smile evolved for a while into a quiet laugh. The softening of her face conveyed a warm and approachable person. I told her in earnest that I appreciated her tolerating my ineptness. Her smile became broader, and her body appeared for the first time to be at ease.

In the process of liberating myself in order to express myself more freely, I became aware that I had been more concerned during the interview with my persona to the professionals present at the conference than in how difficult and shameful this exposure of herself in front of so many strangers must be for her ...

Curiously, as I spoke increasingly of my shameful feelings, she became more responsive to me. She told me, 'Dr Goldberg, I am now willing to talk with you.'[103]

Unless and until counsellors are able to really *be* with counsellees – *being* their authentic selves, rather than falling into *seeming* – the chances of anything really positive and meaningful happening in the counselling relationship are very slim indeed. The lure of presenting an image, of relating through pretence, is strong for most counsellors. Virtually every counsellor succumbs to the temptation at some point. Relating in the 'being' mode is the condition of the possibility of effective help-giving. But, of course, there are many other things that a counsellor needs to do, and one such essential element is what Buber calls inclusion.

Inclusion in the life experience and view of life of the counsellee

We saw above that inclusion involves a bold 'swinging over' into the internal frame of reference of the other. Understanding the inner world of the counsellee is clearly a central aim in the counselling process. In one of her articles on Buber and psychotherapy, Tamar Kron retells a delightful and profoundly wise Hebrew story of the way in which a Zaddik (a Hebrew sage) includes himself in the crazy world of a prince, thereby effecting his healing. It is reproduced below:

> A royal prince once went mad and thought he was a turkey. He felt compelled to sit naked under the table, pecking at bones and pieces of bread like a turkey. All the royal physicians gave up hope of ever curing him of this madness and the king suffered tremendous grief. Then a Zaddik ... came and said: 'I will undertake to try and cure him.' The Zaddik undressed and sat naked under the table next to the prince, picking at crumbs and bones. After a time – maybe days, maybe weeks – the prince asked: 'Who are you? What are you doing here?' 'And you', replied the Zaddik, 'What are you doing here?'
> 'I am a turkey', said the prince. 'I am also a turkey', answered the Zaddik. They sat together like this for some time without speaking a word, until they became good friends. One day, the Zaddik said to the prince: 'What makes us think that a turkey can't wear a shirt? We can wear shirts and still be turkeys.' The prince agreed and the Zaddik signaled the king's servants to throw them some shirts.
> After a while, the Zaddik said: 'What makes us think that we can't be turkeys if we wear pants? We can wear pants and still be turkeys.' The prince agreed and the Zaddik signaled to the servants and they threw them some pants.
> They continued to sit together under the table, and finally the Zaddik said: 'What makes us think turkeys must sit under the table? Even turkeys can sit at the table.' The prince agreed to sit at the table, and

the Zaddik continued in this manner until the prince was completely healed.[104]

Reflecting on this old Hebrew tale takes my mind to the incarnation. The Son of God came into our crazy world for a time and 'sat under the table with us'. Admittedly, much of the theological work on the incarnation does not help us to make this kind of connection. In both the historical and contemporary contexts, philosophical debates over what constitutes the best articulation of the precise relationship between Christ's human and divine natures have tended to dominate. The language of hypostatic union and communication of attributes takes us quite a distance from the concept of divine inclusion in human experience. There are, however, a number of theologians who contend for a central place for metaphors such as 'empathy' and 'participation' in the conversation. Richard Mouw and Douglas Sweeney have called for 'a more compassionate Christology', one that is grounded in the notion of divine empathy.[105] For Mouw and Sweeney, it is not only the fact that God has suffered in Christ on the cross that is significant, but rather that God has chosen to participate fully in the human experience. They contend that a central aspect of the incarnational ministry of Jesus is that 'a member of the divine Trinity came to earth to understand – from the "inside" of our humanness – what it is like to be one of us in our frailty'.[106]

Full participation in the human experience is also the main focus of Charlene Burns's book, *Divine Becoming*.[107] Burns uses 'participation' as an umbrella category that takes in the terms 'entrainment', 'attunement', 'sympathy', and 'empathy'. Her understanding of these dynamics in human relational experience is informed by a study of developmental and social psychology. Entrainment, first, is something that occurs very early in human development. It is an innate biological response that allows the organism to synchronize with the surrounding environment. In the case of the human infant, entrainment with caregivers involves physiological synchronizing of biological responses such as heart rate and breathing.

Attunement refers to the natural tendency to match the emotional state of the other. For example, if a person excitedly tells me the news of a recent success, my face will naturally 'light up' to match that of the other person.

Entrainment and attunement provide the biological or physical basis for the emotional experience of sympathy. In a sympathetic response, we experience the emotions of another as if they were our own.

Empathy, finally, is 'a somewhat removed way of responding to others'.[108] It is a conscious and linguistic means of participating in the lifeworld of the other. One connects cognitively and emotionally with the other person, while maintaining a clear sense of self as distinct from the other. Let us note in passing that this notion of setting ourselves at a distance, while drawing close to others, is not held by all theorists of empathy. This fact will become important in the discussion on the relationship between empathy and inclusion that follows.

In Burns's reading of the incarnation, Jesus entrained, attuned, sympathized and empathized with the human condition. Thus, the relationship Jesus established with humanity was one of full participation. 'Jesus was the Logos of compassion, the Logos of participation, in that his life was a fulfilment of God's plan, sowed in him at birth. Jesus, as Logos and revealer, was able to mediate between humanity and God such that he, in time, was rightfully and authentically understood to be the presence of God on earth.'[109]

Divine healing of the human condition involved participation in our lifeworld. That one needs to include oneself in the inner world of thought, emotion and experience of the other to facilitate healing and growth is universally recognized in the psychotherapeutic community. In becoming acquainted with Buber's thinking on inclusion, a person engaged in this community would likely connect it with empathy. Carl Rogers was certainly one who made this association. For Rogers, empathy is one of the core conditions of therapy. In an early attempt (1957) to define it, he wrote:

> To sense the client's private world as if it were your own, but without ever losing the 'as if' quality – this is empathy, and this seems essential to therapy. To sense the client's anger, fear, or confusion as if it were your own, yet without your own anger, fear, or confusion getting bound up with it, is the condition we are endeavoring to describe.[110]

Despite the fact that inclusion and empathy may seem to be almost identical concepts, Buber is quick to say that there are in fact important differences between the two. He sees empathy as a process in which one 'transposes' oneself to the place of the other. This transposition 'means the exclusion of one's own concreteness, the extinguishing of the actual situation of life'.[111] In inclusion, on the other hand, a person does not forfeit 'anything of the felt reality of his activity, [and] at the same time lives through the common event from the standpoint of the other'.[112]

The 'as if' quality Rogers stresses puts his understanding of empathy very close to Buber's idea of inclusion. Thinking and feeling oneself into the inner world of the counsellee, the counsellor is careful not to identify with it. Counsellors go over in their imagination to the other side, but nevertheless maintain their personal boundaries, their own particularity and concreteness. In a later (1980) definition of empathy, though, Rogers shows himself to be much less concerned about the possibility of identification. To enter the private world of the client

> means that for the time being, you lay aside your own views and values ... In some sense it means that you lay aside yourself; this can only be done by persons who are secure enough in themselves that they know they will not get lost in what may turn out to be the strange and bizarre world of the other, and that they can comfortably return to their own world when they wish.[113]

A clear distinction can be drawn between this definition of the empathic way of being, containing as it does the idea of laying oneself aside, and Buber's description of imagining the real. As we have seen, Buber insists on the importance of maintaining the actual situation of one's life when attempting to enter the experience of the other. For him, there is an important difference between empathy and inclusion. It is not simply a desire for terminological precision that motivates him here. The reason he insists on the need for people to maintain their own concreteness is that this is absolutely necessary if they are going to confirm the concreteness of others.[114] We can only confirm others in their particularity from our own particular life situation. It is not possible to affirm others while 'lost' in our own world. Rogers also stresses the importance of affirmation or, as he calls it, *acceptance*. He would, of course, agree that in order to communicate unconditional positive regard people must first return to their own world. Nevertheless, it is not the case, as we are about to see, that confirmation and acceptance can simply be equated.

Confirmation of counsellees as the individuals they are at present and as the people they have the potential to become

Along with Buber's approach to inclusion, Rogers was interested in the idea of confirming others in their uniqueness. He considered that in this concept there was something quite close to his own idea of acceptance or unconditional positive regard. It is evident that what we are dealing with are fundamental aspects of the counselling process, and clearly we need to tease out the precise nature of the relationship between the two. It is interesting to note in this regard that during their dialogue at the Midwest US Conference in 1957, Rogers wanted to establish just how Buber saw the connection between the two concepts. He, Rogers, began by explaining how acceptance works in the therapeutic relationship: 'I feel a real willingness for this other person to be *what he is*. I call this 'acceptance' … I am willing for him to possess the feelings he possesses, to hold the attitudes he holds, to be the person he is.'[115]

Buber responded by commenting that all genuine relationships must begin with acceptance, with communicating to the other that 'I take you just as you are'.[116] But he also felt compelled to point out that confirmation is actually a step beyond acceptance. Buber shared his conviction that it is possible to see in the other his God-given *potential*: 'I can recognize in him, know in him, more or less, the person he has been (I can say it only in this word) *created* to become.'[117] Seeing the potential is a movement beyond acceptance, and it implies the need to *act* with the other: 'And now I not only accept the other as he is, but I confirm him, in myself, and then in him, in relation to this potentiality that is meant by him and it can now be developed … He can do more or less to this scope but *I can, too, do something*' [emphasis added].[118] Imagining the potential of the other and helping in the realization of that potential constitute for Buber the critical points of distinction between acceptance and confirmation.

Rogers reacted by asserting that in therapy he accepts not only individuals in their current emotional states but also their potentiality.[119] This unconditional positive regard is the 'strongest factor' in promoting change. Buber found himself unable to find the same level of confidence as his discussion partner in the power of acceptance alone to produce growth. His experience is that often one must struggle with others *against* themselves. That is, others know the direction they should take, but for some reason they find themselves moving in another direction, or not moving at all. For Buber, a human being can best be understood as a polar reality:

> [T]he poles are not good and evil, but rather yes and no, rather acceptance and refusal. And we can strengthen, or we can help him strengthen, the one positive pole. And perhaps we can strengthen the force of the direction in him because this polarity is very often directionless.[120]

It is only possible, according to Buber, to help the other move through ambivalence on the basis of a distinction between accepting and confirming.[121] This seems right. Given the fact that there is often this struggle between 'yes' and 'no' in the other, a more active approach than acceptance is required. Here Buber's image of 'unfolding' comes into play. We struggle with others against themselves not to impose a direction, but to facilitate a release of that which is latent in them. Friedman captures well the nature of this wrestling with the other while respecting that person's autonomy and independence:

> You'll never be confirmed by me simply by my putting myself aside and being nothing but a mirror reflecting you. Confirming you may mean that I do *not* confirm you in some things, precisely because you are not taking a direction. It is not just that you are wrestling with yourself; I am wrestling with you. There is an added factor here that is not what one calls being *empathic*, which strictly speaking means temporarily leaving my ground to enter into yours. It is not just that I am watching you wrestle with yourself; I am also entering into the wrestling ... I may not, of course, impose myself on you and say, 'I know better than you'. It is only insofar as you share with me and as we struggle together that I can glimpse the person you are called to become.[122]

The skill of appropriately and sensitively challenging counsellees to grow into their God-given psychological, moral and spiritual potentialities is of vital importance in faithful and effective pastoral counselling. It is the subject of a later discussion (Chapter 7), in which we will take our lead from Søren Kierkegaard's method of indirect communication.

Summary

We have seen that Martin Buber's dialogical philosophy has been a source of inspiration and guidance for a relatively large number of psychotherapists in developing their particular practice models. These therapists cover virtually the entire spectrum of psychotherapeutic approaches. What unites them is their conviction that while theories of personality and particular therapeutic interventions play an important role, the really decisive factor in the healing and growth process is the quality of the relationship developed between the therapist and client.

In reviewing Buber's dialogical philosophy, we have identified three central elements in the pastoral counselling process. The first is *offering a genuine presence to the counsellee*. To be authentically present to the other involves a willingness to drop image and pretence. Buber refers to this as relating to the other in the being rather than in the seeming mode. The second element is *inclusion in the life experience and view of life of the counsellee*. For Buber, including oneself in the world of another involves a bold 'swinging over' into the lifeworld of the other. One needs to imaginatively project into the inner world of that person's thoughts, feelings, fears, hopes, strengths, weaknesses and values. Lastly, in pastoral counselling the aim is *confirmation of counsellees as the individuals they are at present and as the people they have the potential to become*. Buber envisions a more active role for the counsellor than does Rogers. Pastoral counsellors struggle with others to help them grow into their God-given potential. There is no suggestion here of taking a paternalistic stance; it is not a matter of imposing one's personal view of what is good for the counsellee. Rather, the intention is to help the potential of the counsellee to unfold.

We have now completed the section on attitudes and skills, and in the next part of the book we give attention to interventions and strategies. A significant focus in this first half was on developing a comprehensive model of relational humanness. As important as this aspect of the ministry of care is, influential pastoral theologians have been saying quite emphatically for some time now that relational humanness needs to be complemented with relational justice. Given that socio-political systems, structures and policies impact negatively on the personal well-being of a significant number of those who come to us for help, pastoral ministry needs to include interventions such as advocacy and engaging in joint action for justice. It is to a discussion of this important shift in perspective that we now turn.

Notes

1 M. Buber, 'Healing through Meeting', in J. B. Agassi (ed.), *Martin Buber on Psychology and Psychotherapy* (Syracuse, NY: Syracuse University Press, 1999), pp. 17–21, p. 19.

2 M. Buber, *The Knowledge of Man*, trans. M. Friedman and R. Gregor Smith (London: George Allen & Unwin, 1965), p. 71.

3 See I. Yalom, *Existential Psychotherapy* (New York: Basic Books, 1980), p. 102.

4 Yalom, *Existential Psychotherapy*, p. 3.

5 Yalom, *Existential Psychotherapy*, p. 4.

6 See C. Rogers, *A Way of Being* (Boston, MA: Houghton Mifflin, 1980), p. 41.

7 C. Rogers, *Freedom to Learn* (Columbus, OH: Charles E. Merrill Publishing Company, 1969), p. 232.

8 See C. Rogers, 'A Client-centered/Person-centered Approach to Therapy', in H. Kirschenbaum and V. Land Henderson (eds), *The Carl Rogers Reader*, 1st edn (New York: Mariner Books, 1989), pp. 135–56.

9 Rogers, 'A Client-centered/Person-centered Approach to Therapy', p. 135.

10 Along with *Existential Psychotherapy*, see Yalom's engaging and illuminating work, *Love's Executioner and Other Tales of Psychotherapy* (New York: Basic Books, 2012).

11 See, for example, R. May, *The Discovery of Being* (New York: W.W. Norton, 1983).

12 See, for example, J. F. T Bugental, *The Art of the Psychotherapist* (New York: Norton, 1987).

13 See, for example, J. Lantz, 'Mystery in Family Therapy', *Contemporary Family Therapy* 16, no. 1 (1994), pp. 53–66, and J. Lantz, 'Marcel's "Availability" in Existential Psychotherapy with Couples and Families', *Contemporary Family Therapy* 16, no. 6 (1994), pp. 489–501.

14 May, *The Discovery of Being*, p. 156.

15 May, *The Discovery of Being.*, p. 21.

16 Bugental, *The Art of the Psychotherapist*, p. 46.

17 See Bugental, *The Art of the Psychotherapist*, p. 27.

18 R. Hobson, *Forms of Feeling: The Heart of Psychotherapy* (London: Tavistock Publications, 1985), p. 194.

19 See J. C. Gunzburg, *Healing through Meeting: Martin Buber's Conversational Approach to Psychotherapy* (London: Jessica Kingsley Publishers, 1997), pp. 32–3.

20 See H. Kohut, *The Analysis of the Self* (New York: International Universities Press, 1971); H. Kohut, *The Restoration of the Self* (New York: International Universities Press, 1977); and H. Kohut, *How Does Analysis Cure?* (Chicago, IL: University of Chicago, 1984).

21 See R. Stolorow, D. Brandchaft and G. E. Atwood, *Psychoanalytic Treatment: An Intersubjective Approach* (Hillsdale, NJ: The Analytic Press, 1987).

22 See Stolorow, Brandchaft and Atwood, p. 10.

23 Stolorow, Brandchaft and Atwood, p. 11.

24 See C. Goldberg, 'Healing Madness and Despair through Meeting', *American Journal of Psychotherapy* 54, no. 4 (2000), pp. 560–73.

25 Goldberg, 'Healing Madness and Despair', p. 566.

26 Goldberg, 'Healing Madness and Despair', p. 566.

27 See M. Friedman, *The Healing Dialogue in Psychotherapy* (New York: Jason Aronson, 1985); M. Friedman, *Dialogue and the Human Image: Beyond Humanistic Psychology* (London: Sage, 1992); M. Friedman, 'Buber's Philosophy as the Basis for Dialogical Psychotherapy and Contextual Therapy', *Journal of Humanistic Psychology* 38, no. 1 (1998), pp. 25–40; and M. Friedman, 'Buber and Dialogical Therapy: Healing through Meeting', *The Humanistic Psychologist* 36 (2008), pp. 298–315.

28 See R. Hycner, *Between Person and Person: Toward a Dialogical Psychotherapy* (Highland, NY: The Gestalt Journal, 1990).

29 M. Buber, *A Believing Humanism* (London: Humanities Press International, 1990), p. 142. First published in 1967.

30 Friedman, 'Buber and Dialogical Therapy', p. 299.

31 See Hycner, *Between Person and Person*, p. 56.

32 See A. L. Adame and L. M. Leitner, 'Dialogical Constructivism: Martin Buber's Enduring Relevance to Psychotherapy', *Journal of Humanistic Psychology* 51, no. 1 (2011), pp. 41–60.

33 Adame and Leitner, 'Dialogical Constructivism', p. 44.

34 Adame and Leitner, 'Dialogical Constructivism', p. 43.

35 M. Friedman, cited in K. P. Kramer, *Martin Buber's I and Thou: Practicing Living Dialogue* (New York/Mahwah, NJ: Paulist Press, 2003), p. 15.

36 See M. Buber and C. Rogers, Appendix: 'Dialogue Between Martin Buber and Carl R. Rogers', in Buber, *The Knowledge of Man*.

37 See K. Plant, 'The Two Worlds of Martin Buber', *Theology* 88, no. 2 (1985), pp. 282–87. Plant suggests that the I–Thou world 'could plausibly be regarded as

an escapist world, with religious belief forming an escape from everyday hardships, drudgery and drabness' (p. 285). It is this 'residue' of the ordinary and the mundane which makes up the I–It world (p. 284).

38 Cf. L. Silberstein, *Martin Buber's Social and Religious Thought: Alienation and the Quest for Meaning* (New York: New York University Press, 1989), pp. 104–22. Silberstein traces the theme of actualization vs alienation through a wide selection of Buber's early writings.

39 See F. Tönnies, *Community and Association*, trans. C. Loomis (London: Routledge & Kegan Paul, 1955), pp. 37–116, esp. pp. 37–41. First published as *Gemeinschaft und Gesellschaft* in 1887.

40 See M. Buber, *Daniel: Dialogues on Realization*, trans. M. Friedman (New York: Holt, Rinehart and Winston, 1964), pp. 74–78.

41 Buber, *Daniel*, p. 78.

42 See M. Buber, *Pointing the Way*, trans. M. Friedman (London: Routledge & Kegan Paul, 1957), pp. 5–10.

43 Buber, *Pointing the Way*, p. 8.

44 See G. Wehr, *Martin Buber: Leben – Werk – Wirkung*, Kindle Edition (Gütersloh: Gütersloher Verlagshaus, 2010). Wehr makes this comment: 'So meint Buber [mit »Ich-Du«] ein Mit-Sein. Er meint, was das Ich im Verhältnis zu seinem personalen Gegenüber ist, also nicht, was es dabei »erlebt«. An einer Ich-Du-Psychologie ist er nicht interessiert' (p. 128). ('So Buber means [by I–You] a being-with. He means, what the I in the relationship to his personal counterpart is, thus not what is thereby "experienced". He is not interested in an I–You psychology.')

45 Cf. Silberstein, *Martin Buber's Social and Religious Thought*, p. 127.

46 See Buber, *I and Thou*, trans. W. Kaufmann (Edinburgh: T&T Clark, 1970), p. 112.

47 Buber, *I and Thou*, p. 54.

48 Buber, *I and Thou*, pp. 62–3.

49 Buber, *I and Thou*, p. 53.

50 Buber, *I and Thou*, p. 54.

51 Buber, *I and Thou*, p. 55.

52 Buber, *I and Thou*, p. 59.

53 Cf. Silberstein, *Martin Buber's Social and Religious Thought*, p. 144.

54 See M. Buber, *Between Man and Man*, trans. R. G. Smith (London: Routledge & Kegan Paul, 1947), p. 23.

55 Buber, *Between Man and Man*, pp. 8–10.

56 Buber, *I and Thou*, p. 57.

57 Buber, *I and Thou*, p. 150.

58 Buber, *I and Thou*, p. 151.

59 Buber, *I and Thou*, p. 67.

60 Buber, *Between Man and Man*, p. 3.

61 See Buber, *I and Thou*, p. 85.

62 G. Marcel, 'I and Thou', in P. A. Schilpp and M. Friedman (eds), *The Philosophy of Martin Buber* (LaSalle, IL: Open Court, 1967), pp. 41–8, p. 46.

63 Buber, *I and Thou*, p. 69.

64 Buber, *I and Thou.*, p. 82.

65 Buber, *I and Thou*, pp. 63–4.

66 Buber, *I and Thou*, p. 63.

67 Buber, *I and Thou*, p. 81.

68 See Wehr, *Martin Buber: Leben – Werk – Wirkung*, p. 129. Wehr expresses it this way: 'So stark Bubers menschlich-mitmenschliches Interesse auch sein mag, es erschöpft sich keineswegs in der mitmenschlichen Sphäre. Denn in, mit und unter der Ich-Du-Beziehung verwirklicht sich für ihn die Gottesbeziehung.' ('As strong as Buber's human-interpersonal interest might be, it in no way exhausts itself in the interpersonal sphere. Rather, in, with, and under the I-You relation he sees the God-relation as actualizing itself.')

69 Buber, *I and Thou*, p. 123.

70 Buber, *I and Thou*, p. 124.

71 Buber, *I and Thou*, p. 127.

72 Buber, *I and Thou*, p. 127.

73 Buber, *I and Thou*, p. 163.

74 See M. Buber, 'Distance and Relation', *Psychiatry* 20 (1957), pp. 97–104.

75 Buber, 'Distance and Relation', p. 97.

76 Buber, 'Distance and Relation', p. 97.

77 Buber, 'Distance and Relation', p. 98.

78 Buber, 'Distance and Relation', p. 99.

79 Buber, 'Distance and Relation', p. 99.

80 Buber, 'Distance and Relation', p. 99.

81 See M. Friedman, 'Reflections on the Buber-Rogers Dialogue', *Journal of Humanistic Psychology* 34, no. 1 (Winter 1994), pp. 46–65, p. 58.

82 Buber, *Between Man and Man*, pp. 61–2.

83 See Buber, 'Distance and Relation', p. 102.

84 See M. Buber, 'Elements of the Interhuman', *Psychiatry* 20, no. 2 (1957), pp. 105–13, p. 110.

85 Buber, *Between Man and Man*, pp. 23–4.

86 See Buber, 'Elements of the Interhuman', p. 110.

87 See Buber, 'Distance and Relation', p. 103; and Buber, 'Elements of the Interhuman', p. 110.

88 Buber, 'Elements of the Interhuman', p. 110.

89 See Buber, *Between Man and Man*, pp. 83–103, p. 96.

90 See Buber, *Between Man and Man*, p. 96.

91 See Buber, 'Distance and Relation', p. 103.

92 See C. Gunton, *The Promise of Trinitarian Theology*, 2nd edn (Edinburgh: T&T Clark, 2003), ch. 6.

93 See Buber, 'Elements of the Interhuman'.

94 Buber, 'Elements of the Interhuman', p. 107.

95 Buber, 'Elements of the Interhuman', p. 108.

96 See Goldberg, 'Healing Madness and Despair'.

97 See Goldberg, 'Healing Madness and Despair', p. 567.

98 See Goldberg, 'Healing Madness and Despair', p. 568.

99 See Goldberg, 'Healing Madness and Despair', p. 568.

100 See Goldberg, 'Healing Madness and Despair', p. 568.

101 See Goldberg, 'Healing Madness and Despair', p. 568.

102 See Goldberg, 'Healing Madness and Despair', p. 570.

103 See Goldberg, 'Healing Madness and Despair', p. 571.

104 T. Kron, 'Self/no-self in the Therapeutic Dialogue According to Martin Buber's Dialogue Philosophy', in D. Mathers, M. E. Miller and O. Ando (eds),

Self and No-Self: Continuing the Dialogue between Buddhism and Psychotherapy (London: Routledge, 2009), pp.165–174, pp. 172, 173.

105 See R. J. Mouw and D. A. Sweeney, *The Suffering and Victorious Christ: Toward a More Compassionate Christology* (Grand Rapids, MI: Baker Academic, 2013).

106 Mouw and Sweeney, *The Suffering and Victorious Christ*, p. 48.

107 See C. P. E. Burns, *Divine Becoming: Rethinking Jesus and Incarnation* (Minneapolis, MN: Fortress Press, 2002).

108 Burns, *Divine Becoming*, p. 104.

109 Burns, *Divine Becoming*, p. 127.

110 C. Rogers, 'The Necessary and Sufficient Conditions of Therapeutic Personality Change', in Kirschenbaum and Land Henderson (eds), *The Carl Rogers Reader*, pp. 219–235, p. 226.

111 Buber, 'Education', in Buber and Rogers, Appendix: 'Dialogue between Martin Buber and Carl R. Rogers', p. 97.

112 Buber, 'Education', p. 97.

113 C. Rogers, *A Way of Being* (Boston, MA: Houghton Mifflin, 1980), p. 143.

114 Cf. Friedman, *Dialogue and the Human Image*, p. 52.

115 C. Rogers, in Buber and Rogers Appendix: 'Dialogue between Martin Buber and Carl R. Rogers', pp. 169–170.

116 Buber, 'Appendix: Dialogue', p. 181.

117 Buber, 'Appendix: Dialogue', p. 182.

118 Buber, 'Appendix: Dialogue', p. 182.

119 See Buber, 'Appendix: Dialogue', p. 182.

120 Buber, 'Appendix: Dialogue', p. 180.

121 See Buber, 'Appendix: Dialogue', p. 183.

122 Friedman, 'Reflections on the Buber–Rogers Dialogue', pp. 63–4.

PART 2

Fundamental Interventions and Strategies

5

'Relational Humanness' *and* 'Relational Justice', or Caring for Two Worlds[1]

The model of the personal and interpersonal style of the pastoral counsellor that I have been developing in the early part of this book is closely aligned with what John Patton refers to as 'relational humanness'.[2] In order to give a sense of what he means by this term, Patton identifies the kinds of questions that ministers involved with the American Association of Pastoral Counselors would ask themselves when reviewing the person and work of a counsellor seeking accreditation: 'Is this person present, alive and available to his or her counselee and to us as a committee? Is he or she able to use the counseling relationship as a means for learning and growth? Has the counseling process moved from talking about problems "out there somewhere" to experiencing them "between us" or within the relationship?'[3]

Patton also draws upon essential elements in the Christ story – his life, death and resurrection – to flesh out the meaning of 'relational humanness'. The first element, the life of Christ, leads us in the direction of neighbour-love. Christ's love for his neighbours reminds us that we are people who have needs and who are called to help others in need.

The second element, the death of Christ, reminds us of our fallibility and weaknesses. Good neighbours are patient, loving and generous with their time and gifts. But too often we fall short of the ideal; we relate to others in destructive ways. Instead of healing we wound, in place of love there is hate, where there should be peace there is violence. Christ suffered and died on the cross to set us free from the darkness in us. In and through Christ's suffering, in and through his healing love, we are saved for a life shaped by love. Further, the suffering of Christ itself has a relational structure. Here Patton follows the lead of Jürgen Moltmann (although Moltmann does not use the term 'relational' in the context of the suffering love of Christ). Not only did Jesus suffer physically, he also suffered a much deeper pain as a result of his sense of 'godforsakenness'. The Father, for his part, suffered the ineffable grief of one who has abandoned his son to the agony and disgrace of the cross. Relational humanness, then, is forged through entering into the pain of life. That is, those who are fully present to others in their pain will themselves have been through a time of suffering.

The third element in Christ's experience is the resurrection. Resurrection refers to hope, renewal and the promise of eternal life. It also reminds us that Christ is at work to bring life into relationships that are dying. 'New life in Christ involves grace in spite of suffering ... relationship when relationship seems impossible, the experience of life when nothing is evident but death.'[4]

Patton provides a rich and insightful description of relational humanness. I especially appreciate the way in which he incorporates personal experience, humanistic psychology and theology. Though relational humanness is foundational in the ministry of pastoral care and counselling, it needs to be complemented with 'relational justice'.[5] There are limits on what a one-to-one counselling ministry can achieve. In a significant number of cases, a contributing factor to the suffering a person is experiencing is the impact of unjust socio-political systems, structures and policies. A fully developed pastoral ministry includes both relational humanness and relational justice. With this kind of thinking in mind, there has been a move over the past three decades to broaden the horizon of pastoral theology and practice to include social analysis, critique, advocacy and activism. A holistic pastoral ministry involves both care of persons and care of society.

Pastoral theology needs to take cognisance of the fact that there are forces of dominance and oppression in the social order. Pastoral care, then, is not only concerned with reorganizing intra- and interpersonal dynamics, but also with seeking to undermine oppression and injustice. Very early on, the American pastoral theologian Charles Gerkin argued for a 'widening of the horizons' of pastoral care to include shaping the consciousness and ethos of local communities and, beyond that, the care of society as a whole.[6] We find this concern with social transformation developed much more fully in the work of fellow Americans such as Larry Graham,[7] James Poling[8], Bonnie Miller-McLemore,[9] Pam Couture,[10] Barbara McClure[11] and Nancy Ramsey.[12] They argue that since those of us committed to pastoral care are concerned with the relief of suffering, and given the fact that oppressive social structures and policies contribute substantially to human distress, we need to set ourselves the task of resisting evil and working for the transformation of all that is unfair and oppressive within our society. On the UK scene, we have seen important works by Peter Selby,[13] Elaine Graham,[14] and Stephen Pattison[15] with the same emphasis.

Before we get to a fuller discussion of representative approaches to relational justice, an overview of major philosophical thinking on social justice will be given. The discussion over the nature of social justice is a contested one. Unfortunately, it is quite common in presentations of social justice counselling to either completely sidestep the issue of defining the term 'social justice' or, if it is addressed, the treatment is only cursory. The discussion that follows will indicate some of the complexities around pinning down the concept of social justice. In particular, we will see that while some philosophers construe justice exclusively in terms of distribution of benefits and burdens, others also connect it to oppression and domination. The latter emphasis is particularly important for the models of relational justice that pastoral theologians have developed.

A brief conceptual history of social justice[16]

In the nineteenth century, there was a definite shift in the way philosophers conceived of justice. For the first time, the question of the manner in which social institutions distributed benefits and burdens occupied centre stage. The question exercising the minds of a band of nineteenth-century philosophers was this: What are the clear principles that will guide a just distribution of rights and privileges, of benefits and burdens, among the citizenry? Two main proposals were offered in answering this key question – namely, the principle of desert and the principle of need.

In relation to the former principle, Henri de Saint-Simon and Karl Marx both contended that in order to ensure that the rewards people receive are proportional to the contributions they make to society, it is necessary to have impartial authorities who make judgements about the relative allocations. Moving to the principle of need, the place to begin is with a notion held by both Thomas Hobbes and David Hume. These philosophers took the view that nearly all human beings are approximately equal in terms of their innate capabilities. Hobbes, for example, wrote that '[n]ature has made men so equal in the faculties of body and mind as that ... when all is reckoned together the difference between man and man is not so considerable as that one man can thereupon claim to himself any benefit to which another may not pretend as well as he'.[17] On this view, nature has made all individuals roughly equal; it is education and socialization that account for differences in skills and achievements. Neither Hobbes nor Hume, however, contended that because all have roughly equal talents, justice requires that all should enjoy equal material possessions and be entitled to have their needs met equally. But there were other important thinkers who put forword the proposition that if by nature everyone is endowed with approximately the same level of capability, there is no justification for an unequal distribution of material goods. Still others put the spotlight on equality of worth rather than equality of talent. They argued that regardless of what may be the case in terms of equality of capacities and talents, since everyone is equal in their worth, justice requires equal satisfaction of needs.

Marx construed the principle of desert as a socialist one. But for him socialism is not the final destination; it is a staging post on the way to communism. He had this to say: 'Between capitalist and communist society lies a period of the revolutionary transformation of the one into the other. Corresponding to this is also a political transition period in which the state can be nothing but the revolutionary dictatorship of the proletariat.'[18]

In Marx's view, the distributive principle is defective and therefore must ultimately be replaced with the principle of need. He was inspired, along with a number of other social reformers of the time, by the adage 'from each according to his ability; to each according to his needs'.

There is an obvious problem associated with this debate over distributive justice: the two principles are necessarily at odds with each other. The principle of desert favours the talented who achieve much in their lives, while the principle of need is tilted towards the less well off.

In the distributive justice area, the political philosopher John Rawls[19] is a major figure. Rawls was aware of the issues and problems around the desert and need perspectives, but his main concern was to expose the shortcomings of utilitarianism when it comes to a theory of justice. Jeremy Bentham was a pioneer in utilitarian philosophy. He thought that the principle of social utility furnishes objectivity and certainty in moral thought. 'Nature has placed mankind under the governance of two sovereign masters, *pain* and *pleasure*. The *principle of utility* recognizes this subjection ... An action may be said to be conformable to the principle of utility ... when the tendency it has to augment the happiness of the community is greater than any it has to diminish it.'[20]

The basic criterion of what is morally right, wrong or obligatory in utilitarian theories is the *consequences* that flow from particular rules or acts. That is, they have a teleological frame of reference. The ultimate end posited is the greatest general good. A rule or action is right if and only if it can be assessed as likely to produce at least as great a balance of good over evil for the community as a whole as any alternative. It is important to recognize that the good referred to here is non-moral good: food, shelter, health, etc.

Against this commitment to the principle of utility, deontologists such as Rawls argue that there are other considerations that take precedence over the goodness or badness of consequences. That is to say, there are certain universal principles that establish what is right or obligatory. It is therefore possible, they argue, for an action or a rule to be morally right or obligatory even if it doesn't promote the greatest possible ratio of good over evil.

In relation to the justice question, Rawls was dissatisfied with utilitarianism because of its failure to posit the fair distribution of benefits and burdens as the central issue. Utilitarian theories focus on aggregate human well-being rather than justice. For Rawls, questions of justice are the most important ones in relation to social institutions.

The subject of Rawls's theory is the 'basic structure' of society. By this term he means 'society's main political, social, and economic institutions, how they fit together into one unified system of social cooperation'.[21] Rawls's concern is to develop a theory of how these institutions should operate in order to ensure fairness in society. This is captured in this statement in *A Theory of Justice*: '[T]he principles of social justice ... provide a way of assigning rights and duties in the basic institutions of society and they define the appropriate distribution of the benefits and burdens of social cooperation.'[22]

A central plank in Rawls's theory is a view of a just society as one that operates according to a fair system of social cooperation between free and equal persons over time. That is, in such a society the benefits produced through everyone's endeavours are fairly acquired and distributed from one generation to the next. The key question that must be answered here is this: What defines a fair system of cooperation? Given that society is a partnership that people have entered into for the sake of mutual benefit, an adequate social justice theory needs to specify exactly how it is possible to ensure a fair distribution of benefits among the participants in the social partnership.

The leading nineteenth-century proposals concerning social justice, as we have seen, consisted either of a prescription for contributions members should make to society and for benefits they should receive (the principle of needs), or of an approach that connected benefits that individuals are entitled to with the contributions they make (the principle of desert). In contrast, Rawls's theory focuses on benefits, while setting to one side the issue of contributions.

In addressing the issue of what a fair distribution of benefits across society would look like, Rawls offers his famous hypothetical 'veil of ignorance'. He asks his readers to imagine that each member of society is represented by an agent in a condition he calls 'the original position'.

This position is a hypothetical state of affairs in which agents assemble to reach consensus on the terms on which society operates. Their task is to come up with a set of principles for social justice in relation to distribution of benefits in society.

Now these imaginary agents are reasonable people. They appreciate the fact that they must be prepared to reach agreement with one another by pursuing what is fair. To ensure their reasonableness, Rawls ask us to imagine that the parties in the original position have been placed behind a 'veil of ignorance'. Sitting behind this veil, they are unable to know the abilities, social positions, or indeed the identity of the members they represent. In this way, Rawls sets up a scenario in which impartial agents scrupulously employ the principle of fairness to the distribution of benefits and thereby identify what a perfectly just society looks like.

Despite the widespread acclaim for the rigour and cogency in Rawls's theory of justice as fairness, there have been a number of criticisms levelled at it. For our purposes, the most significant one is that the theory confines justice to distribution and overlooks the central roles that privilege and oppression play. According to the political philosopher Iris Marion Young, when oppression is brought into the frame, issues of decision-making, division of labour and culture all come to the fore. This wider perspective also leads to recognition of the impact of social group differences;[23] some groups are privileged while others are oppressed. The advancement of social justice requires, first, acknowledging these group differences and, second, joining in collective action aimed at undercutting oppression.

Young contends that when it comes to understanding the dynamics of oppression and domination and what is required to undermine them, the leftist social movements in the USA – democratic socialist, environmentalist, black, Hispanic, indigenous American, gay liberation, feminist, disability advocacy, and more – have been particularly helpful. Her aim in her book, *Justice and the Politics of Difference*, is to investigate the conceptions of justice undergirding these movements, and the way in which they revise traditional conceptions of justice.

Young is particularly critical of the ideal of impartiality that is considered by many political philosophers to be 'the hallmark of moral reason'.[24] This ideal is the result of a search for a universal, objective moral point of view. The problem is that the impartial transcendental subject represses difference. In particular, she takes aim at Rawls and his 'veil of ignorance'. In the end, the impartiality approach supports cultural imperialism by unwittingly presenting the perspective of privileged groups as the universal one.

In her more recent book entitled *Responsibility for Justice*,[25] Young once again takes up the issue of structural injustice, but this time focusing on responsibility. She argues that social structure is the subject of justice, and that structural injustice is distinct from wrongs associated with certain individual actions or policies. People are the victims of structural injustice when the unfortunate circumstances they find themselves in do not result primarily from their own choices and actions. They are largely the victim of circumstances beyond their control.

Young then moves on to the central question of her book – namely, who bears responsibility for structural injustice? She proposes a 'social connection' model of responsibility. According to this model, 'all those who contribute by their actions to structural processes with some unjust outcomes share responsibility for the injustice'.[26] The consequence of bearing such responsibility is that one is morally obligated to join forces with others who also bear responsibility in transforming the structural forms and processes such that their outcomes are more just.

It is this attention to oppression and structural injustice that sits at the centre of the approaches to social justice counselling that important figures such as Stephen Pattison and Larry Graham developed in the early 1990s. They both contend that it is unhelpful and irresponsible to focus exclusively on the intrapsychic and interpersonal dynamics in pastoral care. One eye must also be cast on what can be done to undermine the oppression that is contributing significantly to the personal suffering.

In his book entitled *Pastoral Care and Liberation Theology*, Stephen Pattison is critical of the fact that most pastoral theologians and pastoral caregivers fail to give attention to the impact that structural and policy factors have on individual suffering. What is required is robust criticism of the injustice associated with social structures and policies. But since the political dimension of personal suffering is not on the radar screen of pastoral theorists and practitioners, there is an inevitable failure in this regard.

Pattison offers an extended case of mental illness and the practice of chaplains working in mental health facilities to make his point. He is critical of the fact that an almost total reliance on the therapeutic paradigm results in a failure to notice the socio-political context that so influences the experience of mental illness. Pattison reports on the evidence for large inequalities in relation to access to and provision of healthcare, personal services and welfare benefits. He notes that the poor in the UK are a significantly dispossessed class and that those suffering from mental illness are even further disadvantaged and marginalized. The level and form of care they receive is far from adequate.

Pattison contends that the well-known critique of most systematic theology as being individualistic and apolitical in its focus applies equally to the theology and practice of pastoral care. Pastoral care and counselling is too often limited to ameliorating the suffering associated with social injustice; it needs to expand its horizon by challenging the lack of fairness and equity at the systemic, structural and policy levels.

In a liberation model of pastoral care, attention is given to the inter-relationship between low socio-economic status and ill health, the power that the medical and psychiatric professions possess in relation to determining patient treatment, and the impact of inequalities associated with gender, race and class in relation to the provision of care and treatment. Pastoral care that addresses the exclusion and invisibility of those without power and voice takes an interventionist and preventative stance. In this model of care, practitioners join with others who share their perspective in criticizing unfair structures and inequitable power dynamics in healthcare relationships, and in working for change.

As I indicated in an earlier note, the name that Larry Graham gives to this model is 'relational justice'. He contrasts it with relational humanness. Graham's major statement of the idea of relational justice is presented in his book *Care of Persons, Care of Worlds*. There he uses the slightly different term, 'redemptive justice'. Further, in that book he does not use the term 'relational humanness', but instead applies the generic description, an 'existential-anthropological model of care'.[27] Graham characterizes this model as individualistic. For practitioners guided by this approach, '[c]ontext is background; personhood foreground'.[28] That is, Graham is claiming that they do not pay sufficient attention to the role of familial, social, political and cultural contexts. He advocates a systemic approach. In such an approach, there is an understanding that the various personal, ecclesial, social, political and ecological sub-systems exert mutual influence and determine the nature and functioning of the system. Thus, when a caregiver works with a careseeker, that work needs to involve interpretation of, and action on, the psyche, the family of origin, the current family, the work environment, social and political institutions, and ecology. Straightaway it is evident that this is a complex and challenging model of care. Graham describes his 'psycho-systemic' approach to care in this way:

> [My aim] is to demonstrate the ongoing, permanent, and reciprocal interaction between the psyches of persons and the larger environments that are bringing psyches into being and influencing their nature. It is my conviction that psyches create systems and systems create psyches. The relationship between them is synaptic, or spiritual, characterized by mutual reception, rejection, struggle, and creative accomplishment.[29]

In this approach, an important function of care is to work for transformation of the larger structures – the socio-political structures – that mitigate personal well-being. 'Religious ministry', writes Graham, 'is understood as the totality of strategic activities engaged in by the religious community and its individual members to increase the love of self, God, and neighbour, and to promote a just social order and a liveable environment.'[30] The ministry of care, in particular, involves offering support and encouragement, on the one hand, and developing change strategies, on the other, in the face of the destructive consequences of lovelessness, injustice and ecological irresponsibility. It is 'the task of pastoral caretaking to increase the capacities for the love of self, God, and neighbour, and the abilities to work for a just social order and a liveable environment on the part of careseekers'.[31]

The smaller and larger structures – that is, the family and work environment on the one hand, and social and political systems and institutions on the other – are responsible, in part, for the suffering of the individual. But individuals must themselves take some responsibility for the crises they find themselves in. But there are also significant external factors. In order for healing and growth to take place in a person, there needs to be a strategy and a subsequent course of action aimed at positive change. The caregiver and the careseeker need to see themselves as co-workers for change. Together, and in concert with others with similar values and goals, they need to work for transformation. The project of care has the goal of 'redemptive justice'.

In his later article, entitled 'From Relational Humanness to Relational Justice', Graham reiterates his view that a concern with liberation from domination and oppression should be central in pastoral care. Whereas the aim of promoting healing and growth through therapeutic intervention was once seen as the beginning and end of pastoral care and counselling, the new approach incorporates advancement of justice and ecological integrity. Graham notes the link with those concerned with liberation for oppressed groups such as women, gays and lesbians, and ethnic minorities and goes on to describe a ministry committed to relational justice:

Rather than perpetuating the domination and subordination which seem so pervasive in our political and moral economy, relational justice seeks to correct power imbalances. A caregiver seeks relational justice in the paradigm I am developing by working to replace domination and subordination with cooperation. The caregiver promotes conditions in which power is accountable and flexible, rather than exclusive, hidden, or inaccessible. These conditions promote self-determination and fulfillment, full participation in the social order, and nurture of individuals and cultural groups. Relational justice calls for a thorough-going revision of our value systems, transactional patterns, and the way we organize the institutions of our world.[32]

In order to illustrate his approach to relational justice, Graham uses the experience of Connie, a lesbian and a Christian. Connie grew up in a family that did not recognize or understand her sexual orientation. She also experienced certain difficulties as a result of living in a predominately Mormon area. In her early years, her church could not help her embrace her sexuality, but later in life she encountered both Christian communities and a secular therapist who encouraged her to affirm her lesbianism and to advocate for wider acceptance of homosexuality. Graham says of Connie's experience that '[o]ne simply cannot comprehend the full dimensions of the care provided to her without appropriating a foundational concept of relational justice or emancipatory liberation'.[33]

More recently, Nancy Ramsey has made an important contribution to this new way of thinking about pastoral care and counselling.[34] Ramsey also argues for the urgent need for pastoral theorists and practitioners to escape from the psychological captivity that has been a prominent feature for so long. The practice of separating love from justice needs to stop. According to Ramsey, '[t]he transformative energy of love [is] obscured by confining it to an individual and existential focus'.[35] Like both Larry Graham and Iris Marion Young, she argues that much can be learned from the theory and practice in various emancipatory movements when it comes to exposing the asymmetry in power relations and the impact these have on both the privileged and the oppressed. In this new vision, adequate care requires attention to the way in which the socio-political context impacts on the suffering and distress that many individuals are experiencing today.

The metaphor that Ramsey employs, following Bonnie Miller-McLemore and others, is the living human web. There is a social web of systems, structures and policies that individuals are tangled up in. In the old therapeutic model, this web is invisible. The pastoral counsellor works with an individualistic paradigm, blithely ignorant of the relational and systemic ecology that is so significant in relation to the careseeker's suffering.

Ramsey refers to the 'highly ecological anthropology'[36] that is in play. She contends that it is vitally important to give attention to the way in which gender, race, class and other factors impact on personal experience.

In her most recent work, Ramsey uses intersectional theory to illumine the nature of this ecological anthropology.[37] Intersectionality is a theory that addresses the individual, relational, structural and ideological aspects of oppression and privilege. It gives attention to the way in which differences in gender, race, class and sexuality are associated with power differentials that result in dominance over, and control of, socially valued resources. In particular, the theory focuses on the fact that differences such as gender, race, class and sexuality are simultaneous, interrelated systems of inequality. The goal of the theory is to point up effective pathways to social justice. That is to say, the aim is to empower those experiencing inequality and oppression, especially through supporting strategic action by coalitions.

Ramsey suggests that pastoral theologians and care practitioners committed to the relational justice paradigm can profit from integrating intersectionality into their theoretical models. Its main strength is that it points up the way in which various types of difference often intersect one another. Oppressed people may be, for example, simultaneously female, persons of colour, and have low socio-economic status. They find themselves caught up in related systems of inequality and domination. Pastoral counsellors committed to relational justice who are working with such individuals can profitably employ intersectionality in shaping their liberative practices.

Summary

Over the past three decades we have seen a host of influential pastoral theologians in the UK and in the USA arguing that relational humanness needs to be supplemented with relational justice. The suffering that many individuals experience is to a significant degree the result of the impact of dominance and oppression associated with unjust social systems, structures and policies. An individualistic focus and reliance on therapy alone constitutes an inadequate pastoral response. Pastoral ministry in such cases requires social analysis, critique, advocacy and action for change. A holistic ministry of care incorporates both relational humanness and relational justice.

What this means in the context of this book is that while the subject matter in the chapters that follow is very largely interventions and strategies in one-to-one counselling, it is essential to keep in mind that this kind of work needs to be complemented with awareness of socio-political context and a commitment to work for the undermining of oppression and injustice. It must never be thought that one's pastoral ministry starts and finishes with a facility with an array of therapeutic, spiritual and ritual techniques. Working with these psychological and spiritual resources needs to be supplemented with working for justice and a liveable environment.

Notes

1 The two 'worlds' I refer to are the intrapsychic-interpersonal domain and the socio-political world.

2 See J. Patton, *Pastoral Counseling: A Ministry of the Church* (Nashville, TN: Abingdon Press, 1983), ch. 1.

3 Patton, *Pastoral Counseling*, p. 21.

4 Patton, *Pastoral Counseling*, p. 27.

5 The term is used by Larry Graham in his article 'From Relational Humanness to Relational Justice: Reconceiving Pastoral Care and Counseling', in P. Couture and R. Hunter (eds), *Pastoral Care and Social Conflict* (Nashville, TN: Abingdon Press, 1995), pp. 220–34.

6 See C. Gerkin, *Widening the Horizons: Pastoral Responses to a Fragmented Society* (Philadelphia, PA: Westminster Press, 1986).

7 See L. Graham, *Care of Persons, Care of Worlds: A Psychosystems Approach to Pastoral Care and Counseling* (Nashville, TN: Abingdon Press, 1992); and Graham, 'From Relational Humanness to Relational Justice'.

8 See J. Poling, 'An Ethical Framework for Pastoral Care', *The Journal of Pastoral Care* 42, no. 4 (Winter 1988), pp. 299–306; and J. Poling, *Deliver Us From Evil: Resisting Racial and Gender Oppression* (Minneapolis. MN: Fortress Press, 1996).

9 See B. Miller-McLemore, 'The Living Human Web: Pastoral Theology at the Turn of the Century', in J. Stevenson-Moessner (ed.), *Through the Eyes of Women: Insights for Pastoral Care* (Minneapolis, MN: Fortress Press, 1996), pp. 9–26; and B. Miller-McLemore, 'Pastoral Theology and Public Theology: Developments in the U.S.', in E. Graham and A. Rowlands (eds), *Pathways to the Public Square: Practical Theology in an Age of Pluralism* (Münster: Lit Verlag, 2005), pp. 95–105.

10 See P. Couture, *Blessed are the Poor? Women's Poverty, Family Policy, and Practical Theology* (Nashville, TN: Abingdon Press, 1991); P. Couture, 'The Family Policy Debate: A Feminist Theologian's Response', *Journal of Pastoral Theology* 3 (1993), pp. 76–87; and P. Couture, 'Pastoral Care and the Social Gospel', in C. H. Evans (ed.), *The Social Gospel Today* (Louisville, KY: Westminster John Knox Press, 2011), pp. 160–196.

11 See B. J. McClure, *Moving Beyond Individualism in Pastoral Care and Counseling* (Eugene, OR: Wipf & Stock, 2010).

12 See N. Ramsey, 'Contemporary Pastoral Theology: A Wider Vision for the Practice of Love', in N. Ramsey (ed.), *Pastoral Care and Counseling: Redefining the Paradigms* (Nashville, TN: Abingdon Press, 2004), pp. 155–176; and N. Ramsey, 'Intersectionality: A Model for Addressing the Complexity of Oppression and Privilege', *Pastoral Psychology* 63 (2014), pp. 453–69.

13 See P. Selby, *Liberating God: Private Care and Public Struggle* (London: SPCK, 1983).

14 See E. Graham, *Transforming Practice: Pastoral Care in an Age of Uncertainty* (London: Mowbray, 1996).

15 See S. Pattison, *A Critique of Pastoral Care*, 2nd edn (London: SCM Press, 1993), esp. ch. 5; and S. Pattison, *Pastoral Care and Liberation Theology* (Cambridge: Cambridge University Press, 1994).

16 Useful discussions on the historical development in philosophical thinking on social justice are as follows: B. Jackson, 'The Conceptual History of Social Justice', *Political Studies Review* 3 (2005), pp. 356–73; D. Johnston, *A Brief History of Justice* (New York: Wiley, 2011), chs 7 and 8; W. P. Pomerleau, 'Western Theories of Justice', *Internet Encyclopedia of Philosophy*, available at http://www.iep.utm.edu/justwest/; and J. T. Jost and A. C. Kay, 'Social Justice: History, Theory, and Research', in S. T. Fiske, D. T. Gilbert and G. Lindzey (eds), *Handbook of Social Psychology* vol. 1 (New York: Wiley, 2010), pp. 1122–65.

17 T. Hobbes, *Leviathan*, ch. 13. Cited in M. Hoelzl and G. Ward (eds), *Religion and Political Thought* (London: Bloomsbury Academic, 2006), p. 108.

18 K. Marx, 'Critique of the Gotha Programme', in D. McKellan (ed.), *Karl Marx: Selected Writings*, 2nd edn (Oxford: Oxford University Press, 2000), p. 611.

19 See J. Rawls, 'Justice as Fairness', *Philosophical Review* 64, no. 1 (1955), pp. 3–32; J. Rawls, *A Theory of Justice* (Cambridge MA: Belknap Press, 1971); and J. Rawls, 'Justice as Fairness: Political not Metaphysical', *Philosophy and Public Affairs* 14, no. 3 (1985), pp. 225–52.

20 J. Bentham, *An Introduction to the Principles of Morals and Legislation* (London: Athlone Press, 1970), ch. II, p. xiv. Cited in H. Kainz, *Ethics in Context* (London: Macmillan Press, 1988), p. 78.

21 Rawls, 'Justice as Fairness: Political not Metaphysical', p. 225.

22 Rawls, *A Theory of Justice*, p. 4.

23 The link between social justice and social group differences is a major theme in I. M. Young's book, *Justice and the Politics of Difference* (Princeton, NJ: Princeton University Press, 1990).

24 Young, *Justice and the Politics of Difference*, p. 99.

25 See I. M. Young, *Responsibility for Justice* (New York: Oxford University Press, 2011).

26 Young, *Responsibility for Justice*, p. 96.

27 See Graham, *Care of Persons, Care of Worlds*, p. 32ff.

28 See Graham, *Care of Persons, Care of Worlds*, p. 33.

29 See Graham, *Care of Persons, Care of Worlds*, p. 41.

30 See Graham, *Care of Persons, Care of Worlds*, p. 43.

31 See Graham, *Care of Persons, Care of Worlds*, p. 45.

32 Graham, 'From Relational Humanness', pp. 230–31.

33 Graham, 'From Relational Humanness', p. 230.

34 See Ramsey, 'Contemporary Pastoral Theology: A Wider Vision for the Practice of Love'; and Ramsey, 'Intersectionality: A Model for Addressing the Complexity of Oppression and Privilege'.

35 Ramsey, 'Contemporary Pastoral Theology', p. 161.

36 Ramsey, 'Contemporary Pastoral Theology', p. 162.

37 See Ramsey, 'Intersectionality'.

6

Revising Faulty Thinking, or a Socratic Approach to Healing 'Belief-Sickness'

As indicated in the introduction, I envision a broad scope for pastoral counselling. It consists of offering compassion, understanding, support, guidance and challenge to those struggling with various intrapsychic, interpersonal, spiritual and moral issues. A significant reason for people experiencing emotional and/or spiritual distress, or misconstruing the nature of the good, is that they suffer from what I like to call 'belief-sickness'. Unhealthy beliefs fall into the three categories I have just identified – namely, the psychological, the spiritual, and the moral.[1] Beliefs sometimes elude neat categorization, but there is usually one dimension that is most prominent. A belief-sickness is defined as a take on self, others, life or God that is unrealistic, unhealthy or unfaithful, and that causes significant emotional and spiritual distress, and/or militates against personal well-being, positive interpersonal relating, and movement towards spiritual maturity.

In placing a focus here on belief-sickness, I do not wish to give the impression that I think that all the pain and distress that pastoral counsellors encounter can be traced back to faulty thinking. I certainly do not think that helping a counsellee to challenge distorted patterns of thinking is the centre of gravity for pastoral ministry. While assisting with cognitive reframing is an important skill for counsellors to master, there are a number of other skills that well-rounded counsellors need in their kitbags. Some of these have already been discussed; others will be explored in the chapters that follow.

I was led to the metaphor of belief-sickness through my engagement with certain great philosophers. Indeed, the medical metaphor has featured for a very long time in the history of Western philosophy.[2] Among the Hellenistic philosophers, for example, we find the idea that the pupils in this school of thought were infected with certain unhealthy beliefs that were common in the existing society. The role of the teacher was construed as offering a cure. We find a more modern version of it in the approach of Søren Kierkegaard. According to Kierkegaard, the pastor should view the whole world as 'a giant hospital', in which people are waiting for their 'wounded souls' to be completely healed.[3]

There were two general and quite distinct approaches to philosophical doctoring: indoctrination in the (healthy) beliefs of the teacher and his school, and promotion of healing through self-doctoring. This latter approach – one that was advanced by certain Stoics – is naturally enough the one that will be advocated here.

Self-doctoring aligns in a general way with the approach of contemporary psychotherapists such as Christine Padesky, James Overholser, Patricia Calvert and Christine Palmer. They use the term 'guided discovery' to capture a strategy that values client autonomy and self-guided action.[4] These authors identify the 'Socratic method' or 'Socratic questioning' as very helpful in promoting guided self-discovery. But as we shall see, there is a gap between what these therapists construe as the Socratic method and what is presented in the Platonic Dialogues. Despite this technical flaw, they do actually offer a useful process for guiding the cure of unhealthy beliefs. However, the method of guided discovery needs to be adapted to fit the central aim of challenging faulty beliefs. The emphasis in Rational Emotive Behaviour Therapy (REBT) on disputation and helping the counsellee philosophize more effectively is recommended for this purpose. Further, the line of Socratic questioning needs to be broadened beyond the psychological domain; it needs also to extend to the spiritual and moral areas.

This chapter is structured as follows. First, we consider the question of personal belief systems or schemas from the perspective of psychology, theological ethics and the Bible. This is followed by a general discussion on the philosophical approach of healing the false beliefs (belief-sickness) people commonly hold. Third, the idea of self-doctoring is covered. This leads into a discussion of the use of Socratic questioning in the counselling process in order to promote self-discovery and reframing faulty thinking. In the last section, the Socratic questioning technique is applied to work in the psychological, spiritual and moral domains.

Personal belief systems

Every individual has a set of beliefs about the nature of self, others, life and the world. For some, included in this set are beliefs about God and the spiritual life. In psychology, a set of personal beliefs is often referred to as a schema. Mozdzierz *et al.* refer to a schema as 'a "map", a *construct*, or a systematic theory of how the world works' [emphasis in the original].[5] According to these authors, our personal templates or maps serve as a guide as we negotiate life in the world. Further, we tend to follow our schemas loyally and with little change; in this way we secure the assets of stability, continuity and predictability.

Life, with all of its associated intellectual, emotional, moral and spiritual challenges, is exceedingly complex. No one is able to map a perfect route through it. No one has the capacity to take in all the relevant data, make the necessary assessments and evaluations, and come up with a set of beliefs that fit perfectly with the way the world works and, from a theological point of view, with God's will and purpose for human life. It is therefore a question of more or less adequate interpretations of self, others, life, and God.

The idea of schemas has a long history in psychology. Alfred Adler referred to 'private maps'.[6] He distinguished between neurotics who live according to their maps of 'private intelligence', and well-adjusted people who operate out of 'common sense'. Those who possess 'common sense' evaluate self, others and the world through employing reason. The fact that rational evaluations and interpretations are behind the personal vision of those in the common sense camp means that these visions are ones that will make sense to others, and therefore they are widely shared. Adler has this to say about facilitating cure for the ills associated with 'private intelligence':

> For the neurotic, coming to understand his own picture of the world – a picture which he built up early in childhood and which has served as his 'private map', so to speak, for making his way through life – is an essential part of cure. When one is attempting to redirect his life to a more nearly normal way of living, he will need to understand how he has been seeing the world. He will have to re-see the world and alter his private view in order to bring it more into harmony with a 'common view' of the world – remembering that by common view we mean a view in which others can share.[7]

A similar idea is found in the work of George Kelly. Kelly set the notion of personal constructs at the centre of his theory of personality. He observed that human beings view the world through 'transparent patterns or templates' which they create in an attempt to make sense of life in the world and to guide thinking and behaviour. He called these templates 'constructs' and discussed their purpose as follows: 'They are ways of construing the world. They are what enables man, and lower animals too, to chart a course of behaviour, explicitly formulated or implicitly acted out, verbally expressed or utterly inarticulate, consistent with other courses of behaviour or inconsistent with them, intellectually reasoned or vegetatively sensed.'[8]

A vision of life is also a central concept in moral philosophy and theological ethics. While the moral life certainly involves decision, choice and action, it may be that vision is even more important. Stanley Hauerwas has made a strong case for this position. 'The moral life', he suggests, 'is not first a life of choice – decision is not king – but is rather woven from the notions that we use to see and from the situations we confront. Moral life involves learning to see the world through an imaginative ordering of our basic symbols and notions.'[9] Hauerwas argues that Christian ethics has allowed itself to be shaped by the dominant philosophical view of the human as actor and self-creator. According to this view, human beings construct themselves through a 'willful' actualization of the choices and decisions that they have made. Individuals decide on the significant actions and plans that will give the desired shape to their lives and then engage their wills to ensure that these are realized.

I readily acknowledge that decision-making has a role in ethical theory and practice. But I contend that decisions and actions are based on a vision of what is most real, meaningful and worthwhile.[10] When we make assessments about the moral life, we do not look only to the choices that people make and the decisions they enact. Rather, we look to something that is much more difficult to grasp but that is also more important and more fundamental – namely, a 'total vision of life'.[11] This total vision is shown in our ways of speaking and relating, in our assessments of others, in the way we think about our own lives and of the world around us, and in what we judge to be noble and of worth. What we are grasping for here is a total way of viewing self, others, life and God that informs and moulds all our thoughts, desires, words and actions.

When it comes to theology, there is of course a fundamental schema that is discernible in the Bible. This schema consists of creation, fall, redemption, and the final transformation of heaven and earth with the return of Christ. Even when stating the biblical schema in this very general way, one cannot avoid the issue of individual interpretation. For example, there are those who construe the fall in historical terms and those who view it in a symbolic way. Whatever interpretation one brings to this broad schema, it is clear that the New Testament conveys the message that God was at work in Christ reconciling the world to Godself. Christ came to establish a new kingdom or realm. The old aeon was dominated by evil, idolatry, hatred, violence and injustice. Through Christ's life, death and resurrection a new age was ushered in – one characterized by generosity, love, compassion, righteousness, reconciliation, peace and justice. This Realm is both a present and future reality. God in Christ, through the power of the Holy Spirit, has won a victory over evil. But the complete victory will only come at the end of time when Christ returns in glory. In the meantime, those who follow Christ are called to a life of worship, witness and service as they join with Christ's cause of extending God's reign.

Schemas operate at the global level; they provide the map that guides people in their way of life. What I am calling belief-sickness is located at the street level, if you will. At this lowest level, there is a cluster of rules and principles that people embrace. Though the vast majority of Christians will likely accept the broad depiction of the biblical schema I have offered, there are almost countless interpretations that individuals bring to the various elements in it. It is when we get to the level of the specifics that we find significant disagreements. In this contested area, there are both healthy and diseased perspectives. Belief-sickness has taken hold of certain Christians because they have a faulty understanding of some of the specific psycho-spiritual and moral elements associated with the big scriptural picture. Here are some examples that I encounter on a regular basis:

- The view that since Christians are filled with the joy and the resurrection power of Christ, they should not be troubled by anxiety or depression.
- Taking the line that if we are not a complete success (in life generally but in the spiritual life in particular) we are complete failures.
- A tendency to believe relatively small failures or negative events are catastrophic.
- Believing that a particular construal of a situation or event must be true because one feels it strongly (judging on the basis of emotion).
- A readiness to forgive means that we would be letting transgressors get off too lightly.
- A misunderstanding of the place of material things in the life of a Christian, characterized by an overvaluation of their importance and contribution to personal happiness.
- Paying lip service to finding identity and personal value in Christ and in God's gracious acceptance, while really believing that self-worth is tied to success and personal achievement.
- The belief that Christian humility means thinking you are nothing and never asserting yourself.
- An interpretation of the ideal of Christ-like love as never thinking of oneself and always acting self-sacrificially.
- Believing that masturbation is sinful and sleazy.

- Viewing gays, lesbians, bisexual and transgender persons as sinful and perverted.
- The view that what's going on in the socio-political world has nothing to do with faith and practice.
- The idea that social injustice is so entrenched that it is futile to seek to do anything about it.
- The conviction that women flourish under male headship.
- The view that Christians are called to be mild-mannered and nice, and should therefore refrain from any form of speech, no matter how true and necessary it may be, that is hard, confronting and uncomfortable for oneself and for others.
- The belief that a strong faith and obedience to God is insurance against bad things happening.
- Thinking that the ideal for holiness is perfection.

We have noted that belief systems or schemas have psychological, moral and theological dimensions. As indicated above, I am aligned with those pastoral counselling theorists who contend that all three dimensions need to be fully attended to in working with people of faith.[12] Daniël Louw has made an important contribution in this regard. In an article on philosophical counselling, he identifies a network of existential categories that draws in psychology, ethics, and spirituality. He presents it in table form;[13] and an adapted version is presented below. In reviewing it, it will be obvious to the reader that associated with the existential realities and the 'Christian spiritual dimensions' that Louw identifies, there are particular schemas, and also that behind the 'compulsions' and pathological levels in the 'existential issues' sit various forms of belief-sickness.

In attending to belief-sickness, pastoral counsellors need to focus on all three dimensions (the psychological, the moral and the theological). What is particularly helpful in Louw's network approach is that he makes it abundantly clear that the various existential issues that we all face are intimately connected to these three domains. We will return to this focus below.

Existential issues: The threat to dignity	Compulsions: Excessive human quests	Existential life needs and being needs: Courage to be	Christian spiritual dimensions: Spiritus
Anxiety: experience of loss or rejection	To be acknowledged and validated; seeking honour and pride (Plato)	Intimacy; affirmation and self-actualization	Grace: unconditional love; role of God-images
Guilt or shame	To be perfect; success; achievement (avoid failure)	Freedom or deliverance	Forgiveness or reconciliation
Despair or doubt	The quest for absolute security, safety or certainty	Anticipation: meaning and trust	Eschatological realm of hope determined by the belief in the cross and resurrection of Christ
Helplessness or vulnerability	To be independent and in control (power: to dominate or abuse)	Support system	Fellowship, *koinonia* or *diakonia*
Frustration or anger	To possess and to have (greed)	Life fulfilment or direction or transformation	Gratitude and joy or promissio- therapy or ethics

Philosophical therapy for belief-sickness

Philosophers throughout the ages have also observed, unsurprisingly, that individuals construct a personal philosophy or worldview. They have noted, too, that some worldviews are based on faulty reasoning; the result is suffering in the soul. In assessing the corrective role that philosophy is able to play, use is sometimes made of a medical analogy.[14] For example, Epicurus wrote this about the role of philosophical argument: 'Empty is that philosopher's argument by which no human suffering is therapeutically treated. For just as there is no use in a medical art that does not cast out the sickness of bodies, so too there is no use in philosophy, if it does not throw out suffering from the soul.'[15] If we turn to the Stoics, Epictetus has this to say on healing unhealthy desires before they really take hold of a person: '[W]hen once you conceive a desire for money, if reason is applied to make you realize the evil, the desire is checked and the Governing Principle recovers its first power; but if you give it no medicine to heal it, it will not return to where it was, but when stimulated again by the appropriate impression it kindles to desire quicker than before.'[16]

The Epicureans and the Stoics observed that there were many people in society whose souls are sick because they are driven by unhealthy desires. Everywhere they looked, they saw people feverishly chasing after money, after fame, after various luxuries, after passionate love.[17] These sick souls were driven by the false belief that if only they could attain the desires of their hearts they would be happy and fulfilled. A false belief about the world and about the source of value generates the wrong kind of desire – an empty one.[18] The philosopher's calling was construed as the conversion of pupils suffering from distorted beliefs through engaging them in a process of rational argumentation.

Plato similarly observed the close connection between disorder in the affective life and false opinion. When a person is dominated by an irrational appetitive power, the problem can be traced back to faulty thinking.[19] The metaphor of the Cave in the *Republic* points to the radical enslavement of the total person. The prisoners in the Cave are fettered by something more than a lack of enlightened thinking. There is disorientation of the mind under the impact of the irresistible push of disordered desire. There needs to be a radical conversion in belief and desire if a person is to be liberated. Robert Cushman correctly suggests that Plato's understanding of the role of philosophy is essentially therapeutic.[20] The philosopher, on a Platonic view, tends the soul in such a way that its vision is gradually purified, thus allowing it to see what is best. Having attained a clear and true vision, a person needs then to change those habitual actions that are not aligned with it.

Moving to an era closer to our own, Søren Kierkegaard refers to a 'sickness unto death' that can only be healed through inwardness and subjectivity. Attempts to address the problem of despair, he contends, must always bear 'some resemblance to the address which a physician makes beside the bedside'.[21] It is sometimes the case that a particular individual feels quite healthy; that person is not experiencing any signs or symptoms of illness. Such individuals are therefore quite shocked when a doctor diagnoses them as ill. Kierkegaard draws an analogy with the spiritless people in the existing society who are blithely unaware of the sickness in their souls.[22] He is aiming to expose the folly in the confident judgement that we are competent assessors of our own spiritual health.[23]

When we turn to Kierkegaard's upbuilding discourses, we also find the medical metaphor being employed. According to him, the world is full of sick people who are rushing about frenetically trying to procure all the wrong things – a problem that, as we have just seen, was also a major concern for the Hellenistic philosophers. Kierkegaard suggests that if he were a physician, he would prescribe a dose of stillness – a quiet space in which the word of God can be heard.[24]

Kierkegaard was deeply distressed by the spiritual malaise suffered by so many in nineteenth-century Denmark. The 'aesthetes' and 'philistines' in society were afflicted by 'spiritlessness' and despair. In these social categories we find all kinds of people, including the educated and the successful. These are the ones who think that they are in command of their destiny. They are convinced that they are persons of substance and purpose. But in fact, says Kierkegaard, they only skate across the surface of life, tranquillizing themselves in trivial ideas and pursuits.[25]

Kierkegaard took an indirect route in his confrontation of deluded thought and behaviour (something we will attend to in much more detail in Chapter 7). He realized that to tackle head-on the superficiality and despair that plagued many of his fellow Danes would be worse than useless. He therefore opted for an indirect means of communication in which his readers were presented with a variety of perspectives and value systems. Kierkegaard's thinking was that in using this strategy his audience would be presented both with a position they knew very well – namely, their own – and others containing different and better perspectives. In this way, he hoped to wake up their souls and provoke self-reflection.

In the twentieth century, this idea of the philosopher being in the business of offering therapy for false beliefs was picked up by Ran Lahav and others in the philosophical counselling movement. Lahav is the main proponent of 'worldview interpretation' in this counselling approach.[26] He begins by observing, as we also have, that everyone has a 'personal philosophy'.[27] We have a view of what constitutes a right and good way to live: how to secure personal happiness, what the meaning and purpose in life are. We use this framework to navigate our way through life. The totality of beliefs and perspectives about how one's life should be lived, about what constitutes a fair, honourable and happy existence, Lahav calls a 'worldview'. The aim of philosophical counselling as he construes it is to provoke and facilitate an interpretation of a personal worldview. The kinds of things that people typically suffer from – boredom, loss of meaning and purpose, anxiety, depression – can be traced back to problematic elements in the worldview that a person holds. Lahav refers to these problematic components as 'contradictions or tensions between the conceptions about how life should be lived, hidden presuppositions that have not been examined, views that fail to take into account various considerations, over-generalizations, expectations that cannot realistically be satisfied, fallacious implications, and so on'.[28]

Lahav notes that philosophers are experts in analysing conceptions of the world. Through sponsoring critical investigation of a personal worldview, the philosophical counsellor helps the client identify problematic elements associated with the current feelings of distress, dissatisfaction and frustration so that these unhelpful components may ultimately be replaced with better ones.

Self-doctoring as the preferred option

We have just seen that in certain traditions of philosophy, rational argumentation is viewed as therapy for sick souls. We have also seen that often a medical analogy is employed in this regard. When the image of the physician is appropriated, a certain asymmetry is immediately suggested. It is commonly accepted that 'doctor knows best'. That is to say, doctors are established as medical authorities, and patients, if they know what is good for them, should rely on their expertise and assiduously comply with their recommended treatment regime. It is this implication in the metaphor that was appropriated within the Epicurean community. Pupils were instructed not to trust themselves, but rather to place themselves under the wisdom of teachers and to follow their guidance. The cure involved converting the suffering person through the use of argumentation and a process of memorization, confession of false beliefs, and inculcating summaries of correct belief. Martha Nussbaum characterizes the approach as one in which the pupil is 'saturated with the correct ways of thought and kept away from alternative views'.[29] It is amazing that Epicurus actually expected his disciples to memorize his very extensive writings.[30] In recognition of the enormity of the task, he finally decided to provide them with summaries that could be applied in curing false beliefs. A sense of Epicurus' directive approach can be gleaned from the following piece of advice: 'The things which I used unceasingly to commend to you, these do and practice, considering them to be the first principles of the good life.'[31]

This paternalistic approach sits in stark contrast to the method employed by Socrates. He did not aim to fill pupils with wise teachings in order that they might correct their false beliefs. Instead, Socrates acted as the midwife, helping to bring to birth the truth that is already the possession of the pupil. Ernest Barker captures the Socratic approach nicely: 'Socrates had never attempted to instil knowledge ... He desired to awaken thought. He was the gadfly who stung men into a sense of truth; he gave the shock of the torpedo-fish; he practised the art of mid-wifery, and brought thought to birth.'[32]

This Socratic approach is reflected most strongly in the Roman school within Stoicism. Seneca and Epictetus sought to promote self-activity in their pupils. It is certainly true that they are confident in their own arguments and put them strongly. It is also the case that they are usually quite contemptuous of the views of their opponents. Nevertheless, these philosophers do not set themselves up as the authority; the reason of the pupil is posited as the only true authority. They insist, like Socrates, on pupils taking up the challenge of thinking for themselves. They need to take charge of their own lives. Indeed, in one of his letters to Lucilius, Seneca explicitly contrasts his approach with the directive method of the Epicureans:

> We are not subjects of a king: each man claims his own. But among Epicureans everything that Hermarchus said, or Metrodorus, is credited to one man; anything someone in that brotherhood uttered was said under the supreme command and auspices of one leader. I tell you, we cannot, even if we try, detach anything from such a host of consistent thoughts.[33]

When one reads through the letters of Seneca, it is very clear that his message is this: Do not simply memorize the wisdom of others; think it through for yourself and make it your own. To give just one illustration, Seneca, after having given examples of men who had demonstrated mastery over the fear of death, exhorts Lucilius thus: 'Think over all this in your heart, ideas you have often heard and often uttered, but then prove whether you have really heard and uttered them by the result ...' (24, 15).

These Stoic philosophers had no time for subservience; they wanted pupils to teach themselves. Here the spirit of Socratic inquiry is being embraced. In response to Lucilius' complaint that sayings of Epicurus have not been included in recent epistles, Seneca replies by saying that it is better to think for oneself, rather than simply remembering the wise sayings of another. In this way, one creates new knowledge:

'Zeno said this!' And what have you to say? 'Cleanthes said this'. And what have you to say? How long will you move under another's guidance? Take command and say something worth committing to memory, say something of your own creation. So I believe that all those men who are never originators, but always interpreters hiding in another's shadow, have no spark of nobility, and never dared to do what they spent so long learning. They exercised their memory on other men's thoughts, for remembering is different from knowing. Remembering is keeping safe something entrusted to the memory, whereas knowing is making each thing one's own and not depending on the model and constantly looking back to the teacher. 'This is what Zeno said', 'what Cleanthes said.' Let there be some difference between yourself and the book.[34]

Kierkegaard also embraced a Socratic approach. In both his philosophical and his religious writings, the aim is not to correct faulty thinking through instilling knowledge. He sees every person as potentially a 'spirited being'. Growth in maturity and wisdom comes not through indoctrination, but rather through the awakening of inwardness. Kierkegaard's strategy is not 'to convey results as much as to elicit in his reader a self-activity and a process of appropriation'.[35]

Good philosophy, according to our guides, is like the therapeutic work of a physician. But in the end, these philosophers subvert the medical model with its strong focus on the authority of the doctor. What they advocate is actually *self*-doctoring – to use Nussbaum's term.[36] In this method of doing philosophy, the aim is not to indoctrinate, but rather to awaken the soul.

Self-doctoring for counsellees using the socratic method

I have already indicated that Socrates promoted self-doctoring, and his major concern was with how to live the good life. His approach was not to simply indoctrinate his listeners with his version of how life should be lived. Rather, he engaged in a process of interrogation of the views of his contemporaries. During the process, they become acutely aware that they do not know what they think they know. Unable to answer Socrates' sharp, incisive questions, they are brought face to face with their ignorance of an issue that they thought they understood clearly and fully.

A significant number of therapists have made a connection between Socrates' approach and their strategy in working with clients. There are dozens of articles and a number of books on therapy and counselling in which one finds mention of terms such as 'the Socratic method', 'Socratic dialogue' and 'Socratic questioning'. There is a significant amount of confusion about what these terms mean and exactly how the Socratic method should be applied in therapy.[37] Rarely is there any attempt to define the terms. It is virtually never the case that authors discuss the Socratic method as it is revealed in the Platonic dialogues in presenting their 'Socratic' approach.[38]

Were these authors to turn to the Platonic dialogues, they would discover that what they label 'Socratic questioning' or 'Socratic dialogue' in their counselling approach is really quite different to the original version. Socrates' method is usually referred to as the *elenchus*. *Elenchus* involves cross-examination and refutation. In the early dialogues, Socrates interrogates his conversation partners on the topic of virtue. There is usually a concentration on a particular virtue (e.g. bravery in *Laches*; piety in *Euthypro*; and moderation in *Charmides*). Terence Irwin captures the nature of *elenchus* well:

> The basic structure of a typical elenchus is simple. Socrates asks a question, either a request to be told what some virtue is (for instance, 'What is bravery?'), or some other question about a virtue. The interlocutor affirms some proposition p in answer to Socrates' initial question; under Socrates' questioning he agrees that he also believes q and r; and he discovers, under further questioning, that not-p can be derived from q and r; hence he finds that his beliefs commit him to p and not-p. Finding himself in this situation, he is 'at a loss' (aporein) about what to believe.
>
> It is not just the interlocutor who is at a loss. Socrates himself insists that he does not know the answers to the questions that he asks his interlocutors; and so he concludes that they are 'all alike at a loss'.[39]

Socrates begins by claiming ignorance on the topic under investigation. Through this process of interrogation, he brings his interlocutors to the realization that he is in the same state. Both individuals are in a position of not knowing. Therefore, the main Socratic insight is that everyone starts from a position of ignorance.

Meno is a good place to turn in search of the Socratic method. Meno opens the dialogue by inquiring how virtue is learned or acquired. Socrates responds by suggesting that Meno begins with the wrong question. Socrates tells him that if one is to know the attributes of anything (*quale*), it is necessary to first know what its nature or essence (*quid*) is. Thus, he makes the point that the primary question is not how one should go about acquiring virtue, but rather what virtue is.

Meno's starting point carries with it the assumption that both he and Socrates know the essence of virtue. He moves on to ask about one of the attributes of virtue; he wants to know if it is gained by teaching or acquired naturally. Socrates offers a challenge to this unexamined assumption. He tells Meno that he himself knows virtually nothing about virtue, and moreover that he has never met anyone else who is any better off in this regard. Socrates then says that given that he does not know the *quid* of virtue, how can he possibly know the *quale*?

Meno lets the challenge slide by him, however, and simply asserts that he knows what virtue is. When challenged by Socrates to declare his knowledge, Meno boldly and arrogantly claims that this is an easy thing for him. He attempts to do this by using the virtue of a person as illustrative. Socrates objects to this approach to definition because it focuses only on a particular expression of virtue and does not go to what virtue is in and of itself. Through the employment of *elenchus*, cracks in Meno's veneer of certainty concerning his knowledge of virtue are beginning to open up. Through persistent interrogation by Socrates, the cracks widen and deepen. Meno reaches a point of deep perplexity and confusion. He finds himself in an *aporia*: he cannot come up with a definition of virtue that is satisfying to both himself and Socrates.

Obviously therapists and counsellors do not intend to lead their clients through 'Socratic questioning' into an *aporia*. The therapeutic process is not one of leading clients to a point of perplexity and disillusionment in order to bring them to a place of humility and wisdom. As indicated above, the divergence between the Socratic method we find in the Platonic dialogues and in the therapeutic literature is hardly ever recognized or acknowledged. I was therefore struck in reading such a declaration in a report of a panel discussion from the 34th National Conference of the Australian Association of Cognitive and Behaviour Therapy.[40] Christopher Fairburn, from the Centre for Research on Eating Disorders at the University of Oxford, declares that he thinks the term 'Socratic questioning' is actually a misnomer in the therapeutic context:

[I]f you come from Oxford you tend to meet experts in other topics, and I recently had dinner with an international expert on Socrates. From what he told me, Socrates certainly did not engage in what we refer to as Socratic questioning ... He was apparently famously ruthless with his questioning and would pin people to the ground almost with his questioning. He liked to baffle people by asking mysterious questions that were slightly off topic, but he had a target and he would pursue people in his questioning until he could find some flaw in their position or argument. He was famous for being aggressive in his questioning, whereas I think all of us are taking the opposite stance of wanting to be gentle rather than confrontative [sic]. So, the term is probably a misnomer, but it exists.[41]

Given that therapists are not actually using the Socratic method of the Platonic dialogues, is there any real point of connection with the original? I believe that there is but it is a connection at a general level only. When therapists who claim to be using the Socratic method refer to their approach as using carefully crafted questions to guide discovery, they link with the philosopher's technique in a real though generalized manner. Socrates' aim was similarly to provoke self-examination and to guide a process of personal discovery. In the most general terms, the self-discovery is that one is ignorant. In the case of Meno, the ignorance is 'trebled', as Thomas Eisele points out: '(1) He is ignorant as to the nature of Socratic questions and how they need to be answered (or the kind of answer that they expect or require); (2) he is also ignorant as to the nature or essence of virtue ... and (3) he does not know initially that he is ignorant in either of these respects.'[42]

Obviously both the nature of the self-discovery involved and the process of getting there in the modern therapeutic setting are not the same as what we see in Socrates' educative practice. Nevertheless, there is a general point of connection; this explains the decision of certain therapists to appropriate Socrates. The link is the use of skilful, well-targeted questioning to stimulate self-reflection and transformative discovery. It is this adapted rather than pure version of the Socratic method that we take up below.

So what is the 'guided discovery' facilitated by Socratic questioning that contemporary therapists refer to? Christine Padesky defines it thus:

> Socratic questioning involves asking the client questions which: (a) the client has the knowledge to answer, (b) draw the client's attention to information which is relevant to the issue being discussed but which may be outside the client's current focus, (c) generally move from the concrete to the more abstract so that (d) the client can, in the end, apply the new information to either reevaluate a previous conclusion or construct a new idea.[43]

There are two fundamental principles underpinning the guided discovery paradigm. The first is that the insights that clients/counsellees discover for themselves most often lead to real and lasting change. Second, Socratic dialogue serves to establish in clients/counsellees a habit of critical reflection on personal beliefs, the goal of which is self-improvement.[44] James

Overholser neatly captures the aim of supporting self-discovery: 'Therapy can facilitate autonomy and promote an internal locus for change, often through self-awareness, self-direction, and self-regulation.'[45]

We have been talking about Socratic questioning in general terms. We need now to identify what might be some helpful questions in relation to guided discovery. On Padesky's 'good questions list' are these suggestions: 'Have you ever been in similar circumstances before? What did you do? How did that turn out? What do you know now that you didn't then? What would you advise a friend who told you something similar?'[46] Overholser offers a much more extensive and systematic presentation of helpful questions.[47] Under 'Question Content' he lists questions in the categories of problem definition, generation of coping alternatives, decision-making and implementation. Under 'Questioning Process' he refers to five elements, each with sample questions assigned: the leading question, the explication, the defence, a sequential progression, and the use of short sequences. It is not expedient to summarize this extensive discussion here, and readers are encouraged to read the article for themselves. However, I do want to draw attention to Overholser's important insight that Socratic questioning should be conducted in short bursts and alternated with other forms of dialogue.[48] Over-use of questions limits spontaneity and the client's self-exploration. Moreover, constant questioning will be perceived by the client as interrogation.

A Socratic approach to belief-sickness in the three domains

The guided discovery approach depicted above is a helpful one. However, it has two shortcomings in terms of the particular approach to pastoral counselling that we are developing. First, the set of questions that is commonly used lacks the tight focus on disputing faulty thinking required for an approach involving guiding the healing of belief-sickness. Second, the scope is limited to the psychological domain. In this final section, we see how the general approach can be refined to fit the aim of promoting self-doctoring for belief-sickness.

When it comes to disputing faulty beliefs, the obvious place to turn is cognitive therapy. There are three schools of psychotherapy that are usually included under this banner – namely, the Rational Emotive Behaviour Therapy (REBT) of Albert Ellis, the Cognitive Therapy of Aaron Beck and his associates, and the Cognitive-Behavioural Therapy of Donald Meichenbaum. Ellis's approach attends in the most direct way to the Socratic method; it is therefore the one that we will work with.

The central tenet of REBT is that events alone do not cause people to feel depressed, highly anxious or angry. Rather, it is their (irrational) beliefs about the events that are the major sources for unhealthy feelings and self-defeating behaviours. Ellis defines an irrational belief as the notion that something in life should, ought or must be different from the way it is. He contends that a key to happiness is to challenge these 'foolish', 'crazy' beliefs and to replace them with saner, more rational ones.[49]

REBT works on an ABC approach.[50] A refers to the *activating event*. B indicates the *belief system*, and C stands for the emotional *consequence*. An example of A is the fact that a senior manager has just had a bad month at her job. She has made a series of errors of judgement that have led to negative outcomes for her company. Her belief about it, B, is this: 'This is a disaster. I'm losing it. I don't have what it takes anymore.' The emotional consequence, C, that follows is feelings of anxiety, worthlessness and depression. According to REBT, the activating event, A, in one sense is not all that important. It is of course not insignificant that this manager has messed up at her job. But it is the meaning we assign to events rather than the events themselves that cause upset.

Those who use REBT believe, as virtually all therapists do, that there is value in attending to the emotional consequences, C. The woman feels shame and a sense of inadequacy; she's also very anxious because she has lost confidence in her ability to perform her work at an acceptable level. These feelings need to be acknowledged, but proponents of REBT contend that the most efficacious action is confronting B.

Further, REBT prioritizes attention to the here and now over exploring past traumatic history. It is argued that no matter how defective and traumatic individuals' personal and family histories may have been, the main reason why they are overreacting or underreacting to disagreeable stimuli (A) is because at this present moment they have some dogmatic, irrational and unexamined beliefs (B). Therapists bring dispute, D, into the ABC equation. They dispute irrational thought by challenging clients to marshal their evidence for the validity of their beliefs. Albert Ellis and Debbie Joffe Ellis describe the REBT practitioner as 'an exposing and sceptical scientist'.[51]

A distinction is made between General REBT and Preferential REBT. The former has the aim of inculcating rational and health-promoting behaviours, whereas the latter is focused on teaching the client how to dispute irrational ideas and unhealthy behaviours. Preferential REBT employs a 'one-to-one Socratic-type dialogue' which seeks to help the client 'separate rational (preferential) from irrational (absolutistic) beliefs'.[52] The aim is to break the hold of the magical 'shoulds' and 'oughts' that result in emotional distress. This is clearly exhibited in the following extract from a typical REBT session. The client is a

25-year-old woman who works as the head of a computer programming section. She suffers from heavy guilt and shame feelings, a deep sense both of unworthiness and of insecurity, and is constantly depressed. She overeats and drinks excessively. In this extract, the therapist is disputing her belief that she should have a purpose in life:

T-33: You're perfectly able ... to think – to stop giving up. That's what you've done most of your life; that's why you're disturbed. Because you refuse to think. And let's go over it again: 'It would be better if I had a purpose in life; if I weren't depressed, *et cetera, et cetera*. If I had a good, nice, enjoyable purpose.' We could give *reasons* why it would be better. It's fairly obvious why it would be better! Now, why is that a magical statement, that 'I *should* do what would be better'?

C-33: You mean, why do I *feel* that way?

T-34: No, no. It's a belief. You *feel* that way because you *believe* that way.

C-34: Yes.

T-35: If you believed you were a kangaroo, you'd be hopping around; and you'd *feel* like a kangaroo. Whatever you *believe*, you *feel*. Feelings come from your beliefs. Now, I'm forgetting about your feelings, because we really can't change feelings without changing the beliefs. So I'm showing you: you have two beliefs – or two feelings, if you want to call them that. One, 'It would be better if I had a purpose in life'. Do you agree? (client nods). Now that's perfectly reasonable. That's quite true. We could *prove* it. Two, 'Therefore I *should* do what would be better'. Now those are two different statements. They may seem the same, but they're vastly different. Now, the first one, as I said, is sane. Because we could prove it. It's related to reality. We can list the advantages of having a purpose – for almost anybody, not just for you.

C-35: (calm now, and listening intently to T's explanation): Uh-huh.

T-36: But the second one, 'Therefore I *should* do what would be better' is crazy. Now, *why* is it crazy?

C-36: I can't accept it as a crazy statement.

T-37: Because who said you *should*?

C-37: I don't *know* where it all *began*! Somebody said it.

T-38: I know, but I say whoever said it was screwy!

C-38: (laughs) All right.

T-39: How could the world possibly have a *should*?[53]

While much more could obviously be said about the REBT approach, perhaps enough has been given here to provide a good sense of it. It is presented here not because I give my whole-hearted endorsement to

Ellis's philosophy of life generally and to his approach to psychotherapy in particular. In fact, I think that a critical appraisal raises a number of serious questions.[54]

I suggest that we can profit by taking two things from the REBT method. The first is its aim of helping the counsellee to philosophize more effectively. This is clearly necessary for self-doctoring. The second point – and it is clearly related to the first – is its emphasis on disputation using the Socratic method (loosely conceived, of course). A faulty belief needs to be challenged in order for the person holding it to make a shift. Putting a series of skilful, well-targeted questions can be a powerful tool in this regard.

Obviously the focus in REBT is only on distorted personal psychology. But belief-sickness manifests not only in psychological 'symptoms', but also in spiritual and moral ones. The guided discovery sponsored by pastoral counsellors needs to reach into all three domains. Thus, the scope of the questions they use in facilitating a process of guided discovery needs to be broader than those questions used in the REBT – or a similar – method. I offer below a set of generalized questions to supplement the disputative approach covered above. Clearly, questions that pastoral counsellors use will be tailored to fit individuals and the particular belief that is causing them distress and militating against their quest for spiritual wholeness. All I can do here is work at the general level. The questions work for both a belief-sickness that has a focus in the spiritual life in general, and one that is oriented more specifically to the moral domain:

• How is this belief impacting on your life? On the life of others?
• How does the belief impact on your relationship with others? With God?
• What do you find in the Bible, or in something else you have read, that puts a question mark over this belief?
• What's your warrant for dismissing these alternative views?
• If, after the disputation, you accept that the belief is flawed ... then we're agreed that your belief has its problems. What's a better one?
• Thinking Christianly about this new belief, what supports it?
• What puts a question mark over it?
• What difference would taking up this new belief make in your life?

Summary

In this chapter, we focused on a particular approach to pastoral counselling – namely, facilitating a process of self-doctoring for belief-sickness. We defined sickness of the soul as a take on self, others, life or God that is unrealistic, unhealthy or unfaithful, and which causes significant emotional and spiritual distress and/or militates against personal well-being, positive interpersonal relating, and movement towards spiritual maturity. The idea that a set of personal beliefs causes distress and unhappiness is well established not only in the Bible, but also in psychotherapeutic psychology and in philosophy.

Some schools of philosophy (e.g. the Epicureans) take a paternalistic approach to curing belief-sickness. However, we took a lead from the playbook of Socrates, the Stoics, Kierkegaard, and certain modern schools of psychotherapy in opting for self-doctoring. We also gave attention to the way in which the Socratic method (though this should not be taken to mean the original version) is used in psychotherapy to facilitate a process of guided discovery. It was necessary, finally, to shift the focus to disputing faulty beliefs, and to broaden the dispute approach to incorporate the moral and the spiritual domains.

As I indicated in the introduction to this chapter, it is certainly the case that not all of the work that pastoral counsellors do relates to faulty beliefs. They therefore need skills other than that of using a guided discovery approach to overcoming distorted thinking. In the chapters that follow we will explore facilitation of self-challenge, working with metaphors, and effective use of communal rituals.

Notes

1 As I indicated in the introduction to the book, this way of naming the three domains is not entirely satisfactory. The containers leak into one another. I certainly do not mean to give the impression that spirituality is a discrete category, and that psychology and ethics can somehow be separated out from it.

2 Cf. R. E. Cushman, *Therapeia: Plato's Conception of Philosophy* (London: Transaction Publishers, 2008); M. C. Nussbaum, *The Therapy of Desire: Theory and Practice in Hellenistic Ethics* (Princeton, NJ: Princeton University Press, 1994).

3 On this, see M. Heymel, '"Predigen – die schwierigste aller Künste": Anstöße von Sören Kierkegaard für die heutige Homiletik', *International Journal of Practical Theology* 10 (2006), pp. 34–52.

4 See C. Padesky, 'Socratic Questioning: Changing Minds or Guiding Discovery?' A keynote address delivered at the European Congress of Behavioural and Cognitive Therapies, London, 24 September 1993; J. C. Overholser, 'Collaborative Empiricism, Guided Discovery, and the Socratic Method: Core Processes for Effective Cognitive Therapy', *Clinical Psychology: Science and Practice* 18, no. 1 (2011), pp. 62–6; and Overholser, 'Guided Discovery: Problem-Solving Therapy

Integrated within the Socratic Method', *Journal of Contemporary Psychotherapy* 43, no. 2 (2013), pp. 73–82; and P. Calvert and C. Palmer, 'Application of the Cognitive Therapy Model to Initial Crisis Assessment', *International Journal of Mental Health Nursing* 12 (2003), pp. 30–8.

5 G. J. Mozdzierz, P. R. Peluso and J. Lisiecki, *Principles of Counseling and Psychotherapy* (New York: Routledge, 2009), p. 162.

6 See A. Adler, 'The Underdeveloped Social Interest', in H. L. Ansbacher and R. R. Ansbacher (eds), *The Individual Psychology of Alfred Adler* (New York: Harper Torchbooks, 1964), pp. 250–5, p. 254.

7 Adler, 'The Underdeveloped Social Interest', p. 254.

8 G. A. Kelly, *The Psychology of Personal Constructs*, vol. 1: *A Theory of Personality* (London: Routledge and Kegan Paul, 1991), p. 7. First published in 1955.

9 S. Hauerwas, *Vision and Virtue* (Notre Dame, IN: University of Notre Dame Press, 1981), p. 2.

10 Cf. Hauerwas, *Vision and Virtue*, p. 30.

11 Hauerwas, *Vision and Virtue*, p. 34.

12 See D. J. Louw, *A Mature Faith: Spiritual Direction and Anthropology in a Theology of Pastoral Care and Counseling* (Leuven: Peeters Publishers, and Grand Rapids, MI: Eerdmans, 1999); and D. J. Louw, 'Philosophical Counselling: Towards a "New Approach" in Pastoral Care and Counselling?' *HTS Teologiese Studies/Theological Studies* 67, no. 2 (2011), 7 pages. DOI: 10.4102/hts.v67i2.900; L. Sperry, *Transforming Self and Community: Revisioning Pastoral Counseling and Spiritual Direction* (Collegeville, MN: The Liturgical Press, 2002); N. Pembroke, *Moving Toward Spiritual Maturity: Psychological, Contemplative, and Moral Challenges in Christian Living* (London: Routledge, 2007).

13 See Louw, 'Philosophical Counselling', p. 6.

14 Martha Nussbaum traces this theme in a very comprehensive manner in her fine book *The Therapy of Desire*.

15 Epicurus, Porph. Ad Marc. 31, in H. Usener, *Epicurea* (Leipzig, 1887), p. 209; cited in Nussbaum, *The Therapy of Desire*, p. 102.

16 Epictetus, 'Discourses of Epictetus', Bk II, ch. XVIII, in Whitney J. Oates (ed.), *The Stoic and Epicurean Philosophers* (New York: The Modern Library, 1957).

17 See, for example, Epicurus, 'Fragments' XLIII-LXVII, trans. Cyril Bailey, *Epicurus: The Extant Remains* (Oxford: Clarendon Press, 1926); Epictetus, 'Discourses of Epictetus', Bk II, chs XIV, XVIII.

18 It is a fundamental tenet of Epicurean and Stoic psychology that belief and desire are very closely associated. Cf. C. Gill, 'Psychology', in James Warren (ed.), *The Cambridge Companion to Epicureanism* (Cambridge: Cambridge University Press, 2009), pp. 125–41, p. 132.

19 Cf. Cushman, *Therapeia*, p. 144.

20 Cushman, *Therapeia*, p. 144.

21 S. Kierkegaard, *The Sickness unto Death*, trans. Walter Lowrie (Princeton, NJ: Princeton University Press, 1941), p. 3.

22 See Kierkegaard, *The Sickness unto Death*, p. 32.

23 Cf. G. Connell, 'Knights and Knaves of the Living Dead: Kierkegaard's Use of the Living Death as a Metaphor for Despair', in Patrick Stokes and Adam Buben (eds), *Kierkegaard and Death* (Bloomington, IN: Indiana University Press, 2011), pp. 21–43, p. 38.

24 See Kierkegaard, 'The Mirror of the Word', in *Self-Examination and Judge for Yourselves!* trans. Walter Lowrie (Princeton: Princeton University Press, 1968), p. 71.

25 See S. Kierkegaard, *The Sickness unto Death*, p. 51.

26 See R. Lahav, 'Conceptual Framework', in Ran Lahav and Maria da Venza Tillmans (eds), *Essays on Philosophical Counseling* (Lanham, MD: University Press of America, 1995), pp. 3–24.

27 Lahav, 'Conceptual Framework', p. 3.

28 Lahav, 'Conceptual Framework', p. 9.

29 Nussbaum, *Therapy of Desire*, p. 131. Voula Tsouna contends that Nussbaum overstates the case. Tsouna's view is that Epicurean students actively participated in their own cure, were encouraged to maintain a critical stance, and were engaged in a dialogical process by the teacher. See her essay, 'Epicurean Therapeutic Strategies', in Warren (ed.), *The Cambridge Companion to Epicureanism*, pp. 249–65, pp. 263–5.

30 On Epicurus' demand for memorization, see C. Diskin, 'The Athenian Garden', in Warren (ed.), *The Cambridge Companion to Epicureanism*, pp. 9–28, pp. 20–1.

31 Epicurus to Menoeceus, 122, trans. Bailey, *Epicurus*.

32 E. Barker, *The Political Thought of Plato and Aristotle* (Mineola, NY: Dover Publications, 2009), p. 64.

33 Seneca, *Selected Letters*, trans. Elaine Fantham, 33.4.

34 Seneca, *Selected Letters*, trans. Elaine Fantham, 33, 7–9.

35 Paul Holmer, in his introduction to Kierkegaard, *Edifying Discourses: A Selection*, ed. Paul L. Homer, trans David F. Swenson and Lillian Marvin Swenson (New York: Harper & Row, 1958), p. viii.

36 Nussbaum, *Therapy of Desire*, p. 496.

37 Cf. T. A. Carey and R. J. Mullan, 'What is Socratic Questioning?' *Psychotherapy: Theory, Research, Practice, Training* 41, no. 3 (2004), pp. 217–26.

38 An exception is an essay by Chris Mace on *elenchus* and therapy. See C. Mace, 'Therapeutic Questioning and Socratic Dialogue', in C. Mace (ed.), *Heart and Soul: The Therapeutic Face of Philosophy* (New York: Routledge, 1999), pp. 13–28.

39 T. Irwin, *Plato's Ethics* (Oxford: Oxford University Press, 1995), p. 17; cited in Mace, 'Therapeutic Questioning', p. 18.

40 N. Kazantzis, C. G. Fairburn *et al.*, 'Unresolved Issues Regarding the Research and Practice of Cognitive Behavior Therapy: The Case of Guided Discovery Using Socratic Questioning', *Behaviour Change* 31, no. 1 (2014), pp. 1–17.

41 Kazantzis Fairburn *et al.*, 'Unresolved Issues', p. 6.

42 T. D. Eisele, 'The Poverty of Socratic Questioning: Asking and Answering in the *Meno*', *Faculty Articles and Other Publications*, Paper 36 (1994); http://scholarship.law.uc.edu/fac_pubs/36.

43 Padesky, 'Socratic Questioning', p. 4.

44 Cf. Overholser, 'Collaborative Empiricism', p. 64.

45 Overholser, 'Collaborative Empiricism', p. 64.

46 Padesky, 'Socratic Questioning', p. 1.

47 J. Overholser, 'Elements of the Socratic Method: I. Systematic Questioning', *Psychotherapy* 30, no. 1 (1993), pp. 67–74.

48 See Overholser, 'Elements of the Socratic Method', p. 72.

49 As one would expect, other cognitive therapists provide lists of 'crazy beliefs'. See, for example, J. Beck, *Cognitive Therapy: Basics and Beyond* (New York: The Guilford Press, 1995), p. 119.

50 For a helpful overview, see S. Walen, R. Digiuseppe and W. Dryden (eds), *A Practitioner's Guide to Rational-Emotive Therapy*, 2nd edn (Oxford: Oxford University Press, 1992), pp. 24–6.

51 A. Ellis and D. J. Ellis, 'Rational Emotive Behavior Therapy', in D. Wedding and R. J. Corsini (eds), *Current Psychotherapies*, 10th edn (Belmont, CA: Brooks/ Cole, 2013), pp. 151–91, p. 154.

52 Ellis and Ellis, 'Rational Emotive Behavior Therapy', p. 167

53 Ellis and Ellis, 'Rational Emotive Behavior Therapy', p. 171.

54 For a helpful critique, see S. Jones, 'Rational-Emotive Therapy in Christian Perspective', *The Journal of Theology and Psychology* 17 (Summer 1989), pp. 110–20.

7

Facilitating Self-Challenge, or Learning the Art of Indirection

We all have our blind-spots; it is part of the human condition. There are things about ourselves – our faulty self-interpretation, unrealistic thoughts, self-deception and certain moral inferiorities – that we just cannot see. Now a pastoral counsellor – even the best educated and the most insightful one – is not the fount of all wisdom. To be sure, a pastoral counsellor has the benefit of training in Bible, theology, ethics and pastoral psychology. A good one also has a deep spirituality and possesses keen insight and considerable wisdom. But human beings are necessarily limited. Even a spiritually mature, insightful and well-trained pastoral counsellor will not get it right each and every time. But even an imperfect ability to recognize and appropriately challenge blind-spots is extremely helpful. A blind-spot is something that others can see very clearly, but the individuals concerned entirely miss. The ability to pick up on blind-spots and to help counsellees recognize them is therefore a gift that good counsellors possess.

What we are looking at in this chapter is the other side of the counselling coin. The side that is more comfortable and perhaps instinctive is acceptance and support. Gerard Egan puts in simple terms what every counsellor knows: 'All effective helping is some kind of mixture of support and challenge.'[1] With particular reference to pastoral counselling, Clements and Clinebell refer to this idea as 'the growth formula'. They tell us that a combination of caring and confrontation adds up to personal growth in the counsellee.[2] Caring consists of acceptance, affirmation and grace, while challenging a counsellee requires openness, insight and honesty.

Pastoral counsellors have long been influenced by the non-directive approach of Carl Rogers. As we have seen, Rogers contended that the necessary and sufficient conditions for promoting growth and healing are acceptance, empathy and congruence. But even within the Rogerian movement there have been those who consider that something more is required. In an article entitled 'Confronting Carl Rogers', the person-centred therapist Ralph Quinn points out the limitations in an 'acceptance-only' policy and cites his own clinical experience in support:

> In the last year I have worked with a man who claimed he desperately needed to be more assertive in his life, with a lonely woman who wanted to quit spending all her evenings alone at home, with a student who would do practically anything to stop using marijuana, and with a husband and wife whose constant fighting was 'ruining their marriage.'
>
> With all of these clients at some point in the course of therapy I spent a good deal of time confronting their (largely unconscious) desires to not be assertive, to not be with other people, to keep smoking marijuana, and to maintain the same dysfunctional patterns of fighting.[3]

Virtually all counselling theorists agree that facilitating a process of self-challenge is very often required for the counsellee to instigate real and lasting change.

The thinker who has helped me the most in my reflection on how to subtly and artistically go about confronting people about their blind-spots is Søren Kierkegaard. As we saw in the previous chapter, Kierkegaard was intensely aware of the fact that a direct confrontation aimed at exposing a distorted view of things stirs up defensive reactions, sets the will in opposition, and has the end-result of strengthening the illusion.[4] What the Danish philosopher aimed to do was to use ambiguity and irony to facilitate self-discovery. I suggest that he offers pastoral counsellors an important perspective on their task of promoting self-challenge in the counsellee. His subtle, indirect and ambiguous approach aligns with what some authors call a non-linear approach.[5] The literature on confrontation or challenge in counselling focuses for the most part on relatively direct and straightforward approaches. This is a good place to start; the strategies have been proven to be quite effective. However, Kierkegaard's method of indirection constitutes encouragement for a pastoral counsellor to express intuition and to engage in more artistic approaches to promoting self-challenge. In order to set the scene for a presentation of Kierkegaard's approach, it is necessary to reflect on the blind-spots that we all struggle with.

Common blind-spots

To be human is to have blind-spots. There are certain unrealistic ways of viewing the world, moral inferiorities, biases and prejudices, self-deceptive tendencies, distortions in self-interpretation, and more that we either simply do not see or view in a distorted way. The deficits that accrue from our blind-spots are a weakened ability to identify and manage problem situations on the one hand, and identify and develop opportunities, on the other.[6]

Psychologist Madeleine Van Hecke helpfully identifies ten common blind-spots.[7] Three of these stand out as blind-spots that are especially relevant to the pastoral counselling context. I have in mind the following: (a) lack of awareness of certain personal thoughts, feelings and beliefs; (b) inability to see the self accurately, and (c) failure to see 'my-side bias'.

In discussing the fact that most of us suffer from a lack of awareness of certain aspects of our inner world of thought and experience, Van Hecke makes it clear that she is not referring to Freud's theory of repression. Her focus is on the conscious rather than the unconscious domain. What she is interested in is the fact that we become keenly aware of thoughts, feelings and beliefs at a certain moment, and then they are largely lost to us. The next wave of thought and experience comes along and washes them away.

The second blind-spot has to do with faulty self-interpretations. Psychologists, philosophers, poets and spiritual writers have reflected at great length over the millennia on the nature of the true self. They all agree that every individual has one. This is the self that most truly represents who a particular person is. The problem is that many of us can't see the true self. For example, there are always people who go on talent shows and are genuinely shocked and dismayed when the judges point out what every viewer is thinking: 'Sorry, but you're just not that talented.' Or think of the reverse situation. Some people underestimate themselves. We perhaps all know truly kind, loving and thoughtful people who fail to recognize their goodness and, as a consequence, constantly berate themselves for their moral inferiority. There are many other examples that we could cite.

The last item in our list of common blind-spots – 'my-side bias' – is discussed in a article written by David Perkins and Shari Tishman.[8] The authors refer to empirical research that demonstrates a strong tendency to confirmation bias. Virtually all of us can easily identify and articulate evidence and a rationale that are supportive of our point of view but we find it extremely difficult to come up with data in support of an opposing perspective. Furthermore, this blind-spot is no respecter of persons – that is, my-side bias is not correlated with particular social groupings or level of intelligence. It exists across the board; people with high IQs are as prone to it as people with low IQs.

There is also a tendency in most of us towards what cognitive psychologists call egocentrism. This does not refer to selfishness, but rather to the fact that we unwittingly misattribute our convictions, ideas and feelings to the other person. The reason is that the noise from our personal point of view so fills our heads that we have a great deal of trouble picking up on another person's perspective. Flavell, Miller and Miller put it this way: '[W]e are usually unable to turn our own viewpoints off completely when trying to infer another's viewpoints. Our own perspectives produce clear signals that are much louder to us than the other's, and they usually continue to ring in our ears while we try to decode someone else's perspectives.'[9]

Pastoral counsellors need to attend to moral blind-spots as well as to mental ones. There is an ethico-religious dimension to pastoral care.[10] In their book *Blindspots: Why We Fail to Do What's Right and What to Do about It*, ethicists Max Bazerman and Ann Tenbrunsel point out that many people have an inherent belief in their own moral rectitude, despite evidence that clearly suggests otherwise.[11] In support of their claim, the authors cite a 2008 survey of high school students by the Josephson Institute. Almost two-thirds of the teenagers surveyed admitted cheating in a test in the past year. More than a third confessed to having plagiarized internet sources. A further third reported stealing items from a shop in the past year, and over 80 per cent said that they had lied to a parent about a significant matter. Despite these admissions, 93 per cent of the high school students said they were satisfied with their moral character.

Brazerman and Tenbrunsel also observe the common tendency to maintain a moral value while acting in a way that contravenes it.[12] A very good example of this is provided in a classic psychological study conducted by John Darley and Daniel Batson.[13] The study was conducted at Princeton Theological Seminary. Theological students were led to believe that they needed to hurry over to another building to deliver a sermon that they had been working on. The text for the sermon was the story of the Good Samaritan. Each seminary student was taken on a route to the building past a doorway in which an accomplice of the researchers was slumped over and seemingly unwell. On a number of occasions, seminary students literally stepped over the apparently ill person in their haste to get to their destination where they would deliver their sermons on the Good Samaritan!

The fields of social psychology and behavioural ethics produce findings that show that our ethical behaviour is often inconsistent, and on occasions even hypocritical. The fact that moral hypocrisy is a common phenomenon has been established in a series of psychological experiments conducted by Daniel Batson and his associates.[14] The researchers have a particular version of moral hypocrisy in view. They define it as 'seeking to maximize personal gain by appearing moral while, if possible, avoiding the costs associated with a moral outcome'.[15] This moral style only works if the perpetrators can spin a cover story that they are genuinely good people. Individuals pride themselves on moral action, but in fact they haven't actually acted morally.

The moral dilemma that is set up in the studies by Batson *et al.* is a trivial one. Research participants were given the opportunity to assign themselves and another participant (actually fictitious) to certain tasks. At the start, it was made clear that the other participant would not be told how the tasks were assigned. There were two tasks to be assigned: a 'positive consequences task' in which participants had a chance to earn raffle tickets; and a 'neutral consequences task', which was described as quite dull and uninteresting. The experimenters chose this mundane moral dilemma because, first, they wanted 'to get less scripted responses' and, second, they wanted a situation in which there would be a broad consensus on the morally right approach.[16] The final element in the design is that participants completed a moral responsibility questionnaire prior to the laboratory session.

In order to test for moral hypocrisy, two features were included. First, the experimenters provided an explicit statement on the moral nature of the dilemma, indicating that most people think that the fairest way to assign the tasks is to give both participants an equal chance of being assigned the positive consequences task by, for example, flipping a coin. Also, including the coin introduced a degree of ambiguity. If all participants use the coin in an honest manner, 50 per cent of participants would assign the other participant to the positive consequences task. If there is significant deviation from the 50 per cent result in the direction of assigning oneself to the positive consequences task, it would be evident that there is a motivation to appear moral ('I did the right thing; I flipped the coin') while still serving self-interest ('It's nice that I still ended up with the positive task'). That is, it will have been shown that moral hypocrisy is operating.

Of the 20 participants in the study, 10 flipped the coin and 10 did not. When asked about the most moral way to assign tasks, flipping the coin was the most frequent response from both those who flipped and those who did not. Of the 10 who flipped the coin, 8 said flipping was the most moral action. Of the 10 who did not flip the coin, 6 said flipping was the most moral action.

Of the 10 participants who did not flip the coin, only 1 assigned the other participant to the positive consequences task. What is more revealing is that of the 10 participants who flipped the coin, only 1 assigned the other participant to the positive consequences task. This proportion (.10) is significantly lower than the .50 associated with chance alone. The researchers have this to say about the finding:

Apparently, either ours was a very charitable coin, or with self-interest an issue, flipping the coin introduced enough ambiguity into the decision process that participants could feel moral while still favouring themselves. ('It's heads. Let's see, that means ... I get the positive task.' 'It's tails. Let's see, that means ... the other participant gets the neutral task.') Apparently, some of those flipping the coin took advantage of this ambiguity to hide self-interest in the guise of morality. Aggregating responses across participants, we were able to unmask this moral hypocrisy.[17]

It is evident that self-deception is operating here. A number of the participants wanted the good feeling associated with moral action, but they did not want to pay a price for it. The only way they could convince themselves that they had acted morally, even though they pursued self-interest, was to hide their true motivation from themselves.

In a subsequent study, the experimenters chose to label the coin in order to make it impossible, or at least very difficult, for the participants to deceive themselves.[18] About two-thirds of the 40 participants chose to flip the labelled coin. Of the 12 who chose not to flip the coin, 10 assigned themselves to the positive consequences task, leaving the dull and boring task for the other participant. What is quite remarkable, though, is that of the 28 who chose to flip the coin, only 4 (.14) assigned the other person to the positive consequences task. Remember that if chance is the only factor operating, the proportion would be .50.

A final manipulation used by the researchers is very revealing.[19] In this study, the coin provided was not labelled. The new feature is the addition of a mirror. For some participants, the mirror was set up facing them; for others, it was set up with its back to them. Its use was designed to test the impact, if any, of self-awareness on the morality of the behaviour. Self-awareness manipulations have been associated with increased awareness of discrepancies between behaviour and personal standards, prodding a person to act in accordance with standards.

Approximately half (23) of the 52 participants chose to flip the coin. In the case of those participants not exposed to a mirror, of the 13 who chose not to flip the coin, 11 (.85) assigned themselves to the positive consequences task. More significantly, of the 13 who chose to flip the coin, only 2 (.15) assigned the other person to the positive consequences task. The findings in the earlier study are confirmed here.

What is really interesting is that when the participants were faced with a mirror, the coin was used in a scrupulously fair manner. Ten of the 26 participants chose to flip the coin and, of these, 5 assigned the other participant to the positive consequences task and 5 assigned themselves to it. Six of the 16 who chose not to flip the coin (.38) assigned the other participant to the positive consequences task.

It seems that when I look at myself in the mirror, the sly side of my psyche is decommissioned. A mirror brings me face to face with who I am and with what I am doing. This particular empirical finding points to our pastoral task: we need to help counsellees gaze into a mirror and see themselves truly. Let me use the metaphor of a car's rear-view mirror to make another point. All drivers know that their side mirrors have a blind-spot. Another car is looming up, but the driver can't see it in the mirror. When the other car moves a little closer it comes into view. There is a way to eliminate the blind-spot. One needs to adjust the mirrors far enough outwards so that the viewing angle of the side mirrors just over-laps that of the interior rear-view mirror. When correctly positioned, the mirrors negate a car's blind-spot. The pastoral role involves shifting the mirror that counsellees are using to view the world so that they can see the things that are hidden in the blind-spot. In the next section, we will investigate the indirect method used by Sören Kierkegaard to help his fellow Danish Christians of the nineteenth century recognize their blind-spots. The aim is to learn some lessons for pastoral counselling from Kierkegaard.

Kierkegaard on facilitating self-challenge through indirection

The fundamental problem that Kierkegaard addresses in the totality of his work is that of becoming a Christian.[20] In his writings, he contends that people living in the Danish Golden Age have a large blind-spot. Most are living under the illusion that the lives they lead constitute genuine Christianity. In Kierkegaard's estimation, '[t]o be a Christian has become a thing of naught, mere tomfoolery, something which every-one is as a matter of course, something one slips into more easily than into the most insignificant trick of dexterity'.[21] In the Danish established Christendom of the nineteenth century, people live in the aesthetic realm or at best, in the aesthetic-ethical category.[22] Aesthetes are people who live primarily through the senses. The form of their lives is determined by the natural impulse to seek the pleasurable, the beautiful and the interesting. They are not prepared for the seriousness and self-sacrifice associated with life in the ethico-religious sphere.

The kind of existence that most are living is a cosy and comfortable one. Intent on enjoying life at all costs, they embrace only the externals of the Christian faith. What is required according to Kierkegaard is a 'reduplication' of the witness of Christ.[23] To re-present the love and righteousness of Christ in the world one must live 'absolutely in passion'.[24] Comfortable Christians, to Kierkegaard's mind, have no appreciation of this and are content to 'live in relativities'.[25]

In order to live in the realm of the absolute it is necessary to make the message of Christ one's own. This in turn requires the inwardness of reflection. Religious truth for Kierkegaard is subjective truth. It is a truth that is appropriated by the individual. The quasi-Christian of established Christendom approaches the gospel on the objective level. Such individuals hear the 'facts' of the Christian story presented and give them intellectual assent, but they do not allow the story to penetrate to their deepest level of personal existence.

Kierkegaard, then, contrasts objective and subjective truth. The former is appropriate where 'the positive' in thought is required. That is to say, it has a place in sense perception, historical knowledge and in speculative philosophy.[26] But when the objective mode of appropriation is introduced to Christianity it 'constitutes well-nigh an irreligious exaggeration'.[27] In the ethico-religious sphere, what is required is the subjective reflection of the 'single one' (that is, people who are prepared to think for themselves): 'The world [needs] essential individualities, [persons] artistically interpenetrated with reflection, self-thinking [persons], as distinct from town-criers and docents.'[28]

For Kierkegaard, the way to stimulate people into independent activity is to communicate with them indirectly. It is necessary to 'approach from behind the person who is under an illusion'.[29] A central element in the 'approach from behind' is ambiguity.[30] In much of his writings, Kierkegaard does not come out and say directly and plainly what he thinks the truth of Christianity is. Rather, he uses a range of pseudonyms to present various viewpoints on existence. Turning the pages of Kierkegaard's works, one comes across exotic names such as Johannes Climacus, Johannes de Silentio, Vigilius Haufniensis, Anti-Climacus and Constantine Constantius. Like a playwright, he creates poeticized individuals each with their own particular identity and point of view on life. It is not simply a matter of the characters articulating a particular aesthetic, ethical or religious perspective. Rather, they engage in a dialogue with one another. The essential aim of this fictional and artistic presentation is to provoke a decision. Kierkegaard refuses to tell his fellow Christians what to think; he wants them above all to think for themselves.

Walking into the strange world of Kierkegaardian literature is both an uncomfortable and a captivating experience. One finds oneself in turn getting frustrated, confused, lost, intrigued, illuminated, inspired and challenged. Most of all, one is challenged to *think*. It is very clear that Kierkegaard has no intention of stating his position clearly and directly.

The reader is faced with an array of characters and stances on life. Above all, Kierkegaard wants to provoke a reaction, and this is why he chooses indirect communication. It is not possible to communicate a reaction. All that an author can do is communicate a message that solicits subjectivity – that is, one that calls for personal appropriation.[31]

There is, then, a very serious purpose behind all the poeticized characterization, ironic twists, playfulness, deception, wit and artistic creativity. Kierkegaard is seeking to compel readers to think it out for themselves. Edward Mooney piles adjective upon adjective in order to take us to the heart of the strategy:

> Kierkegaard's use of pseudonyms opens our frustrations, apprehensions, curiosities, alert interests. There is more to this than being coy, exhibitionist or secretive, more than being perverse or provocative, teasing, wicked, or deceptive, more than being playful, jesting, experimental or evasive. We're forced to figure what's going on, to at least partially resolve the whirl, to gather our imaginative capacities and focus them on the matter at hand, the difficult reality impinging.[32]

Kierkegaard tells us that he uses ambiguity to create a 'dialectical knot',[33] and one central strategy that he employs to this end is an attempt to make it impossible for the reader to discern when Kierkegaard is engaging in jest and when he is being serious. He informs us that another example is 'to bring defence and attack together in such a unity that no one can say directly whether one is attacking or defending, so that both the most zealous partisans of the cause and its bitterest enemies can regard one as an ally ...'[34]

Jamie Ferreira shows very clearly how ambiguity functions in Kierkegaard's first work, *Either/Or*.[35] Before getting to this, it is necessary to give a brief overview of the book. *Either/Or: A Fragment of Life* was originally published in two volumes under the same title, with a preface by the editor, Victor Eremita. The first volume consists of a collection of short works involving different genres. There are essays, aphorisms and diary entries. The second volume is made up of three 'letters'. The editor claims to have happened serendipitously upon the collection of papers. He came across a desk for sale in a shop window, and upon returning home with it discovered the papers in a hidden drawer. The two authors are designated by Victor as A and B. We are told that the papers simply reveal A as an aesthete; nothing more is indicated. The second author, B, is identified as William, a magistrate.

In the collection of works by A we find works such as 'The Seducer's Diary', essays on 'The Musical-Erotic', 'The Unhappiest One', 'The First

Love', and dramatic tragedy. The themes that are developed are love, passion, seduction, sorrow and deception.

The second volume consists of B's letters to A. It contains two long letters to A, and a short final letter consisting of a brief introduction to a sermon that B would like A to read. In the first of the two long letters, entitled 'The Aesthetic Validity of Marriage', the proposition is put forward that it is not necessary to simply choose between the aesthetic and the ethical. It should not be assumed that passion, excitement and romance are left behind when two people move into the committed love of marriage. The aesthetic is incorporated into the ethical in marriage. Judge William declares to A: '[T]his is the result I reach: if love can be preserved – and that it can, so help me God – then can the aesthetic also be preserved; for love itself is the aesthetic.'[36]

In the second letter, Judge William avers that choice is the defining characteristic of the ethical. It is not choosing this or that path, this or that course of action, that is the decisive thing, but rather the act of choosing itself.[37] Further, the ethical does not want to annihilate the aesthetic. Living in the ethical sphere of existence constitutes a transfiguration of the aesthetic. It is only when people live ethically that their lives are filled with beauty, truth and meaning. If individuals can find within themselves the energy and earnestness to make a choice, the aesthetic comes back: 'If only the choice is posited, all of the aesthetic returns again, and you will see that only then does existence become beautiful, that only in this way can a [person] succeed in saving his soul and gaining the whole world, can succeed in using the world without abusing it.'[38]

The editor tells us that reading the works of A and B has helped him think through a philosophical problem that has long held his interest – namely, that of the relationship between the inner and the outer.[39] In particular, he is interested in the relationship between a person's external mode of existence and that individual's inner life. The papers he has found confirm his intuition that the external is not the internal. Victor tells us that this 'was especially true about one of them. His external mode of life has been in complete contradiction to his inner life. The same was true to a certain extent with the other also, inasmuch as he concealed a more significant inwardness under a somewhat commonplace exterior.'[40]

As indicated above, Ferreira shows how ambiguity is manifested in *Either/Or*, and identifies a number of aspects to this. First, it is not possible to simply line up A with the aesthetical and B with the ethical. Victor Eremita's assessment of the two men is ambiguous because he does not tell us which figure will correspond to each sphere of existence. To further complicate things, Judge William is presented as being both repulsed by the aesthete and attracted to him. He is turned off by the egoism and corruption that he sees in his 'young friend'. But at the same time he cannot help but feel drawn, albeit reluctantly, to his exuberance and 'aesthetic-intellectual intoxication'.[41]

It is also the case that Kierkegaard is not offering a simple choice between the aesthetic and ethical. For a start, we are told in the preface that in the first part we are not offered a single, unified picture of the aesthetic way of life, but rather a number of different perspectives on it: 'A's papers contain a number of attempts to formulate an aesthetic philosophy of life. A single, coherent, aesthetic view of life can scarcely be carried out.'[42] We are entitled to assume that the same goes for what is presented in the second part. We are offered not so much *the* ethical approach to life, but a number of ethical approaches.

It is also the case that while it may be reasonable to assume that the upper hand in the contest of ideas is assigned to the ethical, even here Victor introduces an element of ambiguity. He counsels the reader, upon having made her way through the collection of papers in its entirety, to pay close attention to the title:

This will free [her] from all finite questions as to whether A was really convinced of his error and repented, whether B conquered, or if it perhaps ended by B's going over to A's opinion. In this respect, these papers have no ending ... When the book is read, then A and B are forgotten, only their views confront one another, and await no finite decision in particular personalities.[43]

Use of irony also has the effect of creating ambiguity. There are two aspects to this relationship between irony and ambiguity in the Kierke-gaardian authorship. First, we have seen that Kierkegaard artistically creates an ensemble of characters, each with his own personality and perspective on life. Commentators routinely suggest that the polyphonic nature of the authorship constitutes a case of ironic indirection.[44] It is also the case, moving now to the second aspect, that Kierkegaard employs irony in a methodical way to create an ambiguous communi-cation. The most common form of irony is saying one thing and meaning another. For example, if an adult offends by acting in a childish manner, one may say, 'Thank you. That was really mature of you.' Along with isolated ironic statements such as this one, we also find in the authorship more extensive employment of the technique. Decoding the message that the pseudonym presents is no simple matter. Constructing a text that is ironic from start to finish is therefore a central technique that Kierke-gaard employs in order to communicate in an indirect, ambiguous way.

Ambiguity is the tool Kierkegaard uses to conceal his subjectivity. In this way, he seeks to provoke what Johannes Climacus refers to in the *Postscript* as 'double reflection'.[45] Objective thinkers can communicate directly the results of their own reflections. They can say, for example, 'In reflecting upon the Gospels and the epistles, important theological works, and my own personal experience and that of others, my understanding of what it is to be a Christian is as follows.' The listener or reader can certainly appropriate this message at the intellectual level. But the act of receiving and understanding the communication cannot in and of itself produce self-discovery, personal appropriation and transformation in one's way-of-being-in-the-world. In order for that to happen, there needs to be a second act of reflection. The listener or reader needs to engage in the kind of deep reflection that the communicator entered into. Indirect communication, loaded as it is with ambiguity, provokes the 'double reflection' that leads to personal transformation. Direct communication can change a mind; only indirect communication can change a life.[46]

What Kierkegaard is attempting to do through employing his techniques of polyphony and irony is to spark in his readers an experience of inwardness and subjectivity. There does not need to be a personal and existential engagement with a statement of fact that is communicated. The person in possession of the following information – that a water molecule is made up of two hydrogen atoms and one oxygen atom – simply explains it to the listener and there is a transfer of objective knowledge. The situation is very different when it comes to moral and religious truths. The one in possession of such a truth can communicate it as clearly and as fully as is humanly possible, but that person cannot thereby guarantee a transfer of that truth. It only becomes a truth for the listener when that individual engages in personal reflection and internalizes it. 'Truth is inwardness; there is no objective truth, but the truth consists in personal appropriation.'[47]

Kellenberger helpfully shows that indirect communication is successful when personal appropriation is a concomitant of a discovery.[48] One discovers the truth in reflection on the indirect communication and internalizes it. This is particularly significant in the context of our investigation of facilitating self-challenge in counsellees. Experienced counsellors sense when counsellees have blind-spots. The goal is to help the counsellee see what the counsellor is seeing.

Kellenberger uses the story of Nathan's confrontation of King David (2 Sam. 12.1–7) to illustrate his point. David finds himself filled with desire for Bathsheba who is the wife of one of his soldiers, Uriah. Clearly Uriah is an impediment to David getting what he wants, so he hatches an evil plan to get rid of his soldier. David sends a message to the commander of his army to put Uriah in the thick of the fighting and then to draw back from him. The outcome is Uriah is killed and David makes Bathsheba his wife. Nathan then goes to David and tells him a parable of two men who live in a certain city. They occupy very different stations in life. One is a rich man with many flocks; the other is poor and has only one ewe lamb. When a traveller visits the rich man, instead of taking one of his own sheep he takes the sole possession of the poor man as an offering for the guest. David, upon hearing Nathan's account, surges with anger against the rich man for his lack of pity. In response, Nathan declares, 'You are the man.'

Kellenberger suggests that here we have an instance of indirect communication. While it is true that Nathan directly *states* the truth to be communicated – 'You are the man' – he does not directly *communicate* it. 'Rather, by his use of the parable Nathan brings David to the point of personally appropriating the truth, and he does so by helping him to see what his moral and sinful state is. This takes a discovery on David's part, one which, be it noted, requires that he not self-righteously denounce any comparison between himself and the rich man.'[49]

Challenging the counsellee

As indicated above, Kellenberger's observation is right on target for the issue that we are interested in. When counsellees have blind-spots, the aim of pastoral counsellors is to facilitate personal discovery. They want to help counsellees see what they cannot see for themselves. Rickey George and Therese Cristiani put it this way: 'Confrontation [is a skill] used to help clients see things as they are rather than perceiving situations on the basis of their needs. In other words, counsellors can help clients attain an alternative frame of reference, enabling them to clear up distortions in experience.'[50]

Inviting self-challenge consists of introducing a discordant note into the melodies that counsellees are playing. It involves disrupting the way counsellees see themselves and their situation. Pastoral counsellors are understandably somewhat reluctant to challenge a counsellee – it is more comfortable and safe to focus on congruency with the person. While this has the important benefit of enhancing the therapeutic relationship, introducing discrepant perspectives is the key to promoting change.[51]

Perhaps the most comprehensive treatment of facilitation of counsellee self-challenge is provided by Gerard Egan in *The Skilled Helper*.[52] He refers to both direct and indirect approaches. However, it is important to note that he is not using the term 'indirect' in a Kierkegaardian sense.

Rather, what distinguishes an indirect approach from a direct one is the presence of tentativeness and refusal of a strong, assertive approach.

The three indirect approaches that Egan identifies are advanced empathy ('sharing the message behind the message'), sharing information, and helper self-disclosure.[53] In discussing the first of these, he takes his lead from Carl Rogers. As we have noted (Chapter 2), Rogers observed that a counsellor who is especially attuned to the client's communication can sometimes intuit meanings of which the client is only dimly aware. In order to facilitate self-discovery, the counsellor looks for answers to these questions: What is the person only half-saying? What is the person hinting at? What is the implicit message behind what is explicitly said?

Given that advanced empathy involves trying to sense something that the client is aware of only in a non-thematic, hazy way, there is always the chance that the counsellor will be wide of the mark. Therefore, it is important to state the challenge in a tentative manner. To illustrate the technique, Egan uses the example of a client who has been discussing ways of getting back in touch with his wife after a recent divorce:

> CLIENT (SOMEWHAT HESITATINGLY): I could wait to hear from her. But I suppose there's nothing wrong with calling her up and asking her how she's getting along.
> COUNSELOR: You've been talking about getting in touch with her, but, unless I'm mistaken, I don't hear a great deal of enthusiasm in your voice.
> CLIENT: To be honest, I don't really want to talk to her. But I feel guilty – guilty about the divorce, guilty about her going out on her own. Frankly, all I'm doing is trying to take care of her all over again. And that's one of the reasons we got divorced. I had a need to take care of her, and she let me do it, even though she resented it. That was the story of our marriage. I don't want to do that anymore.[54]

'Information sharing' is the second of the indirect methods that Egan discusses.[55] The information the counsellor provides offers a perspective that is missing for the client. Egan points out that this can be useful at any stage within the counselling process, but in the early stages it helps clients to know that they are not alone in their suffering. The problem they have is not unique; many others face a similar struggle. In the middle period, clients may be unclear about their goals for growth and healing, or they may not be fully aware of the possibilities open to them. Counsellors can provide a view that helps clients attain a sharper focus and chart a way forward. In the closing stages, information on the roadblocks that people commonly encounter can help clients cope and persevere with their new approach to self and others.

'Helper self-disclosure' is the last of the three indirect approaches that Egan covers.[56] He suggests that a sensitive, appropriate and wise approach to sharing personal experiences, thoughts and feelings can serve to help clients challenge themselves. It is therefore not any old form of personal sharing that Egan has in mind. He is aware of the pitfalls associated with helper self-disclosure. The helper needs to ensure that the personal sharing is culturally appropriate, appropriate in a more general sense, focused and selective, not too frequent, well-timed, and does not result in burdening the client. Egan uses the case of helpers who are former addicts working in substance abuse programmes to make his point:

> [Such helpers] know from the inside the games clients afflicted with addictions play. Sharing their experience is central to their style of counseling and is accepted by their clients. It helps clients develop both new perspectives and new possibilities for action. Such self-disclosure is challenging. It puts pressure on clients to talk about themselves more openly or in a more focused way. [57]

Finally, Egan moves to a discussion of a more direct form of challenging. Remember, first, that he simply means by this a more assertive, blunt approach. There is no reference to a distinction between direct and indirect forms of communication à la Kierkegaard. Egan prescribes the 'stronger medicine' of confrontation to call certain clients to account.[58] Clients who are not true to their word, who fall away from the hard work of honesty, openness and change, violate expectations, or act badly should expect to be confronted.

Facilitation of counsellee self-challenge in a Kierkegaardian key

There is no doubt that an approach to facilitating self-challenge that involves straightforward, plainly worded observations concerning something counsellees are missing, resisting or hiding from themselves – such as Egan and others recommend – is often effective in promoting self-discovery and constructive change. However, I suggest that for those counsellors who feel comfortable with it, a more indirect, playful and creative approach – one that is in line in a general sense with Kierkegaard's authorial strategy – has added benefits. First, I think that Kierkegaard was right in his assessment of the likely outcome of a direct confrontation of his fellow Danes over their blind-spots. Risk factors associated with a direct approach are that it is likely to provoke resistance, mobilize the will in opposition, and result in the illusion becoming even more deeply entrenched. To be sure, any form of challenge runs these risks, but I contend that the risk is lower with an indirect approach. In the second place, I think that an indirect method carries the potential for an even greater impact. It is the ambiguity associated with indirection that is the key to that impact. Ambiguity means that there is a gap in the communicative event that counsellors are asking counsellees to fill. There is a space between the blind-spot counsellors see in counsellees and the intervention they make (telling a story, making a statement) in seeking to address it. It is as if the counsellor opting for an indirect mode of communication is saying, 'Here are two dots. I am inviting you to connect them.' A plain statement of things means that there is no gap; there is simply an invitation to accept or reject the counsellor's perspective. Kierkegaard could, for instance, have communicated his message directly. He could have said something along these lines: 'Those of you in established Christendom think that you are living genuine Christian lives. But this is an illusion. In your heads you know what is required of you, but in practice you have opted for a counterfeit form of Christianity that allows you to maintain your comfortable, aesthetic lifestyles.' Instead, he presents a variety of perspectives on both the aesthetic and ethico-religious spheres of existence and thereby indirectly sponsors self-discovery. The good citizens of Copenhagen are, first, invited to locate themselves in the aesthetic sphere, or at best aesthetic-ethical sphere, of existence and, second, invited to make the move into genuine faith.

When a person is able to make the connection, there is a moment of highly significant self-discovery and transformation. Nathan could have taken a direct route. He could have simply said something like: 'It is a shameful and evil thing that you who have so much have taken from someone who has so little. Furthermore, the fact that you have engaged in this dastardly plot to get Uriah out of the way is unconscionable. Fall on your knees this very moment and repent before Almighty God!' The use of the parable meant that David had to do work beyond simply deciding whether or not he would accept a rebuke from this prophet. Even though Nathan chose a very apt and telling parable, David experienced a blind-spot. He could immediately see the injustice in the wealthy man taking the ewe lamb of the poor man to feed his guest – and even felt a surge of righteous anger – but he could not see that he had done something that closely paralleled it. David was unable to connect the dots. A simple direct statement was required to help him: 'You are that man!' David was immediately overwhelmed with shame, guilt and remorse.

As with many counselling interventions, there are minuses as well as pluses. I can see at least two risk factors associated with the method of indirection. In the first place, a pastoral counsellor may fall into the trap of trying too hard to be clever or witty. Indeed, Kierkegaard has been criticized for self-indulgence and getting carried away with the artful, intricate game he plays. Working too hard on the artfulness of the intervention may well result in counsellees forming the opinion that their counsellors are playing silly games. There is also a danger that the challenge that the counsellor offers may be so subtle and circumspect that the point of it is lost on the counsellee. This potential shortcoming is clearly not as serious as the first one; it can easily be rectified by trying again with a more direct approach.

Having looked at both the positive and negative side of the ledger, it is clear I think that the potential pay-off justifies the risks involved. I would now like to demonstrate the difference in the direct and indirect approaches by working on a case study that Egan uses. He presents it this way:

> In the following example, the counselor is talking with a client who is having trouble with his perfectionism. He also mentions problems with his brother-in-law, whom his wife enjoys having over. He and his brother-in-law argue, and sometimes the arguments have an edge to them. At one point the client describes him as 'a guy who can never get anything right'. Later the counselor says, 'We started out by talking about perfectionism in terms of the inordinate demands you place on yourself. I wonder whether it could be "spreading" a bit. You should be perfect. But so should everyone else.' They go on to discuss the ways his perfectionism may be interfering with his social life.[59]

Clearly, the direct approach that the counsellor takes is useful; it leads to a conversation about the negative impact the client's perfectionism is having on his relationships with others. While there is nothing wrong with the counsellor's way of addressing a blind-spot, I found myself thinking about how I would have responded if I was doing the counselling. Almost immediately the thought came to mind that I would probably have told a story. The story that popped into my head concerned a person whom I once worked with on a committee. I would tell it as follows:

> Your comment just now about your brother-in-law brought to mind for me something out of my own experience. I once worked on a committee with a person who I'll simply call 'Jane'. Jane was a bit like you; she struggled with perfectionism. She was a piano teacher; she gave private lessons. I remember being struck by a story she recounted to me. It said

a lot about her. One of her students obtained a mark of 99 per cent on his piano exam. I thought Jane was going to tell me how excited she was that the young lad had done so well. I thought she was going to tell me how she couldn't wait to give him a big hug and congratulate him. What she said to me instead was that she was disappointed that he had lost a mark. She immediately phoned the examiner and demanded that she be given an explanation for the deduction.

I also remember attending a service of worship with Jane. It was an informal one and, after the Bible readings, the minister invited the congregation to offer their reflections. I can't remember what the readings were about, or a single one of the many comments that were made that night. But I can remember exactly what Jane said. She said this: 'I have learnt only to trust God. He is the only dependable one because he is perfect. Everybody else fails you. Everybody else lets you down.'

Those of us who worked on the committee with Jane found it hard to get close to her. To a certain extent, she was likeable. But the thing that virtually all of us had real problems with, the behaviour that was especially annoying and hard to overlook, was that nothing anyone ever did was good enough for Jane. No matter how hard we worked, no matter how much we tried to be flexible and accommodate her high – I would say unrealistically high – standards, she made it clear that we had fallen short of the mark. We simply didn't measure up. That hurt. It made it difficult for us to get close to Jane.

Those pastoral counsellors who are attracted to the method of indirect communication in facilitating self-challenge will likely resonate with the 'non-linear' approach sponsored by Mozdzierz, Peluso and Lisiecki.[60] The authors describe their method as follows: 'A nonlinear way of thinking does not resemble a straightforward, characteristic, one-dimensional, logical approach to human problem solving but rather the sort of thinking that turns things upside down and inside out – it departs from the linear way of thinking about things.'[61] They supply a case example that captures Kierkegaardian indirection nicely. It's a good note to finish on.

The case features a mother who is having trouble letting go of her adult sons whose careers have taken them far afield. In particular, she reports how upset she is that when they return home they choose to spend most of their time staying in a friend's apartment, affording them the opportunity to catch up with their childhood buddies and 'party' with female friends. While on the one hand the therapist could empathize with the pain the woman felt now that her sons are choosing to spend less time with her, he was also aware that the lads were doing exactly what they should be doing, and that their mother needed to adjust to this new era in her relationship to them. The intervention by the therapist and the client's reaction are recounted in this way:

> The therapist stood up from his desk chair and said, as though pondering something very difficult to figure out, 'Let me see if I have this right. (Gesturing with his right hand as though he were weighing what he was saying.) The boys could spend time with Mom (gesturing with his left hand as though he were weighing and comparing it against what was in his right hand) – or, they could spend time with their friends, drink, party, and enjoy their girlfriends. (Obviously exaggerating, with his hands going up and down as though he were continuing to weigh those options.) They could spend time with Mom, or they could party with their friends. Let's see: Young, energetic men with lots of good friends that they haven't seen in a long time could spend time with Mom (continuing to move his hands up and down, as though he were continuing to weigh something), or they could party with their friends.'
>
> The woman instantly broke into a broad, knowing smile and laughed, recognizing that she had 'exaggerated' her position ... toward her children. Almost instantaneously, she had put things back into balance.[62]

Summary

We began by recognizing that it is part of the human condition to have blind-spots. There are certain things – our faulty self-interpretation, our unrealistic thoughts, our self-deception, and particular moral inferiorities – that we just do not see. Søren Kierkegaard picked up on what he saw as a rather large blind-spot in the vision of his fellow Danish Christians. In their eyes, they were genuine Christians. He, on the other hand, viewed this as simply illusion; they were a long way from engaging in a serious manner with the demands of authentic Christianity. In his various works Kierkegaard took an indirect route to challenging the cosy Christianity that he claimed he saw all round him. Through the use of polyphony and irony, he created an ambiguous communication that forced his readers to figure it out for themselves. He aimed to stimulate subjectivity and personal appropriation.

While it is clear that a relatively straightforward and direct approach to challenging a counsellee is certainly useful – and the option that many, and probably most, pastoral counsellors select – it was suggested above that there are three potential advantages associated with the indirect method. First, the creativity and playfulness associated with an indirect mode of communication resonates strongly with the inclinations and abilities of certain pastoral counsellors. Second, it is less likely than a direct approach to trigger defensiveness, opposition of the will, and stubborn refusal to open the eyes to see what the counsellor sees. And finally, there is the potential for greater impact. This is so because the counsellor creates the conditions for personal discovery rather than simply inviting an endorsement of a plain statement of the blind-spot. However, there are also risk factors associated with it. In the first place, a pastoral counsellor may err by trying too hard to be clever or witty. In this case, it may well seem to counsellees that their counsellors are being supercilious and playing silly games. There is also a danger that the challenge the counsellor offers may be so subtle and circumspect that the point of it is lost on the counsellee. This potential shortcoming is clearly not as serious as the first one; it is possible to simply try again, this time taking a more direct approach. I advocate the indirect approach to facilitating self-challenge, despite the risks involved, because the potential pay-off is big.

The last two chapters have centred on challenging a counsellee. In considering the task of facilitating self-doctoring for belief-sickness, we talked about a disputational style of counselling, and in this chapter we discussed an indirect method of communication that provokes self-discovery. In the next chapter, we shift gears. Our area of interest is working with counsellee metaphors.

Notes

1 G. Egan, *The Skilled Helper: A Problem-Management and Opportunity-Development Approach to Helping*, 10th edn (Belmont, CA: Brooks/Cole, 2014), p. 160.

2 See W. M. Clements and H. Clinebell, *Counseling for Spiritually Empowered Wholeness: A Hope-Centered Approach* (Binghamton, NY: Haworth Pastoral Press, 1995), p. 36.

3 R. Quinn, 'Confronting Carl Rogers: A Developmental-Interactional Approach to Person-Centered Therapy', *Journal of Humanistic Psychology* 33, no. 1 (Winter 1993), pp. 6–23, p. 12.

4 See S. Kierkegaard, *The Point of View for My Work as an Author: A Report to History and Related Writings*, trans. Walter Lowrie (New York: Harper Torchbooks, 1962), p. 25.

5 See G. J. Mozdzierz, P. R. Peluso and J. Lisiecki, *Principles of Counseling and Psychotherapy: Learning the Essential Domains and Nonlinear Thinking of Master Practitioners* (New York: Routledge, 2009).

6 Cf. Egan, *The Skilled Helper*, p. 172.

7 M. L. Van Hecke, *Blind Spots: Why Smart People Do Dumb Things* (Amherst, NY: Prometheus Books, 2007).

8 See D. N. Perkins and S. Tishman, 'Dispositional Aspects of Intelligence', unpublished paper, 1998.

9 J. H. Flavell, P. H. Miller and S. A. Miller, *Cognitive Development*, 3rd edn (Englewood Cliffs, NJ: Prentice–Hall, 1993), p. 181.

10 Up until the early 1970s, the focus of pastoral counselling conducted in mainline Protestant churches in the USA especially, but also in Canada, the UK and Australia, tended to be quite firmly on intrapsychic, interpersonal and developmental issues. At that time, Don Browning spearheaded a movement in pastoral theology aimed at reminding practitioners of the need to attend to the ethico-religious context of pastoral care. On this perspective, see D. Browning, *The Moral Context of Pastoral Care* (Philadelphia, PA: Westminster Press, 1976); J. C. Hoffman, *Ethical Confrontation in Counseling* (Chicago, IL: University Chicago Press, 1979); D. Capps, *Life Cycle Theory and Pastoral Care* (Eugene, OR: Wipf & Stock, 2002), ch. 2 (first published by Fortress Press in 1983); G. Noyce, *The Minister as Moral Counsellor* (Nashville, TN: Abingdon Press, 1989); L. Sperry, *Transforming Self and Community: Revisioning Pastoral Counseling and Spiritual Direction* (Collegeville, MN: Liturgical Press, 2002); and N. Pembroke, *The Art of Listening* (Grand Rapids, MI: Eerdmans, and Edinburgh: T&T Clark, 2002), ch, 5.

11 See M. Bazerman and A. Tenbrunsel, *Blindspots: Why We Fail to Do What's Right and What to Do about It* (Princeton, NJ: Princeton University Press, 2011), p. 62.

12 See Bazerman and Tenbrunsel, p. 4.

13 See J. M. Darley and C. D. Batson, '"From Jerusalem to Jericho": A Study of Situational and Dispositional Variables in Helping Behavior', *Journal of Personality and Social Psychology* 27 (1973), pp. 100–8.

14 See C. D. Batson *et al.*, 'In a Very Different Voice: Unmasking Moral Hypocrisy', *Journal of Personality and Social Psychology* 72, no. 6 (1997), pp. 1335–43; C. D. Batson *et al.*, 'Moral Hypocrisy: Appearing to be Moral to Oneself Without Being So', *Journal of Personality and Social Psychology* 77, no. 3 (1999), pp. 525–37; C. D. Batson, E. R. Thompson and H. Chen 'Moral Hypocrisy: Addressing Some Alternatives', *Journal of Personality and Social Psychology* 83, no. 2 (2002), pp. 330–39.

15 Batson *et al.*, 'In a Very Different Voice', p. 1336.

16 See Batson *et al.*, 'In a Very Different Voice', p. 1337.

17 Batson *et al.*, 'In a Very Different Voice', p. 1342.

18 See Batson *et al.*, 'Moral Hypocrisy: Appearing to be Moral', pp. 527–9.

19 See Batson *et al.*, 'Moral Hypocrisy: Appearing to be Moral', pp. 529–32.

20 See Kierkegaard, *The Point of View*, pp. 5–6.

21 S. Kierkegaard, *Training in Christianity and the Edifying Discourse which 'Accompanied' It*, trans. W. Lowrie (Princeton, NJ: Princeton University Press, 1944), p. 71.

22 See Kierkegaard, *The Point of View*, p. 25.

23 See S. Kierkegaard, *Søren Kierkegaard's Journals and Papers*, vol. 1, ed. and trans. H. Hong and E. Hong (Bloomington, IN: Indiana University Press, 1967), p. 191.

24 Kierkegaard, *Søren Kierkegaard's Journals and Papers*, p. 193.

25 Kierkegaard, *Søren Kierkegaard's Journals and Papers*, p. 192.

26 S. Kierkegaard, *Concluding Unscientific Postscript*, trans. D. Swenson (Princeton, NJ: Princeton University Press, 1941), p. 75.

27 Kierkegaard, *Concluding Unscientific Postscript*, p. 62.

28 Kierkegaard, *Concluding Unscientific Postscript*, p. 62.

29 See Kierkegaard, *The Point of View*, pp. 24–5.

30 A number of Kierkegaard scholars observe that ambiguity is a key element in the method of indirect communication. See, for example, R. E. Anderson, 'Kierkegaard's Theory of Communication', *Speech Monographs* 30, no. 1 (1963), pp. 1–14; V. Rumble, 'To Be as No-One: Kierkegaard and Climacus on the Art of Indirect Communication', *International Journal of Philosophical Studies* 3, no. 2 (1995), pp. 307–21; J. Turnbull, 'Kierkegaard, Indirect Communication, and Ambiguity', *The Heythrop Journal* 50 (2009), pp. 13–22; and K. B. Söderquist, 'Irony', in J. Lippitt and G. Pattison (eds), *The Oxford Handbook of Kierkegaard* (Oxford: Oxford University Press, 2013), pp. 344–64.

31 Cf. J. Kellenberger, 'Kierkegaard, Indirect Communication, and Religious Truth', *International Journal for the Philosophy of Religion* 16, no. 2 (1984), pp. 153–60, p. 154.

32 E. F. Mooney, 'Pseudonyms and "Style"', in Lippitt and Pattison (eds), *The Oxford Handbook of Kierkegaard*, pp. 191–210, p. 206.

33 Kierkegaard, *Training in Christianity*, p. 133.

34 Kierkegaard, *Training in Christianity*, p. 133.

35 See M. J. Ferreira, *Kierkegaard* (Malden, MA: Wiley-Blackwell, 2009), pp. 18–33.

36 S. Kierkegaard, *Either/Or II*, trans. Walter Lowrie (Princeton, NJ: Princeton University Press, 1971), p. 127.

37 See Kierkegaard, *Either/Or II*, p. 180.

38 Kierkegaard, *Either/Or II*, p. 182.

39 See S. Kierkegaard, *Either/Or I*, trans. D. F. Swenson and L. M. Swenson (Garden City, KS: DoubleDay & Co., 1959), p. 3.

40 Kierkegaard, *Either/Or I*, p. 4.

41 Kierkegaard, *Either/Or II*, p. 17.

42 Kierkegaard, *Either/Or I*, p. 13.

43 Kierkegaard, *Either/Or I*, p. 15.

44 On this, see Söderquist, 'Irony', p. 344.

45 Kierkegaard, *Concluding Unscientific Postscript*, p. 69.

46 Cf. D. Lochhead, 'Comment on Nielsen', in A. McKinnon (ed.), *Kierkegaard: Resources and Results* (Waterloo, ON: Wilfrid Laurier University Press, 1982), p. 102.

47 Kierkegaard, *Concluding Unscientific Postscript*, p. 71.

48 See Kellenberger, 'Kierkegaard, Indirect Communication, and Religious Truth', p. 157.

49 See Kellenberger, 'Kierkegaard, Indirect Communication, and Religious Truth', p. 157.

50 R. L. George and T. L. Cristiani, *Counseling: Theory and Practice*, 4th edn (Boston, MA: Allyn & Bacon, 1995), p. 164.

51 Cf. J. G. Treviño, 'Worldview and Change in Cross-Cultural Counseling', *The Counseling Psychologist* 24, no. 2 (1996), pp. 198–215, p. 203.

52 See Egan, *The Skilled Helper*, ch. 6.

53 See Egan, *The Skilled Helper*, pp. 176–87.

54 Egan, *The Skilled Helper*, p. 178.
55 See Egan, *The Skilled Helper*, pp. 182–3.
56 See Egan, *The Skilled Helper*, pp. 183–7.
57 Egan, *The Skilled Helper*, p. 184.
58 See Egan, *The Skilled Helper*, pp. 188–9.
59 Egan, *The Skilled Helper*, p. 181.
60 See Mozdzierz, Peluso and Lisiecki, *Principles of Counseling and Psychotherapy*.
61 Mozdzierz, Peluso and Lisiecki, *Principles of Counseling and Psychotherapy*, p. 5.
62 Mozdzierz, Peluso and Lisiecki, *Principles of Counseling and Psychotherapy*, pp. 377–8.

8

Working with Counsellee Images, or Exploring the 'Metaphors We Live By'[1]

One could be forgiven for thinking that metaphors are simply decorations that add colour to our speech, and many have held this view throughout the ages. In fact, it turns out that we cannot live without them – they are essential to human thought and language. Metaphors are not optional extras; we need them to think and to express ourselves.

It is entirely to be expected, then, that they would feature relatively often in counselling sessions, and this is indeed borne out by experience. Those of us who intentionally work with them report significant benefits in doing so. A number of therapists have written about their experiences, and as a result there is now quite a significant body of literature on the subject.

Some might wonder why this topic is included in a book on foundational issues in pastoral counselling, for it may seem to be more of a specialist theme in the field. On the contrary, it seems that a good case can be made for metaphors to sit right at the centre of things. Not only is metaphor fundamental in human life generally, helping counsellees unpack the images they use connects us with absolutely core issues in counselling. Here I am thinking of matters such as

- understanding and talking about affect
- empathic attunement
- making tacit awareness of issues explicit
- reframing a situation and finding new possibilities.

The structure of this chapter is as follows. First, there is a discussion of the nature of metaphor. Particular attention will be given to the role played by embodiment, culture and personal knowledge in metaphorization. The focus then shifts to the counselling setting. There is a discussion of the link between metaphorical knowing and the change process, and here attention will be given to the four core issues identified immediately above. The third and final section consists of a presentation of a step-by-step approach to supporting and guiding counsellees in working with their metaphors. There is no suggestion that this be used in a mechanical, lock-step manner. It is recommended because it has proven to be very helpful in training counsellors in working with metaphor.

Thinking about metaphor

As already stated, metaphors play an indispensable role in human thought and language, it is certainly the case that scriptural and theological thought lives by metaphor. The fundamental problem that theology is faced with is that it must speak about that which is transcendent. God is infinite and invisible, and therefore ultimately beyond the reach of human thought and language. The biblical writers attest to this basic fact concerning God in relation to humanity:

> Then Manoah said to the angel of the LORD, 'What is your name, so that we may honour you when your words come true?' But the angel of the LORD said to him, 'Why do you ask my name? It is too wonderful' (Judg. 13.17–18).

> For as the heavens are higher than the earth, so are my ways higher than your ways and my thoughts than your thoughts (Isa. 55.9).

In order to say something about this God who is infinite, invisible and transcendent, the biblical writers and the theologians turn to metaphors. But this is not a case of using poetic, decorative expressions to say something about the being and nature of God that could be said in plain language. Aristotle's contention that what is said metaphorically can also be said literally[2] is highly arguable. Modern philosophers and linguists aver that human thought and language are fundamentally metaphorical in nature. Lakoff and Johnson have demonstrated that we structure our everyday lives through a series of metaphors.[3] We say, for example, that argument is war: 'Your claims are *indefensible*'; 'She *attacked every weak point* in my argument'; 'He *shot down* all my arguments'. Lakoff and Johnson's claim is that there is a whole range of implicit metaphors – 'Argument is War' is one of these – that are absolutely essential to the task of thinking about ourselves and the world we live in.

What is metaphor?

We have said that metaphorization is indispensable, but what exactly is a metaphor? The first point to be made is that in metaphorical expression it is not identity that is posited, but a relation of similarity and dissimilarity. As Aristotle puts it in his *Poetics*, '... to make good metaphors implies an eye for resemblances [among dissimilars]'.[4] Thus, when we say that God is mother, we do not mean to say that God is a mother without remainder, but rather that God's mode of relating to human beings shares some of the characteristics of mothering.[5]

If one essential characteristic of metaphorization is the perception of similarity between two dissimilar terms, another is the logical absurdity that it entails. This has not always been clearly seen by philosophers of metaphor. Aristotle states that '[m]etaphor is the application of an alien name by transference either from genus to species, or from species to genus, or from species to species, or by analogy, that is, proportion'.[6] His theory of metaphor is essentially one of substitution: the image has replaced an absent but ordinary word. So in relation to the metaphorical expression 'His lawyer is a shark', the word 'aggressive' has been replaced by the more poetic or decorative one, 'shark'. The work of Richards,[7] Black,[8] Beardsley,[9] Ricoeur[10] and others on metaphor, however, has overturned this approach. Following Richards's lead, the theory of interaction has been adopted as the most adequate understanding of what happens in metaphorization. According to Richards, '[W]hen we use a metaphor, we have two thoughts of different things active together and supported by a single word or phrase, whose meaning is a resultant of their interaction.'[11]

Beardsley and Ricoeur have pointed out that the nature of this interaction is one of logical opposition. That is, there is an inherent tension between the two terms in the metaphorical relation. Beardsley uses the example of 'the spiteful sun'.[12] Two terms that are logically opposed – the sun and spite – are brought into a relation of similarity. It is not logically possible to attribute to a star an emotional expression such as spite. Only human beings (and animals?) can express spitefulness. The genius in this particular metaphor is to perceive that the destructive effects of a burning sun on people, flora, fauna and soil in a parched area can be likened to a spiteful action. The logical opposition makes for the 'metaphorical twist'.

Ricoeur uses the term 'semantic clash'[13] to describe this logical opposition that is at the core of metaphorization. He points out that the difference between a simile and a metaphor is that only in the case of the latter is there a semantic clash.[14] Ricoeur uses the example of the simile 'Jim is as stubborn as a mule' to make his point. All the words retain their meaning in this figure of speech. The representations 'Jim', 'stubborn' and 'mule' remain distinct and coexist without dissonance. That is, there is no incompatibility between the semic units of the sentence. But 'the perception of incompatibility is essential to the interpretation of the message in the case of metaphor'.[15] In the expression 'Jim is an ass', there is this semantic clash. There is a semic incompatibility between 'Jim' and 'ass'.

The clearest explication of the metaphorical twist that I have found is provided by Mary Gerhart and Allan Russell.[16] They use visual images to aid their explanatory work. Metaphor is contrasted with analogy: only in the case of the former is there any twisting of logic. The authors ask us to imagine a map of the world of meanings. This map is drawn on a piece of paper. In the case of analogy, a line is drawn between two locations on the map. Imagine, for example, that we are dealing with the analogical statement 'In his dialectical approach, Socrates torments the citizens of Athens the way a horsefly torments a horse'. There are four terms in play here: Socrates, Athenians, horsefly and horse. On our map of meanings, we can draw straight lines between the sets of terms that show the flow of the logic of the analogy. That is, a straight line can be drawn between the statements 'Socrates is to the Athenians' (A) and 'a horsefly is to a horse' (B). The reason that the line is straight is that a logical relation is operating here. We do not have to effect a distortion in the world of meaning to achieve alignment between these two statements. The connecting line between (A) and (B) is the idea of tormenting.

But the matter is very different in the case of the metaphorical statement 'Socrates is a horsefly'. There is a logical absurdity involved in suggesting that a man is an insect. The only way that we can achieve an alignment between the two terms is to fold our map of meanings in half so that the half with 'Socrates' written on it now sits above the half with 'horsefly' written on it. There is no way that we can draw a straight line between the terms. There is non-logic rather than logic in the relationship between them. Through this visual image, Gerhart and Russell vividly express the fact that metaphor creates a twist in the world of meanings.

Having discussed in general terms what metaphor is, I want now to open up the question of the fundamental ground of metaphor. In other words, what is it in human experience that is the primary source of metaphor? There are three leading candidates: embodied cognition, culture and personal knowledge. Philosophers and linguists argue about which of the three should be assigned primacy. Fortunately, we do not need to enter into that debate. For us, it is sufficient to note that there is clear evidence that all three play an important role.

Embodied cognition and metaphor

If we go back to the 1950s and 1960s, the mind was construed as a
'disembodied logical reasoning device'.[17] The mind works by going to
the relevant filing cabinet, retrieving the information it needs, and then
doing work on the data through the exercise of reason. This approach
had its origins in René Descartes' (in)famous mind–body dualism (we
mentioned this in discussing empathy and embodiment in Chapter 2).
Descartes' theory of the mind and body has been characterized (by
Gilbert Ryle) as 'the ghost in the machine'. Today, thinkers such as Andy
Clark,[18] Jerome Feldman,[19] George Lakoff[20] and Mark Johnson[21] contend for the notion that concepts and reason are embodied. Feldman
points up the contrast well: 'Thought and language are not disembodied
symbol systems that happen to be realized in the human brain through
its computation properties. Instead, thought and language are inherently embodied. They reflect the structure of human bodies and have the
inherent properties of neural systems as well as the external physical and
social environment.'[22]

The basis for the concepts that are fundamental in human reasoning
is categorization. Even an amoeba engages in categorization.[23] It can
tell food from non-food through a chemical process. When it comes to
humans, we engage in categorization in our interaction with objects
in our everyday world. For example, we have categories for particular
kinds of entities (cars, animals, humans); we have categories that involve
degrees (unimportant, moderately important, highly important), and
size (small, large, massive). Consider the hierarchy of categories associated with a chair: furniture → chair → rocking chair. The middle term
in this hierarchy represents a 'basic level category'.[24] That which makes
it a basic level category is essentially two things. First, we are able to
form mental images of the thing. I can imagine a chair; I cannot imagine
generalized furniture. Second, we have motor programmes for interacting with a chair. The same does not apply for furniture in general.
For example, I can move towards a chair, place my hand on its arm, and
sit down in it. In sum, embodiment is the means employed in establishing
that something is a basic category.

Another good illustration of embodied knowing is the colour concept.[25] Colour is not an independent entity that exists out there in the
world. That is, there is no thing called greenness that inheres in a blade
of grass. The experience of colour is created by four factors, two of
which are associated with our bodies. The non-body factors are the
wavelengths of reflected light and the lighting conditions. The contributions of the human body are the colour cones in our retinas and the

complex neural circuits tied into those cones. It is therefore not culture that creates colour. Colour is the result of the interaction between our biology and factors in the physical world.

Finally, the concept of spatial relations illustrates the embodied nature of cognition.[26] Spatial conceptualization is clearly very significant for human existence. We need to be able to make sense of space in order to carry out our everyday endeavours, as well as scientific, artistic and sporting ones. Spatial relation concepts do not exist as entities in the external world. We do not see 'nearness' or 'farness', for example. We see this or that object, and we assign nearness or farness to it on the basis of its relation to a landmark.

Our bodies play a central role in the way we develop spatial relations concepts. The terms 'in front of' and 'at the back of', for example, are projections of the shape of the human body. We have a front. We see from the front. Therefore, we naturally move in a front-facing direction. Our backs are the opposite of our fronts. We develop the concepts of 'in front of' and 'at the back of' through a process of analogical thought grounded in our bodily construction.

Theorists such as Feldman, Lakoff and Johnson contend that metaphor plays a crucial and essential role in learning and working with the huge range of cultural, theoretical and abstract concepts that we all live with.[27] These concepts derive their meaning through mapping, via metaphor, to embodied experiential concepts. In what the authors call 'primary metaphor', a connection is made between a subjective judgement and a sensory motor occurrence. Examples of primary metaphor are *affection is warmth* and *more is up*. The dynamic operating here is that some experience brings together a subjective judgement and a sensory-motor occurrence. In the case of *affection is warmth*, affection is the subjective occurrence and the sensory-motor factor is temperature. The experience that lies behind the linkage that forms the metaphor is cuddling by a parent. In *more is up* (as in 'There was a rise in the stock market today'), the subjective judgement is quantity and the sensory-motor factor is vertical orientation. The experience lying behind the metaphor is observing the level rise when adding a fluid to a glass.

Leonard Talmy has made similar connections in relation to the force dynamics that are a very common part of our sensory-motor experience of the world on the one hand, and a number of metaphors that operate at the intra-psychological and social psychological levels on the other.[28] Talmy observes that we commonly experience two forces opposing each other in the world. We can all remember a common scene in our growing up in which a demanding sibling is pushing on the door to our bedroom and we are pushing back against her or him. At the intra-psychic level this opposition of forces is expressed as 'the divided self'. We use metaphorical expressions such as 'I held myself back from responding'. At the social psychological level, we commonly use or hear metaphors such as 'He's under a lot of pressure to keep silent' or 'The gang pushed him to do things he didn't want to'.

Primary metaphors such as these are used as the building blocks in constructing complex metaphors. Lakoff and Johnson use the example of the complex metaphor 'A purposeful life is a journey' to illustrate the process.[29] The metaphor is grounded in a cultural belief that it is important for people to be purposeful in life, and to act in order to actualize their purposes. The primary metaphors that form the 'atoms' are these: 'Purposes are destinations' and 'Actions are motions'.

The role of culture in metaphorization

Critics of the approach to metaphorization that identifies embodied cognition as the primary factor contend that insufficient recognition is accorded to the place of culture. It is, however, not assumed by these critics that Lakoff and Johnson completely miss the role that cultural constructions play in the way we construct and use metaphors. As soon as anyone thinks about some of the common metaphors people use, it will become evident to the individual that cultural understanding of people, things and life feed into these. Indeed, in their discussion on complex metaphors, Lakoff and Johnson acknowledge this fact. They state that complex, everyday metaphors 'are built out of primary metaphors plus forms of commonplace knowledge: cultural models, folk memories, or simply knowledge or beliefs that are widely accepted in a culture'.[30] The example that we cited – namely, that 'a purposeful life is a journey' – is built on the commonly accepted cultural value that people should have a purpose in life, and that there is something awry if they do not. The argument, then, is not over whether or not culture plays a role in metaphorization, but rather over whether its role is primary or secondary.

Naomi Quinn is convinced that culture is the primary factor in the process of metaphorization.[31] Quinn begins by stating her understanding of culture. It is 'the shared understandings that people hold and that are sometimes, but not always, realized, stored, and transmitted in their language'.[32] Her argument in a nutshell is that 'cultural understanding underlies metaphor use'.[33] She uses her own work on the way in which Americans talk about the nature of marriage – including their use of metaphor – to make her case. Against Lakoff and Johnson, Quinn contends that 'metaphorical systems or productive metaphors typically do not structure understandings de novo'.[34] Rather, metaphors are selected by people because of their ability to express existing cultural understandings. It is the fact that there is a good match between a particular cultural view and the chosen metaphor that is the crucial factor.

John Vervaeke and John Kennedy take a similar approach in critiquing the Lakoff and Johnson construction of metaphor use.[35] They work with one of the so-called implicit metaphors identified by their interlocutors to make their point. This metaphor is associated with expressions such as these: 'He is rooted' and 'She is blooming'. Lakoff and Johnson contend that these expressions and others like them are grounded in the pervasive and influential metaphor 'People are plants'. Vervaeke and Kennedy, however, are troubled by this contention that various groupings of common, everyday sayings can be tied into a set of implicit metaphors. They ask us to consider people metaphors of a different type:[36]

'He's a solid citizen.'
'He is dense.'
'Don't talk to him, he is too heavy.'
'He is so thick.'
'He is many-faceted.'
'He is so durable.'
'He is so hard.'

Someone who has accepted the Lakoff and Johnson theory might look at this list and suggest that the use of these expressions is explained by the implicit metaphor 'People are rocks'. It would presumably be possible to generate another set of expressions that could be grounded in an unconscious, master metaphor. All of this counts as evidence against the view that there is a pervasive, influential, implicit metaphor that explains why we use the people metaphors that we do. Vervaeke and Kennedy's point is that it is the typical cultural thinking about people that generates the metaphorical expressions used of them, rather than an implicit, primary metaphor.

The role of personal knowledge in metaphor use

The focus on culture's role in metaphorization points to the broader issue of context. The context surrounding metaphor use includes, along with the wider culture, the following: (i) the relationship between the participants in the conversation, (ii) the immediate social and physical environments, and (iii) the immediate linguistic context itself. In discussing context, a number of theorists identify personal knowledge as an important factor.[37] I have decided to concentrate on this here, in part because it is clearly quite significant in relation to counselling work. The accuracy and depth with which counsellors interpret the metaphors used by counsellees depend on counsellors' level of understanding of counsellees' personal contexts.

Kövecses provides enlightening examples of the role played by personal knowledge in metaphor construction. The first illustration involves a sporting metaphor.[38] In the Comment section of *The Times*, the author (we are not given a name) is suggesting that David Beckham should be picked for an upcoming international game of soccer. The author of the piece does acknowledge, however, that Beckham is not fully prepared for soccer at this level. The piece continues: 'Beckham is 32. He has not played top-class football since November. Los Angeles Galaxy are sardines not sharks in the ocean of footy.'

Kövecses asks the question: How did the author come up with this metaphor that plays with the terms 'football', 'sardines', 'sharks', and 'ocean'? His answer is as follows: 'In all probability, it is the author's knowledge about David Beckham – the main topic of the discourse – that gives rise to the metaphors. The author (together with us) knows that Beckham plays for the Los Angeles Galaxy, a team located in Los Angeles, which, in turn, is a city on the Pacific Ocean, and the Pacific Ocean contains sardines and sharks.'[39]

The second illustration involves the American news anchorman Dan Rather. In his coverage of the 2001 American presidential elections, Rather opined that 'the presidential campaign is ... still hotter than a Laredo parking lot'.[40] The reference to 'a Laredo parking lot' is drawn from his southern upbringing.

In sum, embodiment, culture and individual experience are all important ideational resources for metaphorization. It is interesting to note that Dennis Tay has examined transcripts of psychotherapeutic sessions and demonstrated that metaphors used by the clients can be tied into all three of these domains.[41] This is not surprising. What we find to be the case for the general population, we would expect to manifest in the therapy/counselling cohort. It is therefore quite natural that embodiment, culture and personal knowledge inform the metaphors that clients/counsellees use.

Having discussed the nature of metaphor, we move now to a consideration of the role of metaphor in the change process within the counselling process. In doing so, we will see that metaphorization is linked in important ways to fundamental aspects of the counselling practice. I will make connections with understanding of and talking about affect, empathic attunement, making tacit awareness of issues explicit and, lastly, reframing and finding new possibilities.

Metaphors in counselling and the change process

If all that the use of metaphors by the counsellee did was add a little colour and vividness to the counselling conversation, not much would be gained by attending to the images. Those theorists and practitioners who advocate for this practice do so because they believe that it makes a significant contribution to facilitating change. It is therefore important for us to come to an understanding of exactly how working with counsellee metaphors leads to healing and growth. A survey of the literature suggests that there are at least four ways in which attending to metaphors facilitates change. They are these:

- helps counsellees understand their emotional experience and articulate it more precisely;
- constitutes empathic attunement and contributes to building the therapeutic alliance;
- shifts awareness of central personal issues from the tacit to the explicit level; and
- facilitates reframing and a move towards new possibilities.

It is to a discussion of each of these important contributions that we now turn.

Expansion of understanding and fuller articulation of affect

The emotions that we feel are significant indicators of our mental state and how we are coping with our psychological challenges, personal pain and the stressors of everyday life. It is quite common for emotions to be unexplored and the role that they play in personal experience to be poorly understood. Moreover, it is quite difficult for virtually all of us to articulate our affective experience. In order to move in the direction of healing and growth, it is essential for counsellees to be aware of, and able to explore, the main emotions connected to their personal issues. It is widely reported that when counsellees/clients use metaphor it has the effect of expanding awareness of emotional experience and facilitating a sharper, clearer expression of it. Ellen Siegelman observes that metaphor flows from emotion because its use is indicative of a felt need to express a deep, inner experience of self and others. She goes on to say that '[i]t typically arises when feelings are high and when ordinary words do not seem strong enough or precise enough to convey the experience'.[42] Raymond Fox suggests that metaphor 'sparks deep and complex responses' and 'expresses hidden emotion-laden content'.[43]

Lastly, Mary Baird Carlsen notes that emotions are 'barometers of meaning' and that metaphors 'serve a very important role in translating the intangibles of emotion into some sort of verbal expression'.[44]

One gets a strong sense of this experience in engaging with the psalms. In reading the psalms of protest, for example, one is immediately struck by both the rawness of emotion displayed and the vivid imagery used to communicate it. Those in distress have reached a point of extremity; the old certainties, along with the feelings of serenity and joy associated with them, have been swept away. In this limit-experience, it is impossible to hold on to a restrained, tame and timid way of communicating with God. There is now no slippage between the agonies of the heart and the primitive, aggressive articulations before God. The images of distress and anguish tumble out in prayer (the italic is my own):

I am the scorn of all my adversaries, a horror to my neighbours, an
   object of dread to my acquaintances;
those who see me in the street flee from me.
I have passed out of mind like one who is dead;
I have become *like a broken* vessel. (Ps. 31.11–12)

[My enemies] *set a net for my steps*; my soul was *bowed down*.
They *dug a pit* in my path,
but they have fallen into it themselves.
(Ps. 57.6)

How long will you assail a person
will you batter your victim, all of you, as you would a *leaning wall,*
   a tottering fence?
(Ps. 62.3)

Your wrath has *spread over* me;
your dread assaults destroy me.
They surround me *like a flood* all day long;
(Ps. 88.16–17)

These ejaculations of anguish, however, do not simply represent a release of emotion. They are manifestations of emotional knowledge. Behind the metaphors is an understanding of the dynamics of the distress. In this theological frame, 'enemies' of various kinds are being allowed by God to press in and wreak havoc. People today feeling something of the same agonies of the soul will easily be able to put their own names on the enemies.

We note, too, that those who cry out to God in these psalms are not lost in a whirl of emotion. They are not paralysed by their distressing circumstances; associated with their cries from the heart are will and directedness. The psalmists are praying a protest. There is a very clear expectation that God should intervene in the current turmoil to bring order, freedom and peace.

The way that the psalmists expressed their emotion through metaphor is something that one encounters frequently today – albeit with expressions most often lacking the poetic flair of the psalmists. In thinking about this fact, 'Terry's' story came immediately to mind:

Terry, a 42-year-old teacher, suffers from low self-esteem, anxiety and mild depression. He is shy, quietly spoken, sensitive and very polite. After listening to his recounting of interpersonal engagements in which he was treated quite shabbily, the fact that he made no mention of feeling slighted or upset stood out like a sore thumb. In response to a query about this, Terry denied taking any offence or feeling annoyed or angry. The issue was pursued, however, and finally he had this to say: 'I guess if I think about it, there are probably some hard feelings there, but I have locked them down pretty tight. I guess I don't want to have to deal with them.' He went on to say that he finds the expression of anger by himself and by others to be 'deeply distasteful, threatening, and really uncomfortable'.

Terry reported that when he has allowed himself to feel angry in the past, he has 'completely blown his top'. 'I don't seem to have a regulator on the expression of my anger. The anger either gets held down, or I explode. There are no half-measures with me.' He went on to say that the reason he doesn't allow himself to acknowledge angry feelings is because he is afraid of the explosion that might follow. 'I'm so afraid of a bad scene that I lock the anger away in the basement. It can't do any damage locked away down there.'

When asked 'What's it feel like having to keep your anger locked down?' Terry had this to say: 'Sometimes I feel completely worn out by it. I feel flat ... full of tension ... and pretty fearful too. I live with the constant fear that maybe the lock won't be strong enough, and the angry beast will break out and wreak havoc.'

That the use of metaphor by counsellees facilitates articulation of affective experience, and reflection on the meaning associated with it, is clearly very significant in relation to the goal of positive change. But equally important is the fact that this dynamic is catalytic for challenging personal constructions of self and others, along with unquestioned ways of thinking and acting. This is very clear in the case of Terry. The fact that his pattern of suppressing angry feelings is exhausting, anxiety-creating, and leaves him feeling down, highlights for him that he needs to rethink and restructure his approach to dealing with conflict and anger. Alan Marlett and Kim Fromme capture the general point well:

> Emotions are presumed to make up 'feeling memories' which in turn furnish individuals with a more or less automatic unconscious reaction repertoire to affectively meaningful stimuli. By providing affectively meaningful stimuli which are incongruous with the individual's current ways of seeing him/herself or situation, metaphor may necessitate structural changes in a person's personal reality system.[45]

This connects with the fourth element we listed above in relation to metaphor and the change process – namely, reframing and identifying new possibilities. A full discussion of this will come later. At this point, we need to attend to the issue of empathic attunement and building the relationship.

Constitutes empathic attunement and builds a stronger counselling relationship

Attending to the metaphors counsellees use, and thus working with their frame of reference, communicates a desire to enter into and understand their inner world of experience. It is vitally important for counsellees to perceive that counsellors are attuned to their self-experience and to honour it (we gave an extended treatment to this in Chapter 2). In his work on metaphor in counselling, Marty Babits helpfully introduces Donald Winnicott's image of the 'holding environment' to capture this.[46] In discussing the approach of the 'good enough' mother, Winnicott identifies as crucial the fact that she holds her baby both physically and emotionally in a tender, caring way. 'Good enough mothering' involves being attuned and attentive to the baby's needs; in this way, the fundamental requirement for healthy mental development is met. The growing infant acquires a sense that the world is a safe, trustworthy and loving environment. Winnicott contends that a psychotherapist needs to establish a symbolic holding environment in therapy. Building on this insight, Babits opines that '[t]he therapeutic metaphor can serve such a holding environment, spawning its own common language, reflecting back to the patient a sense that she can be and/or is understood, that she can be, or is being, "held" adequately'.[47] Let me offer an example based on my own experience of the creation of a shared metaphorical language and empathic communication:

Maria, 30 years of age, was experiencing difficulties in her working relationship with her colleague Tom. They worked closely together on a number of projects. Maria was troubled by what she saw as Tom not pulling his weight. She was of the view that Tom is selfish and inconsiderate, that he wants things 'too much his own way'. She offered this image: 'The working relationship is like a set of scales that are hardly ever in balance. He keeps loading stuff on so that they tilt in his favour.' When asked about her attempts to right the imbalance, she spoke of 'a deeply frustrating cycle'. 'I tell him my view of things; I point out what I see as the lack of fairness; he tells me he can't see that he's being selfish ... We just go round and round. I end up almost at screaming point!' The image that came to mind for me in reflecting on her description of the situation was of Justice holding up a set of scales: 'Justice is blind-folded and holding the scales. But the scales in your working relationship are out of kilter because Tom can't match her objectivity. He just can't see that he's being unfair and that drives you nuts.'

Enables shift in awareness from the tacit to the explicit level

Those who come to see counsellors are not usually keenly self-aware, possessing clear insight into the connections between their cognitions and affect on the one hand, and their experiences and situation on the other. It is unusual for them to be able to identify all the pieces of the puzzle and see how they fit together. Those blessed with such insight and personal awareness do not usually turn to a counsellor for assistance.

Those seeking help are typically aware of certain feelings and cognitive patterns, and there are particular dynamics that they have caught hold of, but there are certain crucial elements that elude their grasp. They cannot fully get a grip on how all the various factors and dynamics fit together. There is a degree of confusion and lack of clarity that is troubling and frustrating. Important information and insight is not too far away, but it cannot easily be grasped. It is sitting at the tacit level. Metaphor gives us a way of speaking about something that is unfamiliar to us through something that is familiar. It is for this reason that its use by counsellees assists in making tacit knowledge explicit.

Babit's case example of 'Justine'[48] illustrates nicely the way in which the use of metaphor enables making connections between cognitions and affect on the one hand, and personal experience and frame of reference on the other. This shift to making the right connections is crucial in relation to unlocking the door that leads to a more positive, free and hopeful future.

Justine was in her mid-twenties and was suffering from depression. She was concerned that without therapeutic help she would harm herself. Justine told her therapist that she felt isolated from her family, which consisted of her mother and her older brother. For the past 18 months she had had no contact with them. The fact that she had not seen them over this period caused her considerable distress.

Justine's parents had separated when she was ten years old; her mother had raised her and her older brother on a very tight budget. Her mother suffered herself from depression and was largely emotionally unavailable to her children when they were growing up. Justine had witnessed on many occasions her father's perpetration of physical and emotional abuse on her mother.

She asked her therapist for help in working through her feelings related to the difficult and painful experiences with her family, and in overcoming difficulties she experienced in forming a lasting relationship with a man. Sexual acting out and drug and alcohol binges were reported as elements in the presenting problem. Babits discusses the way in which the use of the image of being caught in a pit, from which it was impossible to see out, assisted Justine in making important connections:

> [T]he therapist asked Justine if she could say more about what it felt like for her to be depressed. 'I feel like I'm stuck in a pit and can't see out.' When the therapist replied, 'What's preventing you from seeing out?' she had a ready answer. 'The walls are too high and it's dark. There's all kinds of stuff around in there … It's caked on and very frustrating because I can't clean it up, I can hardly move around in it. It's like living with all the clutter of my whole life all around me …'
>
> Although Justine had begun the treatment sharing a burst of information about her depressed and angry feelings, she had then seemed unwilling or unable to make connections between those feelings and central events in her life. For Justine, the events of her life, her feelings about those events, and her feelings about herself appeared to run on separate tracks, lacking coherence. The use of metaphor provided her a sense of freedom which helped her begin making some of these important connections.[49]

It is interesting and instructive to note that the therapist does very little in this exchange with Justine. He simply asks, 'What's preventing you from seeing out?' And yet there is a very large yield produced in terms of insight. Effective counselling, on one level, is about doing not very much. It requires only that the counsellor remain attentive and supportive, and able to offer a few well-timed, apt and probing questions and/

or comments. Of course, the art of the counsellor consists of doing this small number of things exceedingly well. It takes a high level of skill and wisdom to carry that off. Siegelman has it just right when she refers to her work with clients' metaphors as similar to that of a midwife helping to deliver babies.[50] The best midwives are not overly active and intrusive. Mostly they stand by quietly and supportively, and offer some well-timed and well-targeted interventions that make all the difference.

Some of the timely interventions by counsellors are aimed at inviting counsellees to reframe their thinking, acting and way of viewing themselves and others. Metaphors play an important role here, and it is to a consideration of this issue that we now turn.

Reframing and moving into new possibilities

In order for counsellees to experience healing and growth, they need to modify their conceptual frameworks. Without reconstruction of their habitual, taken-for-granted and unhealthy ways of interpreting themselves, their experiences and their relationships with others, they will remain stuck. Metaphor has the potential to play an important role in this reframing; a number of counsellors and therapists report positive experiences in this regard.[51] Setting one's view of oneself and others in a new frame opens the way to a more healthy, free and hopeful experience of life. Tracey Robert and Virginia Kelly sum this up well: '[Metaphors] provide a bridge when literal language does not have a discrete, particular way of describing experience. [They] allow clients and counsellors to explore and elaborate on the images provided and then transform them into a new understanding and way of knowing or being.'[52] Laurence Kirmayer offers three therapy vignettes[53] that demonstrate this point very clearly (they are paraphrased and summarized here):

1 A 54-year-old woman, mother of five adult children, currently divorced and living on her own was deeply depressed. She likened her experience to a completely black room that had no door to get out. The therapist and the client agreed that because the room was totally dark, there might in fact be an opening to the outside that was currently hidden from view. Further, they concurred that she had to slowly feel her way round at various levels looking for an opening. Over time, she was able to pursue new and positive options in terms of changes in attitude and behaviour, and training for employment.
2 A 29-year-old married woman, with no children, was anxious and lacking in self-confidence. She had a vision of herself falling into a bottomless pit. She clung desperately to roots and vines; she was

deeply afraid of the fall. Over time, she gradually felt herself getting closer to the bottom and her fear was mitigated. In fact, when she finally touched the bottom, she felt a sense of relief and her confidence in herself soared.

3   A 33-year-old female, married with two children, was afraid that expressing her feelings would be like sinking into a whirlpool that was impossible to escape from. She was unable to use the image to create a new possibility for herself, so the therapist suggested that therapy was like a rope thrown to her, so that even though she would experience the whirlpool, she would not go under. This significantly reduced her fear of the unknown impact of giving expression to her feelings. As a consequence, she was prepared to take risks with experiencing painful affect.

Working with metaphors in counselling: a step-by-step approach

After reporting at considerable length on 'metaphors of the self' that emerged in two cases of psychotherapy, Ellen Siegelman poses this question: 'What does the therapist need to "do" with these embracing metaphors of the patient's psychological situation?'[54] Her response is this: 'Very little, it seems to me.' She goes on to describe what constitutes 'doing very little': 'My role in these cases was to provide a setting in which such metaphors could flourish. I did this by my interest (not coercive or exclusive) in these products, by encouraging their exploration, by attending to the affect that invariably accompanies them.'[55]

I agree entirely with Siegelman. In my time teaching pastoral counselling to theological students, I found myself saying on numerous occasions, 'You don't need to do all that much to help people. You just have to do what you do really well.' This comment came as part of my response after watching a counselling role play. The trainee counsellor concerned had been overactive and, in his eagerness to be helpful, engaged in a number of useless interventions.

We have just seen that Siegelman offers a brief description of what she does in supporting and guiding clients' 'play' with their metaphors. Richard Kopp and Michael Craw have a more expansive model; they offer a step-by-step approach that picks up Siegelman's intentions and also adds a few extras.[56] Working with counsellees around their metaphors requires artistry, sensitivity and intuition. It is more art than science. This seems to count against the use of a staged process such as these therapists recommend. Indeed, Kopp (in his monograph on metaphor therapy[57]) acknowledges that there does seem to be a contradiction involved here. He also warns against using the steps in a 'mechanical' or 'rigid' manner.[58] The reason Kopp and Craw have taken this approach – rightly I think – is that it has proved to be very effective in training counsellors and therapists unfamiliar with metaphor therapy. I am therefore happy to recommend it. The steps are as follows (Note: I've changed the language from 'clients' to 'counsellees'):

1 Write down counsellees' metaphors verbatim.
2 Invite counsellees to explore their metaphoric images by asking a question such as: 'What does the metaphor look like?'
3 Invite counsellees to reflect on the metaphors as sensory images.
4 Ask counsellees to describe their feelings and experience linked to the metaphors.
5 Encourage counsellees to change the metaphors. ('If you could change the image in any way, what would you do with it?')
6 Invite counsellees to make connections between their images and the problem situations they are experiencing.
7 Ask counsellees if the way in which they changed the images suggests any changes they might make in their current situation.

In the following case study, based on my own experience, all of the steps are involved, but I have not followed the method exactly. As I mentioned above, Kopp and Craw do not intend a rigid application.

In the pastoral conversation, Mitch raised the issue of feeling overwhelmed with personal and professional responsibilities. He was married, had two teenage children, and worked as a university lecturer. Further, he had significant responsibility for the care and support of not only his own parents, but also of his mother-in-law. Mitch's parents and mother-in-law lived in their own homes, but they were failing mentally and physically, and needed help to maintain their independent living situation.

Mitch was experiencing what many in the aptly named 'sandwich generation' struggle with – namely, feeling overwhelmed by the demands from both children and parents, along with his volume of work and other everyday demands. At the university he was under pressure to boost his research output. While his teenage children were, in his words, 'pretty good kids on the whole', they (naturally enough) had moments of behaving badly. Further, they required a good deal of his time for help with homework and being transported to their various weekly activities. Mitch had also taken on a significant responsibility at his local church as Chair of the Church Council.

When he told me his story and communicated to me his feeling that he was 'only just holding it all together', I responded by saying, 'There's constantly a great wave of responsibility coming at you, and you are barely able to cope.' The conversation unfolded as follows:

Mitch: That's it! My life is plugging holes in a dyke wall. Sometimes I feel like I'm barely holding it all together.

Pastoral counsellor: The pressure of feeling like you could be washed away at any minute is not much fun. *(Step 1. The metaphor has been noticed. A decision is made to work with it.)* Tell me how this image of plugging holes in a dyke wall speaks to what's going on for you. *(Steps 2 and 3.)*

Mitch: Hmm ... It's like there's this torrent of responsibility constantly bearing down on me. It's threatening to overwhelm me. The only thing holding it back is the dyke wall with my fingers stuck in there.

Pastoral counsellor: What's it like having to keep your fingers in place?

Mitch: It's an awful pressure. I live with the scary thought that the wall might break at any time.

Pastoral counsellor: That's a really tough situation to be in. What are some of the feelings that go with that? *(Step 4.)*

Mitch: I feel pressure coming from all sides. It's constant. There is no escape. Most of the time there is a gnawing in my guts. When I think about it, there is this constant, low-grade, nervous feeling. There are butterflies fluttering around in my stomach most of the time. I feel the tension in my shoulders, neck, and in my face. I don't laugh as much as I used to. It's like my face is too tight to crack a smile.

Pastoral counsellor: So that awful feeling of tension and stress ... of feeling pretty uptight a lot of the time. That's hard ... really hard. Other feelings you are aware of?

Mitch: I get pretty down sometimes. I feel like I don't have much fun in my life. It's all work and responsibility. I really hate that.

Pastoral counsellor: OK. You're giving me a pretty clear picture of someone under too much strain. It's really stressful having to constantly hold back the torrent. If you could change the image to reflect a better situation, what would it look like? *(Step 5.)*

Mitch: Gee, I don't know ... It would be great to have an extra hand or two to keep the wall intact. I just need a break, you know.

Pastoral counsellor: Of course you do. It's all too much. What concrete action can you take to make the desire a reality? *(Step 7. Mitch has identified how he would like to change the image to improve his situation. But there needs to be action to make it happen.)*

Mitch: It would be really nice if there was someone to share the load. But this is the problem. It's all down to me.

Pastoral counsellor: Really? I can see that that's the case for your university role, and for your parenting. But what about the support you give to your parents and mother-in-law?

Mitch: Not much we can do in relation to Martha [the mother-in-law], but I do have a brother, John. He's never been especially close to our parents. In any case, he's got a fair bit on his plate as well. I think he drops by about once every few months and takes them out for coffee or a meal, and that's it. The week-in, week-out maintenance and help with grocery shopping and what have you is down to me.

Pastoral counsellor: Does it have to be?

Mitch: What do you mean?

Pastoral counsellor: Have you talked with John about the possibility of him taking a bigger role in the weekly support stuff?

Mitch: Not much point. It's really just easier for me to do it.

Pastoral counsellor: But you said that you could do with an extra hand or two. You need a break.

Mitch: (Grabbing his hair with both hands and expressing frustration and tension) Arrgh … This is my problem! On the one hand, I can't stand all the constant demands and pressure. But I have so much trouble asking for help. Maybe it's a pride thing. Probably something to do with me not handling rejection. I dunno.

A conversation followed about why Mitch found it so hard to ask for help from others. Finally, he acknowledged that talking with his brother about sharing the responsibility for supporting his parents was something that he needed to do. The outcome of this conversation with John was that they would each make themselves available on alternate weeks to give support to their parents.

Getting some relief from the pressures of life was naturally helpful for Mitch, but in the end he was still confronted by busyness and a long list of responsibilities. Given that he was not prepared to make significant changes in his life (downsizing and a new lifestyle, for example), it was clear to us both that the main challenge for him was to enhance his coping mechanisms. Hence we talked about the 'stress-busting' strategies that are commonly touted.

My pastoral conversation with Mitch took place very early in my ministry career. At the time, I am sorry to say, my focus in pastoral work was much more on psychology and counselling theory than on the resources of the Church such as prayer and the Bible.

Reading Don Capps's very fine book *Biblical Approaches to Pastoral Counseling*[59] constituted a turning point for me. Capps opened up for me the possibilities in a wise and thoughtful approach of incorporating

Scripture into the ministry of counselling. He shows how the psalms, proverbs and the parables all work with metaphors that speak to an important existential theme – that is, the sense of being disorientated in one's world. Capps goes on to point out that the metaphors in the psalms often reflect a central aspect of this theme: the experience of transition. This is certainly true. However, another very significant theme that crops up time and again is that of deliverance. There are constant pleas for deliverance from enemies, from sickness and the threat of death, from fears, and from troubles of every kind. With this in mind, were I to be supporting Mitch today, I would invite him to pray a psalm with me. Psalm 34 presents as a good choice. I would preface our reading of the psalm with this comment: 'Mitch, sometimes God delivers us *from* our burdens, and sometimes God delivers us *in* our burdens.' The psalm opens as follows:

> I will bless the Lord at all times;
> his praise shall continually be in my mouth.
> My soul makes its boast in the Lord;
> let the humble hear and be glad.
> O magnify the Lord with me,
> and let us exalt his name together.
>
> I sought the Lord, and he answered me,
> and delivered me from all my fears.
> Look to him, and be radiant;
> so your faces shall never be ashamed.
> This poor soul cried, and was heard by the Lord,
> and was saved from every trouble.
> The angel of the Lord encamps
> around those who fear him, and delivers them (Ps. 34.1–7)

Summary

To re-cap, the use of metaphor is not simply a means to add colour and interest to a conversation. It is essential to human thought and language; it is not an optional extra. We need metaphors to think and to express ourselves.

Given the indispensable role metaphorization plays in human thought and expression in general, it is to be expected that it will feature in counselling conversations. Helping counsellees unpack the images they use connects us with core issues in counselling. These issues include understanding of and talking about affect, empathic attunement, making tacit awareness of issues explicit and, finally, reframing a situation and finding new possibilities.

Though working with counsellee images (and with counsellees in general) requires art, intuition and flexibility, there is value in using a step-by-step procedure – especially when one is learning the process. The steps are these:

- Write it down.
- Invite exploration of the image.
- Invite reflection on the metaphor as a sensory image.
- Ask for a description of feelings/experience associated with the metaphor.
- Encourage changing the metaphor.
- Invite counsellees to make connections between the image and the problem situation.
- Ask if the way in which counsellees altered the image suggests any changes they might make.

It is crucially important to recognize that the method is not intended to be employed in a rigid, mechanical and inflexible manner. The procedure simply identifies the kinds of questions, responses and interventions that counsellors experienced in working with images have found to be efficacious.

The final topic to be considered is collaborating with the counsellee to construct rituals that build hope. We will be drawing on the great advantage that a pastoral counsellor has in relation to her secular counterparts – namely, the support of a worshipping community.

Notes

1 Here I employ the title of a well-known book on the philosophy of metaphor. See G. Lakoff and M. Johnson, *Metaphors We Live By* (Chicago, IL: University of Chicago Press, 1980).

2 See Aristotle, *Poetics*, trans. S. H. Butcher (New York: Hill & Wang, 1961), XXII.7.

3 See Lakoff and Johnson, *Metaphors We Live By*, esp. pp. 3–8.

4 Aristotle, *Poetics* XXII.9.

5 Cf. S. McFague, *Models of God: Theology for an Ecological, Nuclear Age* (Philadelphia, PA: Fortress Press, 1987), p. 22.

6 Aristotle, *Poetics* XXI.4.

7 See I. A. Richards, *The Philosophy of Rhetoric* (London: Oxford University Press, 1936).

8 See M. Black, *Models and Metaphors* (Ithaca, NY: Cornell University Press, 1962).

9 See M. C. Beardsley, 'The Metaphorical Twist', *Philosophy and Phenomenological Research* 22, no. 3 (1962), pp. 293–307.

10 See P. Ricoeur, *The Rule of Metaphor: Multi-disciplinary Studies of the Creation of Meaning in Language*, trans. Robert Czerny (London: Routledge, 2003).

11 Richards, *The Philosophy of Rhetoric*, p. 93.

12 See Beardsley, 'The Metaphorical Twist', p. 299.

13 See Ricoeur, *The Rule of Metaphor*, p. 225.

14 See Ricoeur, *The Rule of Metaphor*, p. 220.

15 Ricoeur, *The Rule of Metaphor*, p. 220.

16 See M. Gerhart and A. M. Russell, *Metaphoric Process: The Creation of Scientific and Religious Understanding* (Forth Worth, TX: Texas Christian University, 1984), pp. 109–20.

17 A. Clark, *Being There: Putting Brain, Body, and World Together Again* (Cambridge, MA, and London: The MIT Press, 1997), p. 1.

18 See Clark, *Being There*.

19 See J. A. Feldman, *From Molecule to Metaphor: A Neural Theory of Language* (Cambridge, MA. And London: The MIT Press, 2006).

20 See G. Lakoff, 'A Neural Theory of Metaphor', in R. W. Gibbs Jr (ed.), *The Cambridge Handbook of Metaphor and Thought* (Cambridge: Cambridge University Press, 2008), pp. 17–38; G. Lakoff and M. Johnson, *Philosophy in the Flesh: The Embodied Mind and Its Challenge to Western Thought* (New York: Basic Books, 1999).

21 See Lakoff and Johnson, *Philosophy in the Flesh*.

22 Feldman, *From Molecule to Metaphor*, p. 8.

23 See Feldman, *From Molecule to Metaphor*, p. 96.

24 See Lakoff and Johnson, *Philosophy in the Flesh*, p. 27; Feldman, *From Molecule to Metaphor*, p. 101.

25 See Lakoff and Johnson, *Philosophy in the Flesh,* pp. 23–6; Feldman, *From Molecule to Metaphor*, p. 104.

26 See Lakoff and Johnson, *Philosophy in the Flesh*, pp. 30–6.

27 See Lakoff and Johnson, *Philosophy in the Flesh*, pp. 45–73; Feldman, *From Molecule to Metaphor*, pp. 199–200; Lakoff, 'A Neural Theory of Metaphor'.

28 See L. Talmy, 'Force Dynamics in Language and Cognition', *Cognitive Science* 12 (1988), pp. 49–50.

29 See Lakoff and Johnson, *Philosophy in the Flesh*, pp. 60–2.

30 Lakoff and Johnson, *Philosophy in the Flesh*, p. 60.

31 See N. Quinn, 'The Cultural Basis of Metaphor', in J. Fernandez (ed.), *Beyond Metaphor: The Theory of Tropes in Anthropology* (Stanford, CA: Stanford University Press, 1991), pp. 56–93.

32 Quinn, 'The Cultural Basis of Metaphor', p. 57.

33 Quinn, 'The Cultural Basis of Metaphor', pp. 56–7.

34 Quinn, 'The Cultural Basis of Metaphor', p. 65.

35 See J. Vervaeke and J. M. Kennedy, 'Metaphors in Language and Thought: Falsification and Multiple Meanings', *Metaphor and Symbolic Activity* 11, no. 4 (1996), pp. 273–84.

36 Vervaeke and Kennedy, 'Metaphors in Language and Thought', p. 278.

37 See, for example, D. Ritchie, *Context and Connection in Metaphor* (New York: Palgrave Macmillan, 2006); D. Ritchie, 'Relevance and Simulation in

Metaphor', *Metaphor and Symbol* 24 (2009), pp. 249–62; Z. Kövecses, *Metaphor in Culture* (Cambridge: Cambridge University Press, 2005); Z. Kövecses, 'A New Look at Metaphorical Creativity in Cognitive Linguistics', *Cognitive Linguistics* 21, no. 4 (2010), pp. 663–97.

38 See Kövecses, 'A New Look', p. 675.

39 Kövecses, 'A New Look', p. 675.

40 Kövecses, *Metaphor in Culture*, p. 107.

41 See D. Tay, *Metaphor in Psychotherapy: A Descriptive and Prescriptive Analysis* (Amsterdam: John Benjamins Pub. Co., 2013), ch. 3.

42 E. Y. Siegelman, *Metaphor and Meaning in Psychotherapy* (New York: The Guilford Press, 1990), p. 16.

43 R. Fox, 'What is Meta For?', *Clinical Social Work Journal* 17, no. 3 (1989), pp. 233–34, p. 234.

44 M. B. Carlsen, 'Metaphor, Meaning-Making, and Metamorphosis', in H. Rosen and K. T. Kuehlwein (eds), *Constructing Realities: Meaning-making Perspectives for Psychotherapy* (San Francisco, CA: Jossey-Bass, 1996), pp. 337–67, p. 350.

45 G. A. Marlett and K. Fromme, 'Metaphors for Addiction', *Journal of Drug Issues* 17 (1987), pp. 9–29, p. 22; cited in W. J. Lyddon, A. L. Clay and C. L. Sparks, 'Metaphor and Change in Counseling', *Journal of Counseling and Development* 79, no. 3 (2001), pp. 269–74, p. 271.

46 See M. Babits, 'Using Therapeutic Metaphor to Provide a Holding Environment: The Inner Edge of Possibility', *Clinical Social Work Journal* 29, no. 1 (2001), pp. 21–33.

47 Babits, 'Using Therapeutic Metaphor', p. 26.

48 See Babits, 'Using Therapeutic Metaphor', p. 29.

49 Babits, 'Using Therapeutic Metaphor', p. 29.

50 See Siegelman, *Metaphor and Meaning*, p. 78.

51 See, for example, L. J. Kirmayer, 'Healing and the Invention of Metaphor: The Effectiveness of Symbols Revisited', *Culture, Medicine and Psychiatry* 17 (1993), pp. 161–95; T. Robert and V. A. Kelly, 'Metaphor as an Instrument for Orchestrating Change in Counselor Training and the Counseling Process', *Journal of Counseling and Development* 88, no. 2 (2010), pp. 182–8; Babits, 'Using Therapeutic Metaphor'; Lyddon, Clay and Sparks, 'Metaphor and Change'; Siegelman, *Metaphor and Meaning*, ch. 4.

52 Robert and Kelly, 'Metaphor as an Instrument', p. 186.

53 See Kirmayer, 'Healing and the Invention', p. 176. The therapy vignettes were supplied by Dr Jacqueline Carroll.

54 Siegelman, *Metaphor and Meaning*, p. 77.

55 Siegelman, *Metaphor and Meaning*, p. 78.

56 See R. R. Kopp and M. J. Craw, 'Metaphoric Language, Metaphoric Cognition, and Cognitive Therapy', *Psychotherapy* 35, no. 3 (1998), pp. 306–11.

57 See R. R. Kopp, *Metaphor Therapy: Using Client-Generated Metaphors in Psychotherapy* (New York: Brunner/Mazel, 1995).

58 See Kopp, *Metaphor Therapy*, p. 4.

59 See D. Capps, *Biblical Approaches to Pastoral Counseling* (Philadelphia, PA: The Westminster Press, 1981).

9

Connecting with a Community of Hope, or Pastoral Rituals that Shine a Light

People go to pastoral counsellors in the hope that the particular counsellor they have chosen will facilitate transcendence of their current unsatisfactory and distressing state of affairs. Help-seekers hope for release and relief, and are looking forward to a time when life will be more comfortable and agreeable. Both the present and the future feature here. Hope has the power to enhance an individual's sense of well-being now through an imaginative projection into the future. Further, hope is also intimately connected with a person's past.[1] It is the memory of positive outcomes after a rough patch that funds the hopeful imagination. For people of faith, these turnarounds are associated with God's gracious action.

Much of the current psychological thinking on hope has an individualistic orientation. Those with high hope, according to this thinking, are those who have both the resourcefulness to find ways around blockages and the mental strength to persist until they have reached the end-point. Hope, from this perspective, is something that individuals do. There is another view on hope, however – one that fits much better with the Christian tradition. On this view, hope is something that we do together. Those who are caught up in difficult circumstances benefit significantly from witnesses to their pain and distress supporting them in building hope.

The traditional African philosophy known as *Ubuntu* is currently very much in the forefront of my thinking, thanks to my participation last year in a wonderful conference on this important theme.[2] *Ubuntu* has the communitarian approach to hope at its very centre. Its essence is captured in the Zulu saying *umuntu ngumuntu ngabantu* 'a person is a person through others'. It is a philosophical anthropology that begins and ends with interdependence. It is the responsibility of the community to respond in solidarity and with care and compassion when a person is in need. Sub-Saharan Africans in difficulty and distress are hopeful not primarily because they have the utmost confidence in their personal resources, but rather because they live in a community that is characterized by solidarity, care and compassion.

The psychotherapist Kaethe Weingarten[3] is inspired in her work by *Ubuntu*. She makes use of a community of 'witnesses' in building hope in her clients. Weingarten has found that developing a community ritual is particularly helpful, and this use of ritual connects with the helpful work done on ritual in pastoral care[4] and in psychotherapy.[5] One of the great assets that pastoral counsellors have is access to a community of faith. They are able to work creatively and effectively with help-seekers and their witnesses to hope. Available of course are the resources for hope-building that one finds in a service of worship. In a general way, the prayers, the hymns, the Bible readings, the preaching and the sacramental liturgics all point us to the source of Christian hope: the grace of our Lord Jesus Christ, the love of God, and the communion of the Holy Spirit. However, there is also the possibility of developing personally tailored rituals that employ Christian resources.

In what follows, we begin by trying to get a fix on the true nature of hope. Next, we develop the connections between *Ubuntu* and the role of a community of hope in working with help-seekers. Finally, we see how personalized rituals are employed in building hope. These rituals are co-created by counsellor and counsellee, drawing on the resources of the Church.

A psychology of hope

'Hoping' is one of those experiences that we think we know exactly what it is until we attempt to spell it out. When we try to say precisely what constitutes it, we very quickly come to realize that hope is an elusive phenomenon. Describing it is no easy task, but we can make a start by offering a broad definition. To put it in general terms, hope is an expectancy of good in the future.[6] Or, to be more specific, it is the expectation that future positive feelings will outweigh future negative feelings.[7]

Hope becomes important to us when we find ourselves in a difficult and trying situation. It is a very uncomfortable place to be; we feel distressed and worried. We feel trapped by our circumstances. When this is the case, it is easy to fall into apathy and despair. Hope pushes against the forces dragging us down into the depths. What sustains us is the knowledge and the feeling that there is a way out.[8]

Psychological definitions of hope

Speaking generally about hope provides an entry point into the experience. It is important, though, to make our understanding of it as sharp as possible. Definitions are helpful in this regard. Let us first consider some representative attempts to capture the psychology of hoping:

> Hoping is the perception that what one wants to happen will happen, a perception that is fuelled by desire and in response to felt deprivation.[9]

> To hope is to believe that something positive, which does not presently apply to one's life, could still materialize, and so we yearn for it.[10]

> Hope is ... a predominance of expected future positive feelings over future expected negative feelings. Hope, comprised of both desire and expectation, involves the interaction of affect and cognition.[11]

These definitions suggest that there are at least three central elements in hoping. First, as has already been indicated, hope is associated with an experience of deprivation. When the situation that we find ourselves in is disagreeable, we naturally hope for something better in the future. The philosopher Gabriel Marcel uses the metaphors of darkness and captivity to capture this felt sense of deprivation.[12] Living in the shadowland of illness, loss, depression or failure has the emotional tonality of captivity. The captive suffers through a deep sense of alienation – an alienation of the self from itself. This loss of the integrity of one's selfhood Marcel vividly describes as 'tearing me out of myself.'[13]

The second essential element associated with these definitions is desire. When we feel trapped in an unpleasant and distressing situation, our yearning is for relief and release. William Lynch, a theologian who has engaged in depth with the psychology of hope, refers to this desire as wishing: 'We must take [the human] as essentially a wishing, desiring being who, in this exalted sense, must at all costs be in contact with his own wishes. Where there is no wishing there can be no hope.'[14] Lynch's point is an important one. In the absence of yearning for positive outcomes, there is only apathy and hopelessness. However, his choice of the term 'wishing' is unfortunate as it has the potential to create confusion. Psychologists tend to distinguish 'wishing' from 'hoping'. This is so because the former does not involve the same level of personal investment as the latter.[15] Most often, we are not overly serious about the things we wish for. We make statements like, 'I wish I could play tennis like Novak Djokovic' or 'I wish I could win a million quid and retire to the good life'. We know that the chances of the wish coming true are incredibly slim. It really is a case of wishful thinking.

It is true that we sometimes use the word 'wish' in relation to something that is a distinct possibility and very important to us. For example, I might say, 'I wish that the doctor could find the right treatment for Mum's illness.' This is not genuine wishful thinking, but rather a case of using the word 'wish' to express the experience of hoping. Hoping is associated with those areas of our lives that are intimately associated with our well-being. Included here are such things as our cherished relationships (including our relationship with God), our health and that of those we love, and our financial security. When something is amiss in one or more of these areas, we find ourselves hoping for a positive turn-around. Because these aspects of our existence are so vitally important to us, we naturally invest a great deal of ourselves in them. If our hopes fail, it comes as a great blow. It would be *nice* for our wishes to materialize; we *desperately want* the things we hope for to become a reality.

The final aspect of hope that is highlighted by our definitions is that both affect and cognition are involved. The affective element is usually associated with the desire that we have just been discussing.[16] The person who hopes is gripped by a deep yearning for positive outcomes in the future. Lazarus suggests that the emotional aspect is also evident in the increase in the level of intensity of one's mental state.[17] Hope elevates one's mood. Korner contends that the affective component is best described by the terms 'clinging, holding on to hope'.[18] It is very close, he suggests, to the feeling of faith. When assaulted by fear and doubt, the person who hopes is sustained by the feeling that the light will eventually break in. One wonders, though, whether it is right to assign this type of 'feeling' to the category of affect. Capps seems right to suggest that it is an intuition or a perception rather than an emotion.[19] He refers to the fact that one can have an intuition or a felt sense that what one desires will happen that is so strong that feelings of doubt are overcome.

Hope, according to psychologists, also has a cognitive dimension. For the one who hopes, there is an *expectation* that the current unsatisfactory situation will be superseded by a more agreeable one.[20] One is sustained by the belief that the present distress will eventually pass. The thinking element can be thought of as a 'rationalizing chain' that 'represents a dike against uncertainty, the cognitive support against external doubts, the antidote for the anxiety generated by the possibility of a negative outcome'.[21]

For Christians, the affective and cognitive components of hoping are rooted in the triune God. First, in relation to the affective element, it is clearly the case that because of our faith conviction that God is working in us and for us through the grace of Christ and in the power of the Spirit, we are able to hold on to hope. Because we trust in God's loving kindness, we are confident that our yearning for a more positive situation will be satisfied. We recognize, however, that finding ourselves in a more positive situation may not necessarily mean that our affliction has been lifted. The knowledge that God is acting to help us make sense of what we are experiencing and to bring peace and strength is also a significant source of hope for us. Second in terms of the cognitive element, when our belief that God is acting lovingly and powerfully for our good is strong, we have a corresponding strong expectation that things will improve.

Many psychologists, after reviewing what has been presented so far, would be struck by the failure to include what they take to be the very essence of hope – namely, the pursuit of goals.[22] At the forefront of the goal-based approach to the psychology of hope we find C. R. Snyder and his associates.[23] In their early work, they defined hope as 'a cognitive set that is based on a reciprocally-derived sense of successful agency (goal-directed determination) and pathways (planning to meet goals)'.[24] Here the three essential components in the theory – goals, pathways, and agency – are identified. Now of course one might say that the definitions of hope presented above also suggest that goal-directed behaviour is central. The goal of the person in a situation of deprivation is clear enough: it is to get out of it. That individual feels trapped in the darkness – the aim is to escape into the light. However, this approach will not satisfy Snyder and his associates. They contend that the goals referred to must be quite specific in order to develop an adequate psychology of hope. 'If you recall the historical scepticism aimed at hope,' they write, 'it often appeared to result because it was vague and lacked an anchor. Goals provide the endpoints or anchors of the mental action sequences; they are the anchors of hope theory.'[25] Two different types of goals are identified.[26]

Goals cannot be achieved without a strategic approach. In order to attain the end-points that we desire, we need to plan. That is, we need to map the path that we are going to follow. 'Pathways thinking taps the perceived ability to produce plausible routes to goals.'[27]

Lastly, is the motivational component; it drives people along the routes to their goals. It requires mental willpower to engage in a sustained approach to achieving a desired end-point. Agentic thinking 'provides the spark for a person's goal pursuits'.[28]

Experience indicates that it is not that often that we find a trouble-free, easy or direct route to our cherished goals. Along the journey we usually encounter some obstacles. The high-hope person, Snyder and his associates point out, has both the capacity to envision pathways around a blockage, and the requisite mental strength to keep pushing forward.

One question that immediately presents itself upon reviewing the Snyder *et al.* approach is whether or not the experience they describe is really hope. It seems more like optimism to me.[29] Optimism is usually construed as a feeling or conviction that one will prevail in one's quest, despite the obstacles in one's path. In his survey of the psychology of optimism, Christopher Pearson has this to say: 'Optimism enters into self-regulation when people ask themselves about impediments to achieving the goals they have adopted. In the face of difficulties, do people nonetheless believe that goals can be achieved? If so, they are optimistic; if not, they are pessimistic.'[30]

Given this interpretation of optimism, it is not surprising that Pearson includes the work of Snyder and his associates in his survey. In reviewing their goals-pathways-agency approach, it seems clear that what they are describing is more an optimistic outlook than the experience of hoping. It is important that we do not confuse the two terms. They are closely related, but they can also be distinguished. Gabriel Marcel makes a distinction between hope and optimism that is germane to our area of interest. The differentiation that he posits revolves around the I–We axis. Optimism operates in 'the province of the "I myself"'.[31] In other words, *I* make the judgement that *I* have the personal resources to overcome the roadblocks on the path to my goal. Hope, on the other hand, is sustained in a relational context. Marcel avers that the most adequate expression for hoping is 'I hope in thee for us'.[32] For him, the fact that hope is indissolubly bound up with communion is so true that he wonders 'if despair and solitude are not at bottom necessarily identical'.[33] Marcel views the despairing person as a neighbour, as one who addresses him with a particular appeal for help. He puts it this way:

Assume that [the despairing person] asks the question: 'Do you pretend that it is in my power to hope, although all the exits seem to me closed?' Doubtless I will reply: 'The simple fact that you ask me the question already constitutes a sort of first breach in your prison. In reality it is not simply a question you ask me; it is an appeal you address to me, and to which I can only respond by urging you not only to depend on me but also not to give up, not to let go, and, if only very humbly and feebly, to act as if this Hope lived in you; and that means more than anything else to turn toward another – I will say, whoever he is – and thus to escape from the obsession which is destroying you.'[34]

Optimism and hope are distinct (though closely related) phenomena. I am optimistic because I trust in myself and in the resources at my disposal. I am hopeful because the other has heard my appeal and entered into a loving solidarity with me. Solidarity with one's sisters and brothers who are in need and in distress is of the essence of *Ubuntu*. It is to a discussion of this African philosophy that we now turn.

Ubuntu and solidarity

In what follows, the notion of employing a community of witnesses to support hope will be discussed. In particular, we will consider Kaethe Weingarten's approach – one that is inspired by *Ubuntu*.

In a modern European and North American worldview, persons are essentially individuals who voluntarily enter into a variety of collectives. At the core of *Ubuntu*, on the other hand, is the idea that the humanness of an individual is established in a web of relationships and in the humaneness that characterizes right relations.[35] Whereas in the West, autonomy is highly valued, in sub-Saharan Africa people think in terms of interdependence.

In order to get a sense as to what *Ubuntu* is about, it is helpful to reflect on Desmond Tutu's description of it:

[*Ubuntu* means] we belong in a bundle of life. We say, 'a person is a person through other people'. It is not 'I think therefore I am'. It says rather: 'I am human because I belong'. I participate. I share. A person with *Ubuntu* is open and available to others, affirming of others, does not feel threatened that others are able and good; for he or she has a proper self-assurance that comes from knowing that he or she belongs in a greater whole ...[36]

Also helpful in getting a feel for *Ubuntu* is to engage with stories in which it features. I have chosen one that Augustine Shutte uses in his book *An Ethic for a New South Africa*.[37] It was told to him by the son of a former magistrate in what was at the time Northern Rhodesia.

Traditional courts, presided over by traditional officials, were still allowed to deal with the most serious cases. These courts took place in the villages from which cases came, usually in some central space in the open air. Both sides would be allowed their say, calling friends and witnesses to support them. The courts were open and there was always an audience. At a certain point in the proceedings the audience would be allowed to comment. Sometimes the magistrate would ask the opinion of people in the audience whom he thought may be able to throw light on the subject. Sometimes he would even listen to the opinion of a passer-by.[38]

For those of us who know only the extreme individualism of the Western urbanized milieu, the process of the Rhodesian court presents as totally foreign and most unusual. Having gleaned something of what the traditional African ethic is about through this story, let us go further. The two philosophers who have been at the forefront of writing and thinking about *Ubuntu* are Mogobe B. Ramose and, a scholar whom we have already met, Augustine Shutte. Ramose contends that it is 'the root of African philosophy'.[39] He goes on to say that '[t]he be-ing of an African in the universe is inseparably anchored upon *ubuntu*'.[40] Ramose suggests that from a philosophical point of view, it is helpful to separate out the two words that form the term – namely, the prefix *ubu-* and the stem *ntu*.[41] *Ubu* connotes the notion of be-ing in general. It indicates that something inheres in be-ing before it manifests as a particular being. Here we have two aspects of be-ing: as an individual instance and as an indivisible wholeness. The individual is indissolubly linked to the whole. Ramose notes that this idea is captured in the Zulu maxim *umuntu ngumuntu ngabantu* (one is a person through other persons). He makes this important comment concerning this saying: 'Although the English language does not exhaust the meaning of the maxim ... it may nonetheless be construed to mean that to be a human be-ing is to affirm one's humanity by recognizing the humanity of others and, on that basis, establish humane relations with them.'[42] This recognition of the humanity of others and feeling of connectedness to them is picked up in a reflection by Pumla Gobodo-Madikizela, formerly a member of the Human Rights Violations Committee of the South African Truth and Reconciliation Commission:

> Its essence is about the capacity for empathy with another person. You see, that is the essence of *ubuntu*: that capacity which I think is something we ought to have as human beings, and which is present in all of us, that capacity to connect with another human being, to be touched, to be moved by another human being. That is *ubuntu*. If I walk down the street, and I see someone ... I can see something in his face that says that this person is going through a difficult moment. I do not have time but I turn to him and say: 'How are you today?' That is *ubuntu* because I am connecting to how he seems to be feeling at the moment, and I am reaching out, and I am acknowledging that I see his pain and want to leave him with some kindness as I walk past him.[43]

The empathic attunement and the connection established through the concerned inquiry, 'How are you today?' demonstrates beautifully the heart of this communitarian ethic. Shutte observes that the emphasis in African thought on community is arguably its most central and widely established characteristic.[44] He goes on to state that 'Negro-African society puts more stress on the group than on the individual, more on solidarity than on the activity and needs of the individual, more on the communion of persons than on their autonomy.'[45] Descartes is famous for his dictum 'I think, therefore I am'. The African replaces this with 'I participate, therefore I am'.[46] Shutte draws on Mulago's work on participation to flesh this out. In describing the individual's indissoluble connection to the group, Mulago says that '[p]articipation is the element of connection which unites different beings as beings, as substances, without confusing them. It is the pivot of relationships between members of the same community, the link which binds together individuals and groups ...'[47]

It is important to note here that there is a strong point of connection between the anthropology represented by *Ubuntu* on the one hand, and the trinitarian dynamic of participation on the other. Indeed, South African theologians have noted the *Ubuntu-perichoresis* link.[48] Given that the human being is created *imago Trinitatis*, it is legitimate to claim that the *Ubuntu* and Christian theological views of a person correlate. We were made for participation; it is a virtue that we need to live out in every domain of our existence.

David Cunningham refers to 'participation' as one of the essential trinitarian virtues.[49] In using this descriptor, he indicates that the divine life is first and foremost an event of mutual indwelling. Further, participation is a virtue that we humans are also called to enact. If the doctrine of the Trinity has anything to teach us about authentic existence it is that communion rather than individualism is the goal of human life: '[T]he focus on *participation* suggests that human beings are called to understand themselves, not as "individuals" who may (or may not) choose to enter into relationships, but rather as mutually indwelling and indwelt, and to such a degree that – echoing the mutual indwelling of the Three – all pretensions to wholly independent existence are abolished.'[50] Participation, then, is a trinitarian virtue that marks our human existence.

Hope and witnessing

The one who enters into a loving solidarity with a friend who is feeling trapped in a set of particular circumstances is referred to by the psychotherapist Kaethe Weingarten as a witness.[51] Weingarten is inspired here by *Ubuntu*. She encountered it in orienting herself for a trip as an invited guest of the South African Association of Marital and Family Therapy in Cape Town, and the Institute for Therapeutic Development in Pretoria. Weingarten has this to say:

> The *Weltanschauung* of Ubuntu ... fits me. From the wisdom that sorrow has brought me, I have needed to invent in Boston what is deeply rooted, known, and felt in South Africa. As an outsider to South Africa, it seems to me that Ubuntu creates persons simultaneously as participants and witnesses to everyone else in one's community.[52]

Weingarten draws attention to the shortcomings in the individualistic view of hope sponsored by C. R. Snyder and associates that we discussed above.[53] In making her case, she refers to these two items on the Adult Trait Hope Scale they have developed:

> I meet the goals I set for myself.
> I can think of many ways to get out of a jam.

The items in the Adult Trait Hope Scale are designed to measure people's convictions concerning their ability to reach their desired end-points by relying on their personal resources alone. For Weingarten, as for Marcel, hope is the responsibility of the community. It is something that people do together. She asks us to imagine a Hope Scale that is predicated on the conviction that hope is the work of the community. The items listed above would be revised as follows:

> I can count on the support of others to help me meet my goals.
> Together, my friends, family, colleagues and I can always find ways to get out of a jam.[54]

Weingarten makes the point, as we also have, that optimism and hope are not the same thing.[55] For her, following Václav Havel, optimism refers to a conviction that something will turn out well, whereas hope is the confident feeling that something is meaningful, regardless of how it turns out. Witnessing to the one who feels trapped in an unsatisfactory and distressing situation is first and foremost aimed at helping that person to make sense of it. Weingarten illustrates the work of the witness through an account of an experience she shared with her daughter, Miranda.[56] Miranda was born with a rare genetic disorder, which has unusual symptoms associated with it. The result is that her bodily functioning is unpredictable and unreliable. It goes without saying that she must cope with considerable physical and emotional pain. Weingarten tells the story of witnessing to Miranda this way:

> In March 1995, Miranda dislocated one hip and both her shoulders. Her friends found her situation disturbing and upsetting. They asked, 'Why did it happen when you were just sitting on the couch?' Miranda had no explanation.
>
> People who study narratives talk about whether they are coherent or not: that is, do they make sense to most people ... Miranda's stories about her disorder rarely make sense. They lack coherence. I couldn't bear that this particular feature of her disorder should contribute to the isolation she already felt. I determined to create a context in which the fact that Miranda's narrative of her condition was often incoherent would not matter. I suggested to her that she and I design a ceremony and invite a group of friends and helpers whom she would trust to share the history of her living with her disorder. Open to anything, Miranda agreed.
>
> The ceremony made vivid for us that our family needed to create forms of being with others that more accurately reflected how we conceptualized our experience. Fervently believing that it was 'unjust' for Miranda to bear her pain alone, and disavowing the idea that pain is inherently an individual and personal matter, we expanded the boundaries of our support beyond our family to a community of caring persons ...[57]

Witnessing to hope through ritual

There are a significant number of psychotherapists and counsellors who work with their clients on incorporating ritual into the therapy. It is most often the case that virtually all the burden of therapeutic work is carried by the spoken word. What typically happens in a counselling room is talk-therapy. Ritual, in contrast, is primarily 'act'. In *Liberating Rites*, Tom Driver recalls a speech at the end of *King Lear*: 'The weight of this sad time we must obey. Speak what we feel, not what we ought to say.' Tom goes on to say, 'At such times the impulse toward ritual is not so much to speak as to act: *act* what we feel, not what we ought to do [emphasis in the original].'[58]

I contend that pastoral counsellors make a significant contribution to building the hope of their counsellees through co-creation of rituals that draw in friends, family and members of the community of faith. Some readers may wonder why I suggest the use of ritual. Why not, for example, simply assemble a group for prayer and reading of the Bible? The first thing to be said is that prayer and Bible reading are in fact characterized by ritualization. Prayer has a certain form (even the so-called free or conversational styles of prayer are formulaic). Heads are bowed; eyes are closed; the prayer begins and ends in a certain way. Bible reading, too, is a ritualized activity – or at least this is the case in a communal setting. These are simply interesting observations. The much more significant point is that ritual includes an element of symbolization and is thereby able to complement prayer and the Scriptures in hope-building. The counsellor Alan Basham makes this observation concerning the relationship between symbolism and words in discussing the use of ritual in working with counsellees: 'A *ritual* is a symbolic experience or action that connects individuals to a deeper meaning or truth, enabling them to encounter that for which words alone are insufficient.'[59] Basham's frame of reference is non-theological. Prayer and reading of Scripture remind the participants of the divine promises of grace, peace, healing and blessing; the words spoken do not move simply on the horizontal plane. The human utterance of words draws the listeners deeply into the Word. It is not a matter, clearly, of whether symbol is more potent than words of prayer and Scripture, or vice versa, in supporting hope. They are of course all important avenues through which God's grace works. The rituals of witness to hope that I have in mind combine prayer, Scripture, story-telling, words of comfort and symbol.

We have already started the process of defining a ritual. While it is true that anthropologists, religious studies scholars or liturgists know a ritual when they see one, there is no consensus on how to define the term. The best we can hope for is to come up with a working definition. Miller defines ritual as 'formalized behaviour that draws out certain feelings and provides individuals ways to express their thoughts and feelings in a symbolic fashion'.[60] This interpretation of ritual is clearly oriented to secular psychotherapy; the element of the sacred does not feature. Denzin's definition draws in the element that is of particular concern for people of faith: 'A conventionalized joint activity given to ceremony, involving two or more persons, endowed with special emotion and often *sacred meaning*, focused around a clearly defined set of social objects, and when performed confers upon its participants *a special sense of the sacred and the out of the ordinary* [emphasis added].'[61] When I refer to ritual used in support of the pastoral goal of building hope, I take it to mean the following: *a communal action that has form and structure, incorporates the elements of words, Word, action, and symbol, provides a safe space for expression of thought and feeling, and has the aim of connecting the suffering person to human and divine witnesses to hope.* It is to a discussion of the constitutive elements that we now turn.

In a ritual of hope-building, words are spoken. Words of prayer have a central place. They remind the individual and the group that the witnessing and the hoping ultimately draw their efficacy from the love and grace of God in Christ.

Some of the most important words that are uttered are those of the distressed person. When the story of pain and hurt is held within, buried and hidden away it maintains its toxicity. People keep their narratives of suffering to themselves for a number of reasons. Three common ones are as follows: First, putting the pain into words brings up powerful and frightening emotions. Second, telling their stories makes people very vulnerable; they are unsure how they will be received. Lastly, bringing one's personal history of hurt and psychological dysfunction into the open is shame-inducing. Truth-telling, even when it is addressed to trusted others, calls for great courage. It is an all-important step in hope-building; it allows others to act as witnesses to the struggle and to thereby support the quest for a brighter future. Wyrostok, following Gilligan, captures succinctly the three main elements in the role that witnesses play: They are there to provide emotional support, to ground the suffering person in the present, and to represent their faith in a hope-filled future for that individual.[62]

Sarah suffered childhood sexual abuse.[63] Her therapist worked with her on creating a liberating ritual, and 'telling her story' was a central aspect. In preparation for the ritual, she produced the following reflection on the process in her journal:

> First and foremost, I want to tell my story completely. Why is this so important? In hearing, others will come to know the vulnerable part of me, the part that I have kept locked away, isolating myself from others and from myself. By telling my story, I can relive it, yet change the ending. Instead of having to repress my feelings, I'll find release in their expression, comfort in finally being heard and acknowledged, and ultimately … connection.[64]

Sarah read the following words by way of introduction to telling the story of her childhood abuse. She asks for three things: to be heard, the courage to witness to her pain, and acts of comfort. Sarah here identifies the heart of witnessing to hope:

What I want to do tonight is to tell my story, like I did when I was a child. But unlike when I was a child, today I want to be heard. This time I want to be believed. I want to let go of the pain that I have held inside for so many years. I need you to be brave enough to be a witness to my pain. And I want you to act. I need you to comfort me.[65]

Sarah invited a response from her witnesses. In my experience, after listening to a story of deep hurt, pain and emotional turmoil, what is called for is a simple, brief and sincere acknowledgment. The words need to sound the right note. They do not have to be particularly profound; they simply need to communicate that the person has been heard, that it is a deep privilege to be trusted with the story, and that the sufferer is not alone.

Sarah asked for listening; she also requested action – acts of comfort. In response to Sarah's call, those who listened encircled her and held her with love. She later wrote this about the experience: 'At last, my words are heard and reflected back to me. Written on the faces of my friends is my pain and sadness, and I know that I am not alone.'[66]

We move now in our discussion of rituals of witness from word to Word. At the centre of any Christian community of hope is the Word of God. Hope joins us one to another; Christ is 'the guarantee of the union which holds us together'.[67] The central theme in the grand narrative of the Bible is the self-communication of God. Witnessing can be a passive activity – a person may witness an event and do little or nothing in response to it. God, however, is an active witness. God is *agape* and it is the nature of *agape* to desire the best for others and to actively give of self in securing this desideratum. In the Scriptures we find story after story of God's healing and liberating engagement with individuals and communities.

It is because God is an active witness that the people learn to trust and to hope. All of the major events recorded in the Bible can be construed as witnessing to hope. The Genesis narratives revolving around Abraham, Isaac, and Jacob, should first be read as testimonies to hope.[68] What these stories attest to is that the identity and the future of the people of God are intimately bound up with the promises of God. The people are invited to imaginatively project into a future in which God will ensure a long line of descendants, greatness as a nation, a new land and, through them, a blessing to the nations. They come to know YHWH as the God who is faithful in keeping promises.

That paradigmatic story of hope, the Exodus, began with a cry of pain.[69] After a long period of containment and control, oppressed people come to a point of simply accepting that what they experience is the way life is. They allow themselves to be moulded by the order that has been constructed by their overlords. But something happened to change the situation for the Hebrew slaves in Egypt. They were no longer content to passively embrace the world that had been shaped for them by those in control. In finding a voice for their grievance and distress, they made a start on the road of defiance and protest. There is hope in protest. The situation for the Hebrew slaves was radically changed because they dared to cry out.

The prophetic texts of the eighth to the sixth century BC also centre on the themes of promise, hope and trust. The poems that we find there take us into the future that God has prepared for the people. It is true that many in the community of the time could not see past the order of things that they were caught in. Whether the order was established around injustice and idolatry in the community, or around the oppressive practices and controlling interests of aggressive nations, what is currently in place is what many accepted as the norm – or at least as simply the way things are and will always be. There is nevertheless a shaft of hope that penetrates into the darkness as the prophets declare, 'Behold, the days are coming.' A new order is on the way. The drive into a new and better world, the prophets declare, comes from nowhere else but the mystery of God.

In the New Testament, God-with-us is given an ultimate expression in the person and work of Jesus Christ. The hope of Jesus, our hope, is centred on the coming reign of God. 'Jesus came to Galilee, proclaiming the good news of God, and saying, "The time is fulfilled, and the kingdom of God has come near; repent, and believe in the good news"'(Mark 1.14–15). We have seen that captivity is a central image for the deprivation that necessitates the sustaining power of hope. The reign of God is characterized by the release from all forms of bondage (Luke 4.18–19).

In his healings and exorcisms, in his words of affirmation and forgiveness, in his befriending of the outcasts, in his challenge to unjust and oppressive practices, Jesus inaugurates a reign of love, freedom and righteousness. The hopeless feel trapped; everywhere they look all they see is a 'No Exit' sign. Jesus embodied the *agape* of God. Love takes as its mission showing trapped people the way out. Love takes those who are trapped in sin, suffering and injustice through the door that opens on to a new and brighter future. The resurrection is the definitive statement on this future. It is a foretaste of the glorious existence that awaits us. We hope for a measure of freedom now, but our ultimate hope is for the end time when God 'will wipe every tear from their eyes' (Rev. 21.4).

Most of the narratives that we have just referred to are very long. Obviously the readings from the Word used in a personalized ritual need to be much briefer! In the little book that I often use in my private prayer, the Scripture sections have two readings – one from the Hebrew Scriptures and one from the New Testament. They are each only one verse. I like that. I often think that many of the precious words of Scripture get lost in a long reading. One or two verses, especially when read slowly and from a stance of deep faith and profound appreciation for the message, can be strongly impactful.

We turn finally to the use of symbols that connect with the personal experience of the one seeking help. Psychotherapists have long known that symbols are the tools used by the unconscious to convey meaning. Freud referred to dreams as the 'royal road' to the unconscious. The dream symbols are pointers to repressed contents associated with psychological trauma. Freud distinguished between latent and manifest content in dreams. The manifest meaning is the literal subject matter of the dream. According to Freud, it should not be taken at face value. Rather, it provides a clue to the latent material – that which lies at a level below that which manifests in the dream imagery. Jung rejected the need to look behind the screen of the manifest symbolism to find the real picture of psychic conflict. He was convinced that the symbols that populate a patient's dreams can be reliably interpreted in a straightforward manner. In Jung's view, when one learns to listen to symbols speaking, one hears the wisdom, guidance and purpose contained in the unconscious.

A symbol is rich and powerful because it is polyvocal (it possesses meaning at many levels), points beyond itself, and participates in the meaning and power of that which it symbolizes.[70] A wedding band, for example, speaks of eternal love, of wholeness, of commitment, and more. Its primary purpose is not to draw attention to itself. To be sure, it may be a thing of beauty in its own right, and may therefore attract attention as an object of art. But its deepest value is to be found in its role of pointing to the eternal love it symbolizes. Finally, it possesses an inherent, intrinsic connection to the eternal love that two people make a commitment to. There is no beginning to a circle, and there is no end. True love is similarly eternal. Contrast this with the way signs function. A sign is an arbitrarily chosen marker for a particular message. There is no intrinsic connection between a red light and the message 'Stop!' Signs also do not have the capacity to speak on many levels at the one time. That is the last thing that one would want them to do! They need to communicate clearly and unambiguously. Signs also fail to point beyond themselves to a profound reality: love, reconciliation, death and God. They deal in much more mundane realities.

In a therapeutic context, symbols allow a person to express and engage with meaning at a deeper level than words alone can. Words are the currency of the conscious mind alone. Symbols have the power to also connect us to meaning at the underground level of our psychic life. When a symbol is used in a ritual, those suffering but seeking hope and healing will be able to articulate something of what it means for them and for their quest. But the Spirit of God uses a symbol to also touch a person at the unconscious level. Basham catches this well: 'Much of what captures people in sorrow or in anger lies beyond words and cognitive expression. What is needed is an experience that is symbolic, one that carries a deeper spiritual truth and means of expression than they can readily articulate ...'[71]

In working with counsellees to help them develop rituals of hope and healing, it is important that the symbol chosen connects meaningfully to their experience of pain and distress. Quite a few counsellees are able to come up with their own symbol quite quickly and to choose very appropriately; some need education and guidance. Emily chose a helium balloon.[72] She came to the university counselling centre to process her sense of loss and grief over failing to reconnect with her father, whom she had not seen since he left home after divorce when she was 10. Emily was particularly close to her dad when she was a child. She later discovered that he had tried to contact both her and her brother multiple times after the divorce. Emily's mother did not want a reunion to take place, so she intercepted the letters. The father did successfully re-establish contact with Emily's brother, but Emily rejected his attempts to reunite with her. She had believed her mother's depiction of him as a person of bad character. However, when her brother helped her to see that this portrait was not a fair one, Emily softened and had a strong desire to meet up with him. Tragically, he was killed in a car accident before she could do so. She was crushed by a profound sense of loss; she longed to tell her father how much she loved and missed him. The counsellor suggested that she write her father a letter in which she could fully express her feelings, but this failed to bring the resolution she hoped for. Finally, the counsellor helped Emily create a means of symbolizing an act of communication with her father. She visited her brother and his family to invite them to be witnesses to her loving communication with her father. Emily tied a copy of her letter to a helium balloon, sang a little song that her father taught her when she was a child, and released it up into the heavens.

What is striking about this ritual is that in one sense it deals in the hopeless. Her father is dead. There is no hope of communicating with him. The ritual involves an act that on a literal level has no hope of success. There is no way that the balloon can actually reach heaven.

The material world and the spiritual plane that holds eternal life have no point of intersection. There is therefore no hope of her loving words being read by her father. And yet this simple ritual involving a balloon and a letter is a profoundly hopeful act.

Summary

In the West, there is a tendency to think of hope as something that an individual is responsible for; in *Ubuntu*-inspired communities, in contrast, hope is a work of the people. One of the great assets that pastoral counsellors have is access to a community of faith. The worshipping community is a witness to hope. Everything that happens when the community comes together for worship points to the source of Christian hope: the grace of our Lord Jesus Christ, the love of God, and the communion of the Holy Spirit. However, there is also the possibility of developing personally tailored rituals that employ Christian resources.

In our discussion on ritual used in support of the pastoral goal of building hope, we defined the term in this way: a communal action that has form and structure, incorporates the elements of words, Word, action and symbol, provides a safe space for expression of thought and feeling, and has the aim of connecting the person who is suffering to human and divine witnesses to hope. In such a healing ritual, people in distress are offered a safe and loving space into which they can communicate their personal stories, their deep desires, and their hope for a brighter future in word and in symbolic action. The witnesses not only listen, but also offer the Word, words of prayer, and their personal words/actions of empathy, love and acceptance.

Notes

1 On hope and temporality, see A. Lester, *Hope in Pastoral Care and Counseling* (Louisville, KY: Westminster John Knox Press, 1995), pp. 13–24.

2 I refer to the International Academy of Practical Theology conference, held in Pretoria from 16–20, July 2015. The theme was, 'Practicing *Ubuntu*: Practical Theological Perspectives on Injustice, Personhood and Human Dignity'.

3 See K. Weingarten, 'Witnessing, Wonder, and Hope', *Family Process* 39, no. 4 (2000), pp. 389–402; K. Weingarten, 'Cancer, Meaning Making, and Hope: The Treatment Dedication Project', *Families, Systems, and Health* 23, no. 2 (2005), pp. 155–60; and K. Weingarten, 'Hope in a Time of Global Despair', unpublished paper delivered at the International Family Therapy Association Conference, Reykjavik, Iceland, 4–7, October 2006.

4 See H. P. V. Renner, 'The Use of Ritual in Pastoral Care', *The Journal of Pastoral Care* 23 (1979), pp. 165–6; E. Ramshaw, *Ritual and Pastoral Care*

(Minneapolis, MN: Fortress Press, 1987); N. Pembroke, *Pastoral Care in Worship* (London: T&T Clark International, 2010).

5 See N. Wyrostok, 'The Ritual as a Psychotherapeutic Intervention', *Psychotherapy* 32, no. 3 (1995), pp. 397–404; M. Perlstein, 'A Spiritual Coming Out', *Women and Therapy* 24, nos 3–4 (2002), pp. 175–92; A. R. Bewley, 'Re-Membering Spirituality', *Women and Therapy* 16, nos 2–3 (1995), pp. 201–13; R. J. Parker and H. S. Horton, 'A Typology of Ritual: Paradigms for Healing and Empowerment', *Counseling and Values* 40 (1996), pp. 82-96; R. J. Parker, H. S. Horton and T. Watson, 'Sarah's Story: Using Ritual Therapy to Address Psychospiritual Issues in Treating Survivors of Childhood Sexual Abuse', *Counseling and Values* 42 (1997), pp. 41–54; A. Basham, 'Ritual in Counseling', in C. S. Cashwell and J. S. Young (eds), *Integrating Spirituality and Religion into Counseling: A Guide to Competent Practice*, 2nd edn (Alexandria, VA: American Counseling Association, 2011), pp. 209–23.

6 Cf. K. Herth, 'Fostering Hope in Terminally ill People', *Journal of Advanced Nursing* 15 (1990), pp. 1250–9, p. 1250.

7 Cf. S. R. Staats and M. A. Stassen, 'Hope: An Affective Cognition', *Social Indicators Research* 17 (1985), pp. 235–42, p. 235.

8 Cf. W. F. Lynch, *Images of Hope: Imagination as Healer of the Hopeless* (Notre Dame, IN: University of Notre Dame Press, 1974), p. 32.

9 D. Capps, *Agents of Hope: A Pastoral Psychology* (Minneapolis, MN: Fortress Press, 1995), p. 53.

10 R. S. Lazarus, 'Hope: An Emotion and a Vital Coping Resource against Despair', *Social Research* 66, no. 2 (Summer 1999), pp. 653–78, p. 653.

11 Staats and Stassen, 'Hope', p. 235.

12 See G. Marcel, *Homo Viator: Introduction to a Metaphysic of Hope* (London: Victor Gollancz, 1951), p. 30.

13 Marcel, *Homo Viator*, p. 31.

14 Lynch, *Images of Hope*, p. 25.

15 Cf. I. N. Korner, 'Hope as a Method of Coping', *Journal of Consulting and Clinical Psychology* 34, no. 2 (1970), pp. 134–9, p. 135; and Capps, *Agents of Hope*, p. 59.

16 See Staats and Stassen, 'Hope', p. 235; and Lazarus, 'Hope', p. 663.

17 See Lazarus, 'Hope', p. 663.

18 See Korner, 'Hope as a Method', p. 136.

19 See Capps, *Agents of Hope*, pp. 53–4.

20 See Staats and Stassen, 'Hope', p. 235.

21 Korner, 'Hope as a Method', p. 137.

22 On the centrality of the goal aspect in the psychological literature on hope, see S. E. Hobfoll, M. Briggs-Phillips and L. R. Stines, 'Fact or Artifact: The Relationship of Hope to a Caravan of Resources', in R. Jacoby and G. Keinan (eds), *Between Stress and Hope: From a Disease-centered to a Health-centered Perspective* (New York: Greenwood, 2005), pp. 81–104, p. 94; and J. F. Miller and M. J. Powers, 'Development of an Instrument to Measure Hope', *Nursing Research* 37, no. 1 (1988), pp. 6–10, p. 7.

23 See C. R. Snyder *et al.*, 'The Will and the Ways: Development and Validation of an Individual Differences Measure of Hope', *Journal of Personality and Social Psychology* 60 (1991), pp. 570–85; C. R. Snyder, J. Cheavans and S. C. Sympson, 'Hope: An Individual Motive for Social Commerce', *Dynamics: Theory,*

Research, and Practice 1, no. 2 (1997), pp. 107–18; C. R. Snyder , 'Hypothesis: There is Hope', in C. R. Snyder (ed.), *Handbook of Hope: Theory, Measures, and Applications* (New York: Academic Press, 2000), pp. 3–21; and C. R. Snyder, J. Cheavans and S. T. Michael, 'Hope Theory: History and Elaborated Model', in J. A. Eliott (ed.), *Interdisciplinary Perspectives on Hope* (New York: Nova Science Publishers, 2005), pp. 101–18.

24 Snyder *et al.*, 'The Will and the Ways', p. 571.

25 Snyder, 'Hypothesis', p. 9.

26 See Snyder, Cheavans and Michael, 'Hope Theory', pp. 105–6.

27 Snyder, 'Hypothesis', p. 9.

28 Snyder, Cheavans and Sympson, 'Hope: An Individual Motive', p. 108.

29 Cf. Hobfoll, Briggs-Phillips and Stines, 'Fact or Artifact', p. 85.

30 C. Pearson, 'The Future of Optimism', *American Psychologist* 55, no. 1 (January 2000), pp. 44–55, p. 47.

31 Marcel, *Homo Viator*, p. 34.

32 Marcel, *Homo Viator*, p. 60.

33 Marcel, *Homo Viator*, p. 58.

34 G. Marcel, 'Desire and Hope', in N. Lawrence and D. O'Connor (eds), *Readings in Existential Phenomenology* (Englewood Cliffs, NJ: Prentice-Hall, 1967), pp. 277–85, p. 285.

35 Cf. E. Hankela, *Ubuntu, Migration, and Ministry* (Leiden: Brill, 2014), p. 2.

36 D. Tutu, *No Future without Forgiveness* (London: Rider, 1999), p. 35.

37 A. Shutte, *An Ethic for a New South Africa* (Pietermaritzburg: Cluster Publications, 2001).

38 Shutte, *An Ethic for a New South Africa*, p. 20.

39 M. B. Ramose, *African Philosophy through Ubuntu* (Harare: Mond Books, 1999), p. 49.

40 Ramose, *African Philosophy*, p. 50.

41 See Ramose, *African Philosophy*, p. 50.

42 Ramose, *African Philosophy*, p. 52.

43 Cited in C. B. N. Gade, 'What is *Ubuntu*? Different Interpretations among South Africans of African Descent', *South African Journal of Philosophy* 31, no. 3 (2012), pp. 484–503, 489–90.

44 See A. Shutte, *Philosophy for Africa* (Rondebosch: UCT Press, 1993), p. 47.

45 Shutte, *Philosophy for Africa*, p. 49

46 Shutte, *Philosophy for Africa*, p. 47.

47 V. Mulago, 'Vital Participation', in K. A. Dickson and P. Ellingworth (eds), *Biblical Revelation and African Beliefs* (London: Butterworth, 1971), p. 145; cited in Shutte *Philosophy for Africa*, p. 49.

48 See, for example, J. S. Manganyi, 'Church and Society: The Value of Perichoresis in Understanding Ubuntu with Special Reference to John Zizioulas', unpublished doctoral thesis, University of Pretoria, 2012; D. T. Williams, '*Perichoresis* and the South African Ideal', *Koers – Bulletin for Christian Scholarship* 78, 1. Art #2118, 2013, 7 pages. http://dx.doi.org/10.4102/koers.v78i1.2118.

49 See D. Cunningham, *These Three are One: The Practice of Trinitarian Theology* (Oxford: Blackwell, 1998).

50 D. Cunningham, 'Participation as a Trinitarian Virtue', *Toronto Journal of Theology* 14, no. 1 (1998), pp. 7–25, p. 10.

51 See Weingarten, 'Witnessing'.

52 Weingarten, 'Witnessing', p. 400.

53 See Weingarten, 'Hope in a Time of Global Despair', pp. 2–3.

54 Weingarten, 'Hope in a Time of Global Despair', p. 3.

55 See Weingarten, 'Hope in a Time of Global Despair', p. 5.

56 See Weingarten, 'Witnessing', pp. 399–401.

57 Weingarten, 'Witnessing', p. 400.

58 T. F. Driver, *Liberating Rites: Understanding the Transformative Power of Ritual* (Boulder, CO: Westview, 1998), p. 5.

59 Basham, 'Ritual in Counseling', p. 210.

60 G. Miller, *Incorporating Spirituality in Counseling and Psychotherapy* (Hoboken, NJ: Wiley, 2003), p. 207; cited in Basham, 'Ritual in Counseling', p. 210.

61 N. K. Denzin, 'The Methodological Implications of Symbolic Interactionism for the Study of Deviance', *British Journal of Sociology* 25 (1974), pp. 269–82, p. 272; cited in Wyrostok, 'The Ritual as a Psychotherapeutic Intervention', p. 397.

62 See Wyrostok, 'The Ritual as a Psychotherapeutic Intervention', p. 401.

63 See Parker, Horton and Watson, 'Sarah's Story'.

64 Parker, Horton and Watson, 'Sarah's Story', p. 50.

65 Parker, Horton and Watson, 'Sarah's Story', p. 50.

66 Parker, Horton and Watson, 'Sarah's Story', p. 50.

67 Marcel, *Homo Viator*, p. 60.

68 Cf. W. Brueggemann, *Hope within History* (Atlanta, GA: John Knox Press, 1987), p. 73.

69 Cf Brueggemann, *Hope within History*, pp. 16, 20.

70 Cf. A. Kull, 'How to Ask Questions about Art and Theology? The Example of Paul Tillich', *Baltic Journal of Art History* 7, no. 4 (2014), pp. 59–80, p. 65.

71 Basham, 'Ritual in Counseling', p. 212.

72 See Basham, 'Ritual in Counseling', pp. 213–14.

Concluding Reflection:
It's Also about Personal Spirituality

I wrote a book some years back entitled *Moving Toward Spiritual Maturity: Psychological, Contemplative, and Moral Challenges in Christian Living*.[1] As the title suggests, it explores a developed Christian spirituality from three angles.[2] Shortly after the book was published, I gave an address to a group of chaplains in Brisbane. During my talk I mentioned the work and how the ideas connected with the vocation of pastoral care. Immediately after, the then Director of the Multi-faith Chaplaincy Academy in Brisbane, Ross Pitt, came up to me and said, 'I'm going to buy up as many copies as I can. It will be required reading in our program from now on.' It meant a great deal to me that Ross was so enthusiastic about the approach to the spirituality of the pastoral caregiver that I was presenting. He clearly shared my conviction that personal spirituality is at least as important as, and probably more so than, the therapeutic skills and techniques that the caregiver possesses. In this concluding reflection, I want to briefly discuss five spiritual qualities that play a vital role in pastoral counselling:

- vulnerability
- compassion
- availability
- tenderness
- integrity.

Clearly, there are more elements that could be added to the list. But the ones I have identified are absolutely central, and even if counsellors decided that these were the only ones they would concentrate on, they would have more than enough to keep them challenged for their entire lives.

For a very long time in my pastoral ministry I struggled to come to grips with my own fears, inadequacies and shortcomings. I wished that I could simply throw them off and be the strong, confident, calm, in-control person that I imagined the best counsellors were. Finally, an important moment of insight came: accepting my weaknesses and limitations, embracing my farcical humanity, is a positive. Such an attitude is an asset for the pastoral counsellor. Counsellor and author Jeanne Ellin gives sound advice when she says this: 'Acknowledge your weakness and make it work for you; it can be a source of strength, a resource for you, whether it makes you aware of your humanness or is a source of increased sensitivity to the varied ways in which people respond to painful or stressful situations.'[3]

Henri Nouwen tells the story of taking a group of final-year seminarians on retreat in preparation for their ordination. One of the students, feeling anxious about his future ministry, said, 'I just hope that I'll be strong enough to be a good priest.' To which Nouwen responded, 'I don't think your strength is really the issue. The question is whether or not you are weak enough for priesthood.'

So what did Nouwen mean by this paradoxical reference to weakness as a strength in ministry? Well, for a start, it is evident that he is *not* connecting with the Pauline approach to the value of weakness. Recall what Paul says in 2 Corinthians 12:

> Three times I appealed to the Lord about this, that it would leave me, but he said to me, 'My grace is sufficient for you, for power is made perfect in weakness.' So, I will boast all the more gladly of my weaknesses, so that the power of Christ may dwell in me. Therefore I am content with weaknesses, insults, hardships, persecutions, and calamities for the sake of Christ; for whenever I am weak, then I am strong (vv. 8–10).

Paul is here extolling the virtue in the apostle embracing his weakness in order to manifest the greatness of God. That God can change lives via the vehicle of 'damaged goods' shows just how majestic God is. In this text, Paul is presenting an important gospel truth, but it is not what Nouwen has in mind. Rather, what we have is a theme that comes through quite often in Nouwen's writings, and especially in his classic book *The Wounded Healer*.[4] That theme is that an inflated, unrealistic sense of one's personal strength keeps us apart from others. An unavoidable part of being human is to live in confusion, fear, destructive urges, deceit, failure, shame and guilt. To pretend to ourselves and to others that we are always strong emotionally, intellectually, spiritually and morally is futile, silly, dishonest and destructive. Our weakness is part of our common humanity. It is only when it is acknowledged and accepted that we can relate to others in an honest and real way. Moreover, it is

through being in touch with our weakness that we release within ourselves a flow of compassion and understanding. It is not that counsellors
must have experienced precisely the same kind of suffering or loss as the
other person. Rather, it is that through their own painful experiences,
whatever they may be, they have entered for a time into that place of
shadows which the other person is in. In the pastoral conversation, we
find two fellow travellers who have passed the same way and feel a bond
of communion. Alastair Campbell puts it well when he says that '[t]he
wounded healer heals, because he or she is able to convey, as much by
presence as by the words used, both an awareness and a transcendence
of loss'.[5]

It is when we feel a bond of solidarity with another, borne out of a
common journey into the shadowlands of human existence, that there
is confidence, trust and openness, and beyond that, hope. An important
gift that a counsellor can offer a person in pain, confusion, and despair is
a re-kindling of hope.[6] Those in the depths suffer under the awful burden
of the thought, so powerful and all-pervasive, that they will always be
in the depths of despair. The presence of the counsellor, usually without that individual needing or wanting to make a specific reference to
transcendence of similar experiences, becomes a sign of hope. It is not
that the counsellor comes straight out with, 'I've been there and I came
through it. You can too. Just hang in there.' Rather, the very fact that
counsellors so clearly understand and are prepared to enter into the pain
of the other person witnesses to the fact that they are not strangers to
suffering. To quote Campbell once more:

> Wounded healers heal because they, to some degree at least, have
> entered the depths of their own experiences of loss and in those depths
> found hope again. The wounded healer has learned that it is useless to
> base security on material possessions, on popularity and worldly suc-
> cess, even on the closest and most important of personal relationships.
> The wounded healer has learned (a little at least) from the Son of Man,
> who had nowhere to lay his head ... and has understood the wisdom
> of Job's words: 'Naked I came from my mother's womb, naked I shall
> return ...[7]

I have been alluding to the link between woundedness and a capacity
for compassion. It is now time to explore compassionate presence more
fully.

In the case of compassionate understanding, one draws the pain and
distress of the other into one's own sphere. The biblical writers, in
describing compassion, use the images of the womb, the bowels and the

heart to communicate this. They identify a deeply personal act in which the hurt the other suffers is experienced in that space that is most intimately one's own.

Dianne Bergant observes that in the cluster of Hebrew words for compassion, *rhm* is the most prominent.[8] It has the primary meaning of 'cherishing', 'soothing' or 'a gentle attitude of mind'. It refers to a tender parental love. The word *rehem*, meaning womb, is also derived from this root. Hence Bergant concludes that this Hebrew word-group indicates a bond like that between a mother and the child of her womb.[9]

Xavier Leon-Dufour, unsurprisingly, describes the Hebrew notion of compassion in a very similar way. He suggests that *rhm* 'expresses the instinctive attachment of one person for another'.[10] He observes that this feeling has its seat in the maternal bosom or in the bowels (or, as we would say, heart) of the father. It is a tenderness that drives a person to action on behalf of those in distress.

The New Testament writers often use *éleos* (mercy) when speaking of compassion.[11] A form of the verb *oiktiro* (connoting sympathy) also appears. However, when reference is made to the compassion of Jesus, *splánchnon* is always used. In early Greek usage, the word denotes the 'inward parts' of a sacrifice.[12] Later, it was used to refer to the 'inward parts of the body', and finally to the womb. We also find the noun form used in the *Testaments of the Twelve Patriarchs*. There it denotes 'the centre of feelings' or 'noble feelings'. In one instance the verb is used to indicate mere emotion, but it generally refers to the inner disposition that generates acts of mercy. The adjective *eúsplanchnos* (tender-hearted) denotes human virtue and the disposition of 'pity'.

The noun appears in three of Jesus' parables: the good samaritan, the prodigal son and the unmerciful servant. Of particular interest for our discussion is the way Paul describes compassion. Only the noun occurs in his writings. He uses *splánchna* not merely to express natural emotions but as 'a very forceful term to signify an expression of the total personality at the deepest level'.[13] It occurs twice in Philemon (vv. 7, 20); reference is made to the refreshing of the *splánchna*. In verse 12 of that letter, Paul says that in Onesimus he is, in effect, coming in person with a claim for Philemon's love. Philippians 1.8 contains a unique phrase. Paul declares that 'For God is my witness, how I long for all of you with the compassion [*splánchna*] of Christ Jesus.' The reference is to 'the love or affection which, gripping or moving the whole personality, is possible only in Christ ...'[14]

In these various uses of the word 'compassion' by the writers of the Scriptures, there are a number of key features. First, the idea of tenderness comes out in a number of places. Second, compassion is associated with an instinctive, intimate relationship: it is like the loving, soothing action of a mother or father. Finally, it refers (most clearly in Pauline usage) not just to an emotion, but to the deepest part of one's personality. This depth dimension is indicated by the cluster of inner parts identifying the seat of the emotion – namely, the womb, the bowels and the heart. People today naturally take these organismic references as metaphorical. It seems, however, that the Semite view of emotion was very definitely psychosomatic.

In a study of the foundational role of compassion in pastoral care, the pastoral theologian Arthur Becker identifies both the intensity of emotion and the somatic base we have been discussing. For the writers of the Scriptures, he observes, compassion entails 'a perception of another's pain, hurt, sorrow, longing, so intense and vivid and organismic that you feel it "in your guts"'.[15]

The condition of the possibility of a compassionate presence is personal availability. The term 'availability' refers to a willingness to dispose of oneself for the sake of the other. It indicates a readiness for self-giving in the service of others. The French philosopher Gabriel Marcel rightly says that it is simply another name for the Christian virtue of *caritas*. He also points out that there is a very close link between availability and receptivity to the other's experience – especially when it is pain and distress.[16] Marcel establishes the link between the two terms using the metaphor of 'in-cohesion'. To exist with others, he observes, is to be exposed to influences, and it is not possible to be human without to some extent being permeable to those influences. Permeability, in its broadest sense, is associated with a certain lack of cohesion or density. Thus the fact of being exposed to external influences is linked with a kind of *in-cohesion*. We are 'porous', open to a reality that seeks to communicate with us. Marcel puts it this way: 'I must somehow make room for the other in myself; if I am completely absorbed in myself, concentrated on my sensations, feelings, anxieties, it will obviously be impossible for me to receive, to incorporate in myself, the message of the other. What I called in-cohesion a moment ago here assumes the form of disposability ...'[17]

Disposability, then, is closely associated with receptivity. Receptivity involves a readiness to make available one's personal centre, one's own domain. Marcel uses a different metaphor to capture this phenomenon; he refers to inviting others to be *chez soi* (at home). He observes that we receive others in a room, in a house, or in a garden, but not on unknown ground or in the woods. Receptivity means that I invite the other to 'be at home' with me. A home receives the imprint of one's personality; something of myself is infused into the way my home-space is constructed. Contrast this with 'the nameless sadness' associated with a hotel room; this is no one's home. To share one's home-space is disposability or availability because '[t]o provide hospitality is truly to communicate something of oneself to the other'.[18]

The meaning of hospitality can also be broadened to include receiving into one's self the appeal of another for understanding and compassion. When we open ourselves to the call of others to be with them in their pain and confusion, we are able to spontaneously feel with them. The intonation of our words, posture and facial expressions say to others that we are with them in their suffering.

The fourth quality that one finds in the deeply spiritual pastoral counsellor is tenderness. The term was coined by the person-centred therapist Brian Thorne.[19] Tenderness is that 'which means both vulnerable and warmly affectionate, easily crushed and merciful, not tough and sympathetic. It seems to incorporate both weakness and gentle strength, great fragility and great constancy.'[20] Relating in a tender way to another person involves the whole of one's being: '[I]t is evident in voice, the eyes, the hands, the thoughts, the feelings, the beliefs, the moral stance, the attitude to things animate and inanimate, seen and unseen.'[21] Thorne goes on to specify the other personal characteristics associated with an experience of tenderness:

Secondly, [this quality] communicates through its responsive vulnerability that suffering and healing are interwoven. Thirdly, it demonstrates a preparedness and an ability to move between the worlds of the physical, the emotional, the cognitive and the mystical without strain. Fourthly, it is without shame because it is experienced as the joyful embracing of the desire to love and is therefore a law unto itself. Fifthly, it is a quality which transcends the male and female but is nevertheless nourished by the attraction of the one for the other in the quest for wholeness.[22]

One of the most striking and touching New Testament accounts of tender relations involves the meeting between Jesus and the 'sinful woman' who anointed him (Luke 7.36–50). Implicit in the narrative is a previous experience of forgiveness. The woman comes with a deep feeling of gratitude moving her whole being. Her thankful heart is bursting as she kneels behind Jesus, weeping. A chain-reaction is set in train. Some of her tears fall on to Jesus' feet. Having nothing to hand to wipe the tears, she uses her hair. Spontaneously, her affection and gratitude are expressed through a shower of kisses on the freshly cleaned feet. Finally, the perfume intended for the head, given her proximity to Jesus' feet, is poured out there.

Contrary to the expectations of his host, Jesus graciously receives the intimate, affectionate contact from the woman. He is not preoccupied with her sinful past, but is instead touched by her beautiful display of thankful affection.

The intimate meeting takes place on a number of levels: the emotional, the spiritual and the physical. First, the woman's tears are not simply the tears of joy of a person liberated from a past of degradation and exploitation. Certainly it is the case that her experience of a new life in which she is able to treat her body respectfully has elevated her mood, but it is divine forgiveness that is uppermost in her mind when she comes to express her gratitude. The spiritual dimension of the encounter is primary. Finally, there is the physical dimension. The joy, the relief, the sense of liberation and forgiveness are all gathered together in a bodily expression of gratitude and affection.

This bodily contact is perhaps the most striking feature in the story. Wiping a man's feet with one's hair and smothering them with kisses are very intimate, sensuous actions. The tactile centres of Jesus and the woman were alive in an experience of communion.

The final spiritual quality I will comment on here is integrity: 'To possess integrity is to be incapable of compromising that which we believe to be true ... To possess integrity is to have a kind of inner strength which prevents us from bending to the influence of what is thought expedient, or fashionable or calculated to win praise; it is to be consistent and utterly trustworthy because of a constancy of purpose.'[23] A person of integrity chooses convictions and personal consistency over satisfying the craving for popularity and conflict-free relations.

A number of psychologists refer to the true or authentic self and the false or conforming self. They contend that values are the primary factor in establishing a coherent sense of selfhood.[24] The suggestion is that when people act in accordance with their value structures they feel in touch with their core selves. That is to say, living true to their deepest values leads to a sense of authenticity. Those whose words and actions are congruent with their value structures feel as though they are living out of their true selves. It goes without saying that such authentic living is difficult to enact.

Because there are large benefits that accrue from conforming to the wishes and desires of others, especially popularity and praise, many of us find that over time we lose touch to an extent with our real selves. We have become so used to responding to the question 'What does this person want me to say?' that we too often fail to ask 'What do I really think?' and 'What needs to be said here?' Another way of talking about the virtue of integrity is to say that it belongs to those who live out of their real selves. The following stances are what matter most to persons of integrity. First, they value getting in touch with their own deepest ideas, values and convictions. And second, they put a high priority on putting those ideas and values before others. It is possible to fail at either point. Some of us, for instance, have become so habituated to an inner dialogue dominated by external demands that we no longer have access to our deepest beliefs. In a moment of scary self-discovery, we are hit with the awareness of a loss of self-contact. We realize that we have no immediate contact with a personal centre.

It may be, on the other hand, that people are able to access their personal beliefs quite readily, but are too afraid to speak the truth. In his book *Who is Worthy?*, Father Ted Kennedy opens his deeply challenging reflections on the Church's relationship to gay people and to the Australian indigenous community with this comment: 'Some time ago I suffered a stroke which triggered in me a decision to live the rest of my life as if I were already dead. I am now more inclined to state things as they are, or as I see them, without fear or compromise.'[25] The problem for many of us is that we can't achieve this illusion. We are very aware of being alive, and we are even more aware of the living hell others may wish to create for us!

In the context of pastoral counselling, this conversation reminds us of how crucially important it is to relate honestly and genuinely. There are times when we need to speak 'an inconvenient truth' to a counsellee (we discussed this in Chapter 7). Counsellees love us when we are compassionate, understanding and supportive; they are usually not so appreciative when we confront them about their self-deception and game-playing! It requires integrity to speak the truth as one sees it.

Integrity in pastoral counsellors also refers to their capacity to be 'dependably real', as Carl Rogers so nicely put it. Assuming the persona of the all-knowing and wise one, projecting a saintly presence, mimicking the style of another (admired) counsellor, refusing to acknowledge mistakes and failings, and pretending to be deeply interested when one is actually bored silly are just some of the ways a pastoral counsellor fails the integrity test.

I'm very aware that this discussion on the spirituality of the pastoral counsellor is incomplete and inadequate. This vitally important topic deserves a much fuller treatment, but at least some crucially important dimensions have been covered here.

The decision to close with this conversation flows from my strong conviction that what we bring as individuals contributes at least as much to the quality and effectiveness of our counselling work as does our skilful technique. Conscientious and faithful counsellors constantly work on enhancing knowledge, skills and techniques. But just as importantly, and probably more so, they continually open themselves up to the Spirit of God in the journey into stronger faith, deeper compassion and firmer character.

Notes

1 N. Pembroke, *Moving Toward Spiritual Maturity: Psychological, Contemplative, and Moral Challenges in Christian Living* (London: Routledge, 2007).

2 They featured in Chapter 6 of this book.

3 J. Ellin, *Listening Helpfully* (London: Souvenir Press, 1994), p. 32.

4 See H. Nouwen, *The Wounded Healer* (New York: Image Books, 1979).

5 A. Campbell, *Rediscovering Pastoral Care*, 2nd edn (London: Darton, Longman and Todd, 1986), p. 42.

6 We discussed this in the last chapter.

7 Campbell, *Rediscovering Pastoral Care*, p. 43.

8 See D. Bergant, 'Compassion', in C. Stuhlmueller (ed.), *The Collegeville Pastoral Dictionary of Biblical Theology* (Collegeville, MN: Liturgical Press, 1996), pp. 154–7, p. 154.

9 See Bergant, 'Compassion', p. 154.

10 X. Leon-Dufour, 'Mercy', in *Dictionary of Biblical Theology* 2nd edn, updated, trans. P. Cahill and E. Stewart (London: Geoffrey Chapman, 1988), pp. 351–4, p. 351.

11 See Bergant, 'Compassion', p. 156.

12 This discussion of *splánchnon* in pre-New Testament and New Testament usage is informed by H. Köster, '*Splánchnon*', in G. Kittel and G. Friedrich (eds), *Theological Dictionary of the New Testament*, one-vol. edn, trans. G. Bromiley (Grand Rapids, MI: Eerdmans, 1985), pp. 1067–69.

13 Köster, '*Splánchnon*', p. 1068.

14 Köster, '*Splánchnon*', p. 1068.

15 A. Becker, 'Compassion: A Foundation for Pastoral Care', *Religion in Life* 48 (Summer 1979), pp. 143–52, p. 145.

16 See G. Marcel, *Creative Fidelity*, trans. R. Rosthal (New York: The Noonday Press, 1964).

17 Marcel, *Creative Fidelity*, p. 88.

18 Marcel, *Creative Fidelity.*, p. 91.

19 See B. Thorne, *Person-Centred Counselling: Therapeutic and Spiritual Dimensions* (London: Whurr Publishers, 1991), p. 41.

20 Thorne, *Person-Centred Counselling*, p. 75.

21 Thorne, *Person-Centred Counselling*, p. 76.

22 Thorne, *Person-Centred Counselling*, p. 76.

23 Campbell, *Rediscovering Pastoral Care*, p. 12.

24 See S. Hitlin, 'Values as the Core of Personal Identity: Drawing Links Between Two Theories of Self,' *Social Psychology Quarterly* 66, no. 2 (June 2003), pp. 118–37.

25 T. Kennedy, *Who is Worthy?* (Sydney: Pluto Press, 2000), p. 27.

Bibliography

Adame, A. L. and Leitner, L. M., 'Dialogical Constructivism: Martin Buber's Enduring Relevance to Psychotherapy', *Journal of Humanistic Psychology* 51, no. 1 (2011), pp. 41–60.

Adams, F., 'Empathy, Neural Imaging and the Theory versus Simulation Debate, *Mind and Language* 16, no. 4 (2001), pp. 368–92.

Adler, A., 'The Underdeveloped Social Interest', in H. L. Ansbacher and R. R. Ansbacher (eds), *The Individual Psychology of Alfred Adler* (New York: Harper Torchbooks, 1964), pp. 250–5.

Aitken, D. E.,'The Experiences of Countertransference as Empathy, Attunement, and Mutual Regression in Individual Psychotherapy: An Intersubjective, Psychoanalytic Study', unpublished doctoral thesis, Chicago School of Professional Psychology, 2014.

Alford, C. F., 'Levinas, Winnicott, and Therapy', *The Psychoanalytic Review* 94, no. 4 (2007), pp. 529–51.

Anderson, H. and Goolishian, H., 'Human Systems as Linguistic Systems: Preliminary and Evolving Ideas about the Implications for Clinical Theory', *Family Process* 27 (1988), pp. 371–93.

Anderson, R. E., 'Kierkegaard's Theory of Communication', *Speech Monographs* 30, no. 1 (1963), pp. 1–14.

Anscombe, G. E. M. and von Wright, G. H. (eds), *Zettel* (London: Blackwell, 1967).

Aristotle, *Poetics*, trans. S. H. Butcher (New York: Hill & Wang, 1961).

Babits, M., 'Using Therapeutic Metaphor to Provide a Holding Environment: The Inner Edge of Possibility', *Clinical Social Work Journal* 29, no. 1 (2001), pp. 21–33.

Barker, E., *The Political Thought of Plato and Aristotle* (Mineola, NY: Dover Publications, 2009).

Barnett, M., 'Empathy and Related Responses in Children', in N. Eisenberg and J. Strayer (eds), *Empathy and Its Development* (Cambridge: Cambridge University Press, 1990), pp. 146–62.

Barry, W. and Connolly, W., *The Practice of Spiritual Direction*, rev. edn (San Francisco, CA: HarperOne, 2009).

Barth, K., *The Epistle to the Romans*, trans. Edwyn C. Hoskyns (London: Oxford University Press, 1933).

Barth, K., *Church Dogmatics* II/1 (Edinburgh: T&T Clark, 1957).

Barth, K., *The Humanity of God* (Atlanta, GA: John Knox Press, 1982).

Basham, A., 'Ritual in Counseling', in C. S. Cashwell and J. S. Young (eds), *Integrating Spirituality and Religion into Counseling: A Guide to Competent Practice*, 2nd edn (Alexandria, VA: American Counseling Association, 2011), pp. 209–23.

Batson, C. D. *et al.*, 'In a Very Different Voice: Unmasking Moral Hypocrisy', *Journal of Personality and Social Psychology* 72, no. 6 (1997), pp. 1335–43.

Batson, C. D. *et al.*, 'Moral Hypocrisy: Appearing to be Moral to Oneself without Being So', *Journal of Personality and Social Psychology* 77, no. 3 (1999), pp. 525–37.

Batson, C. D., Thompson, E. R. and Chen, H., 'Moral Hypocrisy: Addressing Some Alternatives', *Journal of Personality and Social Psychology* 83, no. 2 (2002), pp. 330–9.

Bazerman, M. and Tenbrunsel, A., *Blindspots: Why We Fail to Do What's Right and What to Do about It* (Princeton, NJ: Princeton University Press, 2011).

Beardsley, M. C., 'The Metaphorical Twist', *Philosophy and Phenomenological Research* 22, no. 3 (1962), pp. 293–307.

Beck, J., *Cognitive Therapy: Basics and Beyond* (New York: The Guilford Press, 1995).

Becker, A., 'Compassion: A Foundation for Pastoral Care', *Religion in Life* 48 (Summer 1979), pp. 143–52.

Bennett, M., *The Empathic Healer* (Waltham, MA: Academic Press, 2001).

Bergant, D., 'Compassion', in C. Stuhlmueller (ed.), *The Collegeville Pastoral Dictionary of Biblical Theology* (Collegeville, MN: Liturgical Press, 1996), pp. 154–7.

Bewley, A. R., 'Re-Membering Spirituality', *Women and Therapy* 16, nos 2–3 (1995), pp. 201–13.

Biffle, C., *A Guided Tour of René Descartes'* Meditations on First Philosophy, 3rd edn (Mountain View, CA: Mayfield Publishing House, 2001).

Billington, R., *Understanding Eastern Philosophy* (London: Routledge, 1997).

Black, M., *Models and Metaphors* (Ithaca, NY: Cornell University Press, 1962).

Blumenthal, D., *Facing the Abusing God: A Theology of Protest* (Louisville, KY: Westminster John Knox Press, 1993).

Browning, D., *The Moral Context of Pastoral Care* (Philadelphia, PA: Westminster Press, 1976).

Brueggemann, W., *Hope within History* (Atlanta, GA: John Knox Press, 1987).

Brueggemann, W., 'Prerequisites for Genuine Obedience: Theses and Conclusions', *Calvin Theological Journal* 36 (2001), pp. 34–41.

Buber, M., *Between Man and Man*, trans. R. G. Smith (London: Routledge & Kegan Paul, 1947).

Buber, M., *Pointing the Way*, trans. M. Friedman (London: Routledge & Kegan Paul, 1957).

Buber, M., 'Distance and Relation', *Psychiatry* 20 (1957), pp. 97–104.

Buber, M., 'Elements of the Interhuman', *Psychiatry* 20 (1957), pp. 105–13.

Buber, M., *Daniel: Dialogues on Realization*, trans. M. Friedman (New York: Holt, Rinehart and Winston, 1964).

Buber, M., *The Knowledge of Man*, trans. M. Friedman and R. Gregor Smith (London: George Allen & Unwin, 1965).

Buber, M., *I and Thou*, trans. W. Kaufmann (Edinburgh: T&T Clark, 1970).

Buber, M., *A Believing Humanism* (London: Humanities Press International, 1990).

Buber, M., 'Healing through Meeting', in J. B. Agassi (ed.), *Martin Buber on Psychology and Psychotherapy* (Syracuse, NY: Syracuse University Press, 1999), pp. 17–21.

Buchholz, M., 'Patterns of Empathy as Embodied Practice in Clinical Conversation: A Musical Dimension', *Frontiers in Psychology* 5 (2004), pp. 1–20.

Bugental, J. F. T., *The Art of the Psychotherapist* (New York: Norton, 1987).

Burns, C. P. E., *Divine Becoming: Rethinking Jesus and Incarnation* (Minneapolis, NY: Fortress Press, 2002).

Calvert, P. and Palmer, C., 'Application of the Cognitive Therapy Model to Initial Crisis Assessment', *International Journal of Mental Health Nursing* 12 (2003), pp. 30–8.

Cameron, S., 'The Practice of Attention: Simon Weil's Performance of Impersonality', *Critical Inquiry* 29 (2003), pp. 216–52.

Campbell, A., *Rediscovering Pastoral Care*, 2nd edn (London: Darton, Longman and Todd, 1986).

Capps, D., *Biblical Approaches to Pastoral Counseling* (Louisville, KY: Westminster John Knox Press, 1981).

Capps, D., *The Depleted Self* (Minneapolis: Fortress Press, 1993).

Capps, D., *Agents of Hope: A Pastoral Psychology* (Minneapolis, MN: Fortress Press, 1995).

Capps, D., *Living Stories: Pastoral Counseling in Congregational Context* (Minneapolis, MN: Fortress Press, 1998).

Capps, D., *Life Cycle Theory and Pastoral Care*, reprinted edn (Eugene OR: Wipf & Stock, 2002).

Caranfa, A., 'The Aesthetic and the Spiritual Attitude in Learning: Lessons from Simone Weil', *Journal of Aesthetic Education* 44, no. 2 (2010), pp. 63–82.

Carey, A. and Mullan, R. J., 'What is Socratic Questioning?', *Psychotherapy: Theory, Research, Practice, Training* 41, no. 3 (2004), pp. 217–26.

Carlsen, M. B., 'Metaphor, Meaning-Making, and Metamorphosis', in H. Rosen and K. T. Kuehlwein (eds), *Constructing Realities: Meaning-making Perspectives for Psychotherapy* (San Francisco, CA: Jossey-Bass, 1996), pp. 337–67.

Chartrand, T. L. and Bargh, J. A., 'The Chameleon Effect: The Perception-Behavior Link and Social Interaction', *Journal of Personality and Social Psychology* 76 (1999), no. 6, pp. 893–910.

Clark, A., *Being There: Putting Brain, Body, and World Together Again* (Cambridge, MA; and London: The MIT Press, 1997).

Clark, A. J., 'Empathy and Sympathy: Therapeutic Distinctions in Counseling', *Journal of Mental Health Counseling* 32, no. 2 (2010), pp. 95–101.

Clements, W. M. and Clinebell, H., *Counseling for Spiritually Empowered Wholeness: A Hope-Centered Approach* (Binghamton, NY: The Haworth Pastoral Press, 1995).

Connell, G., 'Knights and Knaves of the Living Dead: Kierkegaard's Use of the Living Death as a Metaphor for Despair', in P. Stokes and A. Buben (eds), *Kierkegaard and Death* (Bloomington, IN: Indiana University Press, 2011), pp. 21–43.

Coulehan, J. L., 'Tenderness and Steadiness: Emotions in Medical Practice', *Literature and Medicine* 14, no. 2 (1995), pp. 222–36.

Coutinho, J., Silva, P. and Decety, J., 'Neurosciences, Empathy, and Healthy Interpersonal Relationships: Recent Findings and Implications for Counseling Psychology', *Journal of Counseling Psychology* 61, no. 4 (2014), pp. 541–8.

Couture, P., *Blessed are the Poor? Women's Poverty, Family Policy, and Practical Theology* (Nashville, TN: Abingdon Press, 1991).

Couture, P., 'The Family Policy Debate: A Feminist Theologian's Response', *Journal of Pastoral Theology* 3 (1993), pp. 76–87.

Couture, P., 'Pastoral Care and the Social Gospel', in C. H. Evans (ed.), *The Social Gospel Today* (Louisville, KY: Westminster John Knox Press, 2011), pp. 160–96.

Cunningham, D., *These Three are One: The Practice of Trinitarian Theology* (Oxford: Blackwell, 1998).

Cunningham, D., 'Participation as a Trinitarian Virtue', *Toronto Journal of Theology* 14, no. 1 (1998), pp. 7–25.

Cushman, R. E., *Therapeia: Plato's Conception of Philosophy* (London: Transaction Publishers, 2008).

Darley, J. M. and Batson, C. D., '"From Jerusalem to Jericho": A Study of Situational and Dispositional Variables in Helping Behavior', *Journal of Personality and Social Psychology* 27 (1973), pp. 100–8.

Decety, J. and Lamm, C., 'Human Empathy through the Lens of Neuroscience', *The Scientific World Journal* 6 (2006), pp. 1146–63.

De Jaegher, H., 'Social Understanding Through Direct Perception? Yes, by Interacting', *Consciousness and Cognition* 18 (2009), pp. 535–42.

De Jaegher, H. and Di Paolo, E., 'Participatory Sense-Making: An Enactive Approach to Social Cognition', *Phenomenology and the Cognitive Sciences* 6 (2007), pp. 485–507.

Dekeyser, M., Elliott, R. and Leijssen, M., 'Empathy in Psychotherapy: Dialogue and Embodied Understanding', in J. Decety and W. Ickes (eds), *The Social Neuroscience of Empathy* (Cambridge, MA: The MIT Press, 2009), pp. 125–38.

Delaruelle, J., 'Attention as Prayer: Simone Weil', *Literature and Aesthetics* 13, no. 2 (2003), pp. 19–27.

Denzin, N. K., 'The Methodological Implications of Symbolic Interactionism for the Study of Deviance', *British Journal of Sociology* 25 (1974), pp. 269–82.

Depoortere, K., *A Different God* (Leuven: Peeters Publishers, and Grand Rapids, MI: Eerdmans, 1995).

Dietz, M. G., *Between the Human and the Divine: The Political Thought of Simone Weil* (Lanham, MD: Rowman & Littlefield, 1988).

Diskin, C., 'The Athenian Garden', in J. Warren (ed.), *The Cambridge Companion to Epicureanism* (Cambridge: Cambridge University Press, 2009), pp. 9–28.

Driver, T. F., *Liberating Rites: Understanding the Transformative Power of Ritual* (Boulder, CO: Westview, 1998).

Egan, G., *The Skilled Helper: A Problem-Management and Opportunity-Development Approach to Helping*, 10th edn (Belmont, CA: Brooks/Cole, 2014).

Eisele, T. D., 'The Poverty of Socratic Questioning: Asking and Answering in the Meno', *Faculty Articles and Other Publications*, Paper 36 (1994). Accessed from http://scholarship.law.uc.edu/fac_pubs/36.

Eisenberg, N., 'Emotion, Regulation, and Moral Development'. *Annual Review of Psychology* 51 (2000), pp. 665–97.

Ellin, J., *Listening Helpfully: How to Develop Your Counselling Skills* (London: Condor, 1994).

Ellis, A. and Ellis, D. A., 'Rational Emotive Behavior Therapy', in D. Wedding and R. J. Corsini (eds), *Current Psychotherapies*, 10th edn (Belmont, CA: Brooks/Cole, 2013), pp. 151–91.

Epicurus, *Epicurus: The Extant Remains*, trans. Cyril Bailey (Oxford: Clarendon Press, 1926).

Evans, M. D., 'Appreciative Consciousness: Learning to Go Beyond', *English Quarterly* 36, no. 1 (2004), pp. 10–5.

Fairchild, R. W., 'Guaranteed Not to Shrink: Spiritual Direction in Pastoral Care', *Pastoral Psychology* 31, no. 2 (1982), pp. 79–95.

Feldman, J. A., *From Molecule to Metaphor: A Neural Theory of Language* (Cambridge, MA; and London: The MIT Press, 2006).

Ferreira, M. J., *Kierkegaard* (Malden, MA: Wiley-Blackwell, 2009).

Flavell, J. H., Miller, P. H. and Miller, S. A., *Cognitive Development*, 3rd edn (Englewood Cliffs, NJ: Prentice-Hall, 1993).

Fox, R., 'What is Meta For?', *Clinical Social Work Journal* 17, no. 3 (1989), pp. 233–4.

Friedman, M., *The Healing Dialogue in Psychotherapy* (New York: Jason Aronson, 1985).

Friedman, M., *Dialogue and the Human Image: Beyond Humanistic Psychology* (London: Sage, 1992).

Friedman, M., 'Reflections on the Buber–Rogers Dialogue', *Journal of Humanistic Psychology* 34, no. 1 (Winter 1994), pp. 46–65.

Friedman, M., 'Buber's Philosophy as the Basis for Dialogical Psychotherapy and Contextual Therapy', *Journal of Humanistic Psychology* 38, no. 1 (1998), pp. 25–40.

Friedman, M., 'Buber and Dialogical Therapy: Healing through Meeting', *The Humanistic Psychologist* 36 (2008), pp. 298–315.

Freud, S., 'The Future Prospect of Psychoanalytic Therapy', *Standard Edition of the Complete Psychological Works of Sigmund Freud*, Volume XI [1910] (London: Hogarth Press, 1971), pp. 141–51.

Fuchs, T. and De Jaegher, H., 'Enactive Intersubjectivity: Participatory Sense-making and Mutual Incorporation', *Phenomenology and the Cognitive Sciences* 8 (2009), pp. 465–86.

Gadamer, H. G., *Truth and Method* (London: Sheed & Ward, 1979).

Gade, C. B. N., 'What is *Ubuntu*? Different Interpretations among South Africans of African Descent', *South African Journal of Philosophy* 31, no. 3 (2012), pp. 484–503.

Galbusera, L. and Fuchs, T., 'Embodied Understanding: Discovering the Body from Cognitive Science to Psychotherapy', *In-Mind Italia* V, nd, pp. 1–6. Accessed from http://it.in-mind.org, 7/10/15.

Gallagher, S., 'The Practice of Mind: Theory, Simulation, or Primary Interaction?', *Journal of Consciousness Studies* 8 (2001), pp. 83–108.

Gallagher, S., 'Direct Perception in the Intersubjective Context', *Consciousness and Cognition* 17 (2008), pp. 535–43.

Gallese, V. and Goldman, A., 'Mirror Neurons and the Simulation Theory of Mind-Reading', *Trends in Cognitive Sciences* 2, no. 12 (1998), pp. 493–501.

Gallese, V., Eagle, M. N. and Migone, P., 'Intentional Attunement: Mirror Neurons and the Neural Underpinnings of Interpersonal Relations', *Journal of the American Psychoanalytic Association* 55, no. 1 (2007), pp. 131–76.

Gantt, E., 'Truth, Freedom, and Responsibility in the Dialogues of Psychotherapy', *Journal of Theoretical and Philosophical Psychology* 14, no. 2 (1994), pp. 146–58.

Gendlin, E., 'Thinking Beyond Patterns: Body, Language, and Situations', in B. den Ouden and M. Moen (eds), *The Presence of Feeling in Thought* (New York: Peter Lang, 1991), pp. 22–152.

George, R. L. and Cristiani, T. L., *Counseling: Theory and Practice,* 4th edn (Boston, MA: Allyn & Bacon, 1995).

Gerhart, M. and Russell, A. M., *Metaphoric Process: The Creation of Scientific and Religious Understanding* (Forth Worth, TX: Texas Christian University, 1984).

Gerkin, C., *Widening the Horizons: Pastoral Responses to a Fragmented Society* (Philadelphia, PA: Westminster Press, 1986).

Gill, C., 'Psychology', in J. Warren (ed.), *The Cambridge Companion to Epicureanism* (Cambridge: Cambridge University Press, 2009), pp. 125–41.

Goldberg, C., 'Healing Madness and Despair through Meeting', *American Journal of Psychotherapy* 54, no. 4 (2000), pp. 560–73.

Goldman, A. I., *Simulating Minds: The Philosophy, Psychology, and Neuroscience of Mindreading* (Oxford: Oxford University Press, 2006).

Gopnik, A., 'The Scientist as Child', *Philosophy of Science* 63, no. 4 (1996), pp. 485–514.

Gopnik, A. and Astington, J. W., 'Children's Understanding of Representational Change and its Relation to the Understanding of False Belief and the Appearance-Reality Distinction', *Child Development* 59 (1988), pp. 26–37.

Gopnik, A. and Wellman, H. M., 'Why the Child's Theory of Mind Really *Is* a Theory', *Mind and Language* 7, nos. 1–2 (1992), pp. 145–71.

Gordon, R., 'Folk Psychology as Mental Simulation', in *Stanford Encyclopedia of Philosophy*. Accessed from http://plato.stanford.edu/entries/folkpsych-simulation/.

Graham, E., *Transforming Practice: Pastoral Care in an Age of Uncertainty* (London: Mowbray, 1996).

Graham, L., *Care of Persons, Care of Worlds: A Psychosystems Approach to Pastoral Care and Counseling* (Nashville, TN: Abingdon Press, 1992).

Graham, L., 'From Relational Humanness to Relational Justice: Reconceiving Pastoral Care and Counseling', in P. Couture and R. Hunter (eds), *Pastoral Care and Social Conflict* (Nashville, TN: Abingdon Press, 1995), pp. 220–34.

Gubb, K., 'Craving Interpretation: A Case of Somatic Countertransference', *British Journal of Psychotherapy* 30, no. 1 (2014), pp. 51–67.

Gunton, C., *The Promise of Trinitarian Theology*, 2nd edn (Edinburgh: T&T Clark, 2003).

Gunzburg, J. C., *Healing through Meeting: Martin Buber's Conversational Approach to Psychotherapy* (London: Jessica Kingsley Publishers, 1997).

Halpern, J., 'Empathy: Using Resonance Emotions in the Service of Curiosity', in H. M. Spiro *et al.* (eds), *Empathy and the Practice of Medicine* (New Haven, CT: Yale University Press, 1993), pp. 160–73.

Halpern, J., 'What is Clinical Empathy?', *Journal of General Internal Medicine* 18 (2003), pp. 670–4.

Hankela, E., *Ubuntu, Migration, and Ministry* (Leiden: Brill, 2014).

Harrington, W., *The Tears of God* (Collegeville, MN: Liturgical Press, 1992).

Hauerwas, S., *Vision and Virtue* (Notre Dame, IN: University of Notre Dame Press, 1981).

Heimann, P., 'On Countertransference', *International Journal of Psychoanalysis* 31 (1950), pp. 81–4.

Herth, K., 'Fostering Hope in Terminally ill People', *Journal of Advanced Nursing* 15 (1990), pp. 1250–9.

Heymel, M., '"Predigen – die schwierigste aller Künste": Anstöße von Sören Kierkegaard für die heutige Homiletik', *International Journal of Practical Theology* 10 (2006), pp. 34–52.

Hitlin, S., 'Values as the Core of Personal Identity: Drawing Links Between Two Theories of Self', *Social Psychology Quarterly* 66, no. 2 (June 2003), pp. 118–37.

Hobfoll, S. E., Briggs-Phillips, M. and Stines, I. R., 'Fact or Artifact: The Relationship of Hope to a Caravan of Resources', in R. Jacoby and G. Keinan (eds), *Between Stress and Hope: From a Disease-centered to a Health-centered Perspective* (New York: Greenwood, 2005), pp. 81–104.

Hobson, R., *Forms of Feeling: The Heart of Psychotherapy* (London: Tavistock Publications, 1985).

Hoelzl, M. and Ward, G. (eds), *Religion and Political Thought* (London: Bloomsbury Academic, 2006).

Hoffman, J. C., *Ethical Confrontation in Counseling* (Chicago, IL: University Chicago Press, 1979).

Hojat, M., *et al.*, 'Physician Empathy: Definitions, Components, Measurement, and Relationships to Gender and Speciality', *The American Journal of Psychiatry* 159, no. 9 (2000), pp. 1563–9.

Hycner, R., *Between Person and Person: Toward a Dialogical Psychotherapy* (Highland, NY: The Gestalt Journal, 1990).

Ikemi, A., 'Carl Rogers and Eugene Gendlin on the Bodily Felt Sense: What They Share and Where They Differ', *Person-Centered and Experiential Psychotherapies* 4, no. 1 (2005), pp. 31–42.

Jackson, B., 'The Conceptual History of Social Justice', *Political Studies Review* 3 (2005), pp. 356–73.

Johnston, D., *A Brief History of Justice* (New York: Wiley, 2011).

Jones, S., 'Rational-Emotive Therapy in Christian Perspective', *The Journal of Theology and Psychology* 17 (Summer 1989), pp. 110–20.

Jost, J. T. and Kay, A. C., 'Social Justice: History, Theory, and Research', in S. T. Fiske, D. T. Gilbert and G. Lindzey (eds), *Handbook of Social Psychology*, vol. 1 (New York: Wiley, 2010), pp. 1122–65.

Kainz, H., *Ethics in Context* (London: The Macmillan Press, 1988).

Käsemann, E., *Commentary on Romans* (Grand Rapids: Eerdmans, 1980).

Kazantzis, N., Fairburn, C. G. *et al.*, 'Unresolved Issues Regarding the Research and Practice of Cognitive Behavior Therapy: The Case of Guided Discovery Using Socratic Questioning', *Behaviour Change* 31, no. 1 (2014), pp. 1–17.

Kellenberger, J., 'Kierkegaard, Indirect Communication, and Religious Truth', *International Journal for the Philosophy of Religion* 16, no. 2 (1984), pp. 153–60.

Kelly, G. A., *The Psychology of Personal Constructs*, vol. 1: *A Theory of Personality* (London: Routledge, 1991).

Kennedy, T., *Who is Worthy?* (Sydney: Pluto Press, 2000).

Kernberg, O., 'Notes on Countertransferences', *Journal of the American Psychoanalytic Association*, 13, no. 1 (1965), pp. 38–56.

Kierkegaard, S., *The Sickness unto Death*, trans. Walter Lowrie (Princeton, NJ: Princeton University Press, 1941).

Kierkegaard, S., *Concluding Unscientific Postscript*, trans. D. Swenson (Princeton, NJ: Princeton University Press, 1941).

Kierkegaard, S., *Training in Christianity and the Edifying Discourse which 'Accompanied' It*, trans. W. Lowrie (Princeton, NJ: Princeton University Press, 1944).

Kierkegaard, S., *Either/Or I*, trans. D. F. Swenson and L. M. Swenson (Garden City, KS: DoubleDay & Co., 1959).

Kierkegaard, S., *Either/Or II*, trans. W. Lowrie (Princeton, NJ: Princeton University Press, 1971).

Kierkegaard, S., *The Point of View for My Work as an Author: A Report to History and Related Writings*, trans. W. Lowrie (New York: Harper Torchbooks, 1962).

Kierkegaard, S., *Søren Kierkegaard's Journals and Papers* vol. 1, ed. and trans. H. Hong and E. Hong (Bloomington, IN: Indiana University Press, 1967).

Kierkegaard, S., *Self-Examination and Judge for Yourselves!* trans. W. Lowrie (Princeton, NJ: Princeton University Press, 1968).

Kirmayer, L. J., 'Healing and the Invention of Metaphor: The Effectiveness of Symbols Revisited', *Culture, Medicine and Psychiatry* 17 (1993), pp. 161–95.

Kohut, H., *The Analysis of the Self* (New York: International Universities Press, 1971).

Kohut, H., *The Restoration of the Self* (New York: International Universities Press, 1977).

Kohut, H., *How Does Analysis Cure?* (Chicago, IL: University of Chicago Press, 1984).

Kopp, R. R., *Metaphor Therapy: Using Client-Generated Metaphors in Psychotherapy* (New York: Brunner/Mazel, 1995).

Kopp, R. R. and Craw, M. J., 'Metaphoric Language, Metaphoric Cognition, and Cognitive Therapy', *Psychotherapy* 35, no. 3 (1998), pp. 306–11.

Korner, I. N., 'Hope as a Method of Coping', *Journal of Consulting and Clinical Psychology* 34, no. 2 (1970), pp. 134–9.

Köster, H., *Splánchnon'*, in G. Kittel and G. Friedrich (eds), *Theological Dictionary of the New Testament*, one-vol. edn, trans. G. Bromiley (Grand Rapids, MI: Eerdmans, 1985), pp. 1067–9.

Kövecses, Z., *Metaphor in Culture* (Cambridge: Cambridge University Press, 2005).

Kövecses, Z., 'A New Look at Metaphorical Creativity in Cognitive Linguistics', *Cognitive Linguistics* 21, no. 4 (2010), pp. 663–97.

Kramer, K. P., *Martin Buber's I and Thou: Practicing Living Dialogue* (New York/Mahwah, NJ: Paulist Press, 2003).

Kron, T., 'Self/No-self in the Therapeutic Dialogue According to Martin Buber's Dialogue Philosophy', in D. Mathers, M. E. Miller, and O. Ando (eds), *Self and No-Self: Continuing the Dialogue between Buddhism and Psychotherapy* (London: Routledge, 2009), pp. 165–74.

Kull, A., 'How to Ask Questions about Art and Theology? The Example of Paul Tillich', *Baltic Journal of Art History* 7, no. 4 (2014), pp. 59–80.

Lahav, R., 'Conceptual Framework', in Ran Lahav and Maria da Venza Tillmans (eds), *Essays on Philosophical Counseling* (Lanham, MD: University Press of America, 1995), pp. 3–24.

Lakin, J. L. and Chartrand, T. L., 'Using Nonconscious Behavioral Mimicry to Create Affiliation and Rapport', *Psychological Science* 14, no. 4 (2003), pp. 334–9.

Lakoff, G., 'A Neural Theory of Metaphor', in R. W. Gibbs Jr (ed.), *The Cambridge Handbook of Metaphor and Thought* (Cambridge: Cambridge University Press, 2008), pp. 17–38.

Lakoff, G. and Johnson, M., *Metaphors We Live By* (University of Chicago Press, 1980).

Lakoff, G. and Johnson, M., *Philosophy in the Flesh: The Embodied Mind and Its Challenge to Western Thought* (New York: Basic Books, 1999).

Landau, R. L., 'And the Least of These is Empathy', in H. M. Spiro *et al.* (eds), *Empathy and the Practice of Medicine: Beyond Pills and the Scalpel* (New Haven, CT: Yale University Press, 1993), pp. 103–9.

Lantz, J., 'Mystery in Family Therapy', *Contemporary Family Therapy* 16, no. 1 (1994), pp. 53–66.

Lantz, J., 'Marcel's "Availability" in Existential Psychotherapy with Couples and Families', *Contemporary Family Therapy* 16, no. 6 (1994), pp. 489–501.

Lartey, E., 'Practical Theology as a Theological Form', in J. Patton, J. Woodward and S. Pattison (eds), *The Blackwell Reader in Pastoral and Practical Theology* (Oxford: Blackwell, 2000), pp. 128–34.

Lazarus, R. S., 'Hope: An Emotion and a Vital Coping Resource against Despair', *Social Research* 66, no. 2 (1999), pp. 653–78.

Leon-Dufour, X., 'Mercy', in *Dictionary of Biblical Theology*, 2nd edn, updated, trans. P. Cahill and E. Stewart (London: Geoffrey Chapman, 1988), pp. 351–4.

Leslie, A., 'Pretense and Representation: The Origins of "Theory of Mind"', *Psychological Review* 94, no. 1 (1987), pp. 412–26.

Leslie, A. M., Friedman, O. and German, T. P., 'Core Mechanisms in "Theory of Mind"', *Trends in Cognitive Science* 8, no. 12 (2004), pp. 528–33.

Lester, A., *Hope in Pastoral Care and Counseling* (Louisville, KY: Westminster John Knox Press, 1995).

Levinas, E., *Ethics and Infinity: Conversations with Philippe Nemo,* trans. R. A. Cohen (Pittsburgh, PA: Duquesne University Press, 1985).

Levinas, E., 'Is Ontology Fundamental?', *Philosophy Today* 33, no. 2 (1989), pp. 121–9.

Levinas, E., *Totality and Infinity: An Essay on Exteriority*, trans. A. Lingis (Dordrecht: Kluwer Academic Publishers, 1991).

Levinas, E., 'Transcendence and Height', in A. T. Peperzak, S. Critchley and R. Bernasconi (eds), *Emmanuel Levinas: Basic Philosophical Writings* (Indianapolis: Indiana University Press, 1996), pp. 11–31.

Levinas, E., *Collected Philosophical Papers*, trans. A. Lingis (Pittsburgh, PA: Duquesne University Press, 1998).

Little, M. I., 'Countertransference and the Patient's Response to It', *International Journal of Psychoanalysis* 32 (1951), pp. 32–40.

Lochhead, D., 'Comment on Nielsen', in A. McKinnon (ed.), *Kierkegaard: Resources and Results* (Waterloo, ON: Wilfrid Laurier University Press, 1982).

Louw, D. J., *A Mature Faith: Spiritual Direction and Anthropology in a Theology of Pastoral Care and Counseling* (Leuven: Peeters Publishers and Grand Rapids, MI: Eerdmans, 1999).

Louw, D. J., '"Habitus" in Soul Care: Towards "Spiritual Fortigenetics" (*Parrhesia*) in a Pastoral Anthropology', *Acta Theologica* 30, no. 2 (2010).

Louw, D. J., 'Philosophical Counselling: Towards a "New Approach" in Pastoral Care and Counselling?', *HTS Teologiese Studies/Theological Studies* 67, no. 2 (2011), 7 pages. DOI: 10.4102/hts.v67i2.900.

Lyall, D., 'The Bible, Worship, and Pastoral Care', in P. Ballard and S. R. Holmes (eds), *The Bible in Pastoral Practice* (Grand Rapids, MI: Eerdmans, 2005), pp. 225–40.

Lyddon, W. J., Clay, A. L. and Sparks, C. L., 'Metaphor and Change in Counseling', *Journal of Counseling and Development* 79, no. 3 (2001), pp. 269–74.

Lynch, W. F., *Images of Hope: Imagination as Healer of the Hopeless* (Notre Dame, IN: University of Notre Dame Press, 1974).

Mace, C., 'Therapeutic Questioning and Socratic Dialogue', in C. Mace (ed.), *Heart and Soul: The Therapeutic Face of Philosophy* (New York: Routledge, 1999), pp. 13–28.

Manganyi, J. S., 'Church and Society: The Value of Perichoresis in Understanding Ubuntu with Special Reference to John Zizioulas', unpublished doctoral thesis, University of Pretoria, 2012.

Marcel, G., *Homo Viator: Introduction to a Metaphysic of Hope* (London: Victor Gollancz, 1951).

Marcel, G., *Creative Fidelity*, trans. R. Rosthal (New York: The Noonday Press, 1964).

Marcel, G., 'Desire and Hope', in N. Lawrence and D. O'Connor (eds), *Readings in Existential Phenomenology* (Englewood Cliffs, NJ: Prentice-Hall, 1967), pp. 277–85.

Marcel, G., 'I and Thou', in P. A. Schilpp and M. Friedman (eds), *The Philosophy of Martin Buber* (LaSalle, IL: Open Court, 1967), pp. 41–8.

Marlett, G. A. and Fromme, K., 'Metaphors for Addiction', *Journal of Drug Issues* 17 (1987), pp. 9–29.

May, R., *The Discovery of Being* (New York: W.W. Norton, 1983).

McClure, B. J., *Moving Beyond Individualism in Pastoral Care and Counseling* (Eugene, OR: Wipf & Stock, 2010).

McFague, S., *Models of God: Theology for an Ecological, Nuclear Age* (Philadelphia, PA: Fortress Press, 1987).

McKellan, D. (ed.), *Karl Marx: Selected Writings*, 2nd edn (Oxford: Oxford University Press, 2000).

Meland, B. E., 'Can Empirical Theology Learn Something from Phenomenology?', in B. E. Meland (ed.), *The Future of Empirical Theology* (Chicago, IL: The University of Chicago Press, 1969), pp. 283–306.

Merleau-Ponty, M., *Phenomenology of Perception*, trans. Colin Smith (London: Routledge & Kegan Paul, 1965).

Merton, T., *Seeds of Contemplation* (London: Burns and Oates, 1949, 1957).

Merton, T., *The New Man* (New York: Farrar, Straus and Giroux, 1961, 2000).

Merton, T., *Conjectures of a Guilty Bystander* (New York: Image Books, 1968, 1989).

Merton, T., *Contemplative Prayer* (New York: Image Books, 1971, 1996).

Merton, T., *Entering the Silence: Becoming a Monk and a Writer – The Journals*, vol. 2 (San Francisco, CA: HarperSanFrancisco, 1995).

Miles, R., *The Pastor as Moral Guide* (Minneapolis, MN: Fortress Press, 1998).

Miller-McLemore, B., 'The Living Human Web: Pastoral Theology at the Turn of the Century', in J. Stevenson-Moessner (ed.), *Through the Eyes of Women: Insights for Pastoral Care* (Minneapolis, MN: Fortress Press, 1996), pp. 9–26.

Miller-McLemore, B, 'Pastoral Theology and Public Theology: Developments in the U.S.', in E. Graham and A. Rowlands (eds), *Pathways to the Public Square: Practical Theology in an Age of Pluralism* (Münster: Lit Verlag, 2005), pp. 95–105.

Miller, G., *Incorporating Spirituality in Counseling and Psychotherapy* (Hoboken, NJ: Wiley, 2003).

Miller, J. F. and Powers, M. J., 'Development of an Instrument to Measure Hope', *Nursing Research* 37, no. 1 (1988), pp. 6–10.

Min, A. K., 'Naming the Unnameable God: Levinas, Derrida, and Marion', *International Journal for Philosophy of Religion* 60 (2006), pp. 99–116.

Moltmann, J., *The Crucified God* (London: SCM Press, 1974).

Moltmann, J., *The Trinity and the Kingdom of God* (London: SCM Press, 1981).

Moon, G. W. and Benner, D. G. (eds), *Spiritual Direction and the Care of Souls: A Guide to Christian Approaches and Practices* (Downers Grove, IL: IVP Academic, 2009).

Mooney, E. F., 'Pseudonyms and "Style"', in J. Lippitt and G. Pattison (eds), *The Oxford Handbook of Kierkegaard* (Oxford: Oxford University Press, 2013), pp. 191–210.

Morris, L., *The Epistle to the Romans* (Grand Rapids, MI: Eerdmans, 1988).

Morrison, A. P., 'Shame, Ideal Self, and Narcissism', in A. P. Morrison (ed.), *Essential Papers on Narcissism* (New York: New York University Press, 1986), pp. 348–71.

Morrison, G. J., 'The (Im)possibilities of Levinas for Christian Theology: The Search for a Language of Alterity', in J. De Tavernier *et al.* (eds), *Responsibility, God and Society: Theological Ethics in Dialogue: Festschrift Roger Burggraeve* (Leuven: Peeters Publishing, 2008), pp. 103–22.

Mouw, J. and Sweeney, D. A., *The Suffering and Victorious Christ: Toward a More Compassionate Christology* (Grand Rapids, MI: Baker Academic, 2013).

Mozdzierz, G. J., Peluso, P. R. and Lisiecki, J., *Principles of Counseling and Psychotherapy* (New York: Routledge, 2009)

Murphy, N., *Bodies and Souls, or Spirited Bodies* (Cambridge: Cambridge University Press, 2006).

Murray, L., '"Poet in the Scientist": The Mystical Naturalism of Bernard E. Meland', *Encounter* 68, no. 2 (2007), pp. 19–31.

Nin, A., *The Journals of Anaïs Nin, 1931–1934*, ed. G. Stuhlmann (London: Peter Owen, 1966).

Nouwen, H., *The Wounded Healer* (New York: Image Books, 1979).

Noyce, G., *The Minister as Moral Counselor* (Nashville, TN: Abingdon Press, 1989).

Nussbaum, M. C., *The Therapy of Desire: Theory and Practice in Hellenistic Ethics* (Princeton, NJ: Princeton University Press, 1994).

Oates, W. J. (ed.), *The Stoic and Epicurean Philosophers* (New York: The Modern Library, 1957).

Overholser, J. C., 'Elements of the Socratic Method: I. Systematic Questioning', *Psychotherapy* 30, no. 1 (1993), pp. 67–74.

Overholser, J. C., 'Collaborative Empiricism, Guided Discovery, and the Socratic Method: Core Processes for Effective Cognitive Therapy', *Clinical Psychology: Science and Practice* 18, no. 1 (2011), pp. 62–6.

Overholser, J. C., 'Guided Discovery: Problem-Solving Therapy Integrated within the Socratic Method', *Journal of Contemporary Psychotherapy* 43, no. 2 (2013), pp. 73–82.

Padesky, C., 'Socratic Questioning: Changing Minds or Guiding Discovery?', a keynote address delivered at the European Congress of Behavioural and Cognitive Therapies, London, 24 September 1993.

Parker, R. J. and Horton, H. S., 'A Typology of Ritual: Paradigms for Healing and Empowerment', *Counseling and Values* 40 (1996), pp. 82–96.

Parker, R. J., Horton, H. S. and Watson, T., 'Sarah's Story: Using Ritual Therapy to Address Psychospiritual Issues in Treating Survivors of Childhood Sexual Abuse', *Counseling and Values* 42 (1997), pp. 41–54.

Pattison, S., *A Critique of Pastoral Care*, 2nd edn (London: SCM Press, 1993).

Pattison, S., *Pastoral Care and Liberation Theology* (Cambridge: Cambridge University Press, 1994).

Patton, J., *Pastoral Counseling: A Ministry of the Church* (Nashville, TN: Abingdon Press, 1983).

Peabody, S. A. and Gelso, C. J., 'Countertransference and Empathy: The Complex Relationship between Two Divergent Concepts in Counseling', *Journal of Counseling Psychology* 29, no. 3 (1982), pp. 240–5.

Pearson, C., 'The Future of Optimism', *American Psychologist* 55, no. 1 (2000), pp. 44–55.

Pembroke, N., *The Art of Listening* (Grand Rapids, MI: Eerdmans and Edinburgh: T&T Clark, 2002),

Pembroke, N., *Moving Toward Spiritual Maturity: Psychological, Contemplative, and Moral Challenges in Christian Living* (London: Routledge, 2007).

Pembroke, N., *Pastoral Care in Worship: Liturgy and Psychology in Dialogue* (London: T&T Clark International, 2010).

Perkins, D. N. and Tishman, S., 'Dispositional Aspects of Intelligence', unpublished paper, 1998.

Perlstein, M., 'A Spiritual Coming Out', *Women and Therapy* 24, nos 3–4 (2002), pp. 175–92.

Perrin, J. M. and Thibon, G., *Simone Weil as We Knew Her* (London: Routledge, 2003).

Pirruccello, A., 'Interpreting Simone Weil: Presence and Absence in Attention', *Philosophy East and West* 45, no. 1 (1995), pp. 61-72.

Plant, K., 'The Two Worlds of Martin Buber', *Theology* 88, no. 2 (1985), pp. 282–7.

Poling, J., 'An Ethical Framework for Pastoral Care', *The Journal of Pastoral Care* 42, no. 4 (Winter 1988), pp. 299–306.

Poling, J., *Deliver Us from Evil: Resisting Racial and Gender Oppression* (Minneapolis, MN: Fortress Press, 1996).

Pomerleau, W. P., 'Western Theories of Justice', *Internet Encyclopedia of Philosophy*, accessed from http://www.iep.utm.edu/justwest/.

Premack, D. and Woodruff, G., 'Does the Chimpanzee Have a Theory of Mind?', *The Behavioral and Brain Sciences* 4 (1978), pp. 515–26.

Purnell, D., 'Pastoral Ministry and the Fleshly Body', *Pastoral Psychology* 53, no. 1 (2004), pp. 81–5.

Quinn, N., 'The Cultural Basis of Metaphor', in J. Fernandez (ed.), *Beyond Metaphor: The Theory of Tropes in Anthropology* (Stanford, CA: Stanford University Press, 1991), pp. 56–93.

Quinn, R., 'Confronting Carl Rogers: A Developmental-Interactional Approach to Person-Centered Therapy', *Journal of Humanistic Psychology* 33, no. 1 (Winter 1993), pp. 6–23.

Ramose, M. B., *African Philosophy through Ubuntu* (Harare: Mond Books, 1999).

Ramsey, N., 'Contemporary Pastoral Theology: A Wider Vision for the Practice of Love', in N. Ramsey (ed.), *Pastoral Care and Counseling: Redefining the Paradigms* (Nashville, TN: Abingdon Press, 2004), pp. 155–76.

Ramsey, N., 'Intersectionality: A Model for Addressing the Complexity of Oppression and Privilege', *Pastoral Psychology* 63 (2014), pp. 453–69.

Ramshaw, E., *Ritual and Pastoral Care* (Minneapolis, MN: Fortress Press, 1987).

Ravenscroft, I., 'What Is It Like To Be Someone Else? Simulation and Empathy', *Ratio* XI (1998), pp. 170–85.

Rawls, J., 'Justice as Fairness', *Philosophical Review* 64, no. 1 (1955), pp. 3–32.

Rawls, J., *A Theory of Justice* (Cambridge, MA: Belknap Press, 1971).

Rawls, J., 'Justice as Fairness: Political not Metaphysical', *Philosophy and Public Affairs* 14, no. 3, (1985), pp. 225–52.

Renner, H. P. V., 'The Use of Ritual in Pastoral Care', *The Journal of Pastoral Care* 23 (1979), pp. 165–6.

Richards, I. A., *The Philosophy of Rhetoric* (London: Oxford University Press, 1936).

Ricoeur, P., *The Rule of Metaphor: Multi-disciplinary Studies of the Creation of Meaning in Language*, trans. Robert Czerny (London: Routledge, 2003).

Ritchie, D., *Context and Connection in Metaphor* (New York: Palgrave Macmillan, 2006).

Ritchie, D., 'Relevance and Simulation in Metaphor', *Metaphor and Symbol* 24 (2009), pp. 249–62.

Robbins, J., 'Theological Table-Talk: A Pastoral Approach to Evil', *Theology Today* 44 (January 1988), pp. 488–95.

Robert, T. and Kelly, V. A., 'Metaphor as an Instrument for Orchestrating Change in Counselor Training and the Counseling Process', *Journal of Counseling and Development* 88, no. 2 (2010), pp. 182–8.

Roberts, P., 'Attention, Asceticism, and Grace: Simone Weil and Higher Education', *Arts and Humanities in Higher Education* 10, no. 3 (2011), pp. 315–28.

Rogers, C., 'A Theory of Therapy, Personality, and Interpersonal Relationships as Developed in the Client-centered Framework', in S. Koch (ed.), *Psychology: A Study of Science: Vol. 3. Formulation of the Person and the Social Context* (New York: McGraw-Hill, 1959), pp. 184–256.

Rogers, C., *Freedom to Learn* (Columbus, OH: Charles E. Merrill Publishing Company, 1969).

Rogers, C., *A Way of Being* (Boston, MA: Houghton Mifflin, 1980).

Rogers, C., 'A Client-centered/Person-centered Approach to Therapy', in H. Kirschenbaum and V. Land Henderson (eds), *The Carl Rogers Reader*, 1st edn (New York: Mariner Books, 1989), pp. 135–56.

Rogers, C., 'The Necessary and Sufficient Conditions of Therapeutic Personality Change', in H. Kirschenbaum and V. Land Henderson (eds), *The Carl Rogers Reader*, 1st edn (New York: Mariner Books, 1989), pp. 219–35.

Ross, M., 'Body Talk: Somatic Countertransference', *Psychodynamic Counseling* 6, no. 4 (2000), pp. 451–67.

Rumble, V., 'To Be as No-One: Kierkegaard and Climacus on the Art of Indirect Communication', *International Journal of Philosophical Studies* 3, no. 2 (1995), pp. 307–21.

Scheler, M., *The Nature of Sympathy* (London: Routledge & Kegan Paul, 1954).

Selby, P., *Liberating God: Private Care and Public Struggle* (London: SPCK, 1983).

Shutte, A., *Philosophy for Africa* (Rondebosch: UCT Press, 1993).

Shutte, A., *An Ethic for a New South Africa* (Pietermaritzburg: Cluster Publications, 2001).

Siegelman, E. Y., *Metaphor and Meaning in Psychotherapy* (New York: The Guilford Press, 1990).

Silberstein, L., *Martin Buber's Social and Religious Thought: Alienation and the Quest for Meaning* (New York: New York University Press, 1989).

Smith, S. G., *The Argument to the Other: Reason Beyond Reason in the Thought of Karl Barth and Emmanuel Levinas* (Chico, CA: Scholars Press, 1983).

Snyder, C. R., 'Hypothesis: There is Hope', in C. R. Snyder (ed.) *Handbook of Hope: Theory, Measures, and Applications* (New York: Academic Press, 2000), pp. 3–21.

Snyder, C. R. *et al.*, 'The Will and the Ways: Development and Validation of an Individual Differences Measure of Hope', *Journal of Personality and Social Psychology* 60 (1991), pp. 570–85.

Snyder, C. R., Cheavans, J. and Michael, S. T., 'Hope Theory: History and Elaborated Model', in J. A. Eliott (ed.), *Interdisciplinary Perspectives on Hope* (New York: Nova Science Publishers, 2005), pp. 101–18.

Snyder, C. R., Cheavans, J. and Sympson, S. C., 'Hope: An Individual Motive for Social Commerce', *Dynamics: Theory, Research, and Practice* 1, no. 2 (1997), pp. 107–18.

Söderquist, K. B., 'Irony', in J. Lippitt and G. Pattison (eds), *The Oxford Handbook of Kierkegaard* (Oxford: Oxford University Press, 2013), pp. 344–64.

Sorajjakool, S., '*Wu Wei* (Non-doing) and the Negativity of Depression', *Journal of Religion and Health* 39, no. 2 (Summer 2000), pp. 159–66.

Sperry, L., *Transforming Self and Community: Revisioning Pastoral Counseling and Spiritual Direction* (Collegeville, MN: Liturgical Press, 2002).

Staats, S. R. and Stassen, M. A., 'Hope: An Affective Cognition', *Social Indicators Research* 17 (1985), pp. 235–42.

Stairs, J., *Listening for the Soul: Pastoral Care and Spiritual Direction* (Minneapolis, MN: Fortress Press, 2000).

Stolorow, R., Brandchaft, D. and Atwood, G. E., *Psychoanalytic Treatment: An Intersubjective Approach* (Hillsdale, NJ: The Analytic Press, 1987).

Talmy, L., 'Force Dynamics in Language and Cognition', *Cognitive Science* 12 (1988), pp. 49–50.

Tay, D., *Metaphor in Psychotherapy: A Descriptive and Prescriptive Analysis* (Amsterdam: John Benjamins Publishing Company, 2013).

Thorne, B., *Person-Centred Counselling: Therapeutic and Spiritual Dimensions* (London: Whurr Publishers, 1991).

Tönnies, F., *Community and Association*, trans. C. Loomis (London: Routledge & Kegan Paul, 1955).

Treviño, J. G., 'Worldview and Change in Cross-Cultural Counseling', *The Counseling Psychologist* 24, no. 2 (1996), pp. 198–215.

Tsouna, V., 'Epicurean Therapeutic Strategies', in James Warren (ed.), *The Cambridge Companion to Epicureanism* (Cambridge: Cambridge University Press, 2009), pp. 249–65.

Turnbull, J., 'Kierkegaard, Indirect Communication, and Ambiguity', *The Heythrop Journal* 50 (2009), pp. 13–22.

Tutu, D., *No Future without Forgiveness* (London: Rider, 1999).

Underwood, R. L., *Pastoral Care and the Means of Grace* (Minneapolis, MN: Fortress Press, 1993).

Van Hecke, M. L., *Blind Spots: Why Smart People Do Dumb Things* (Amherst, NY: Prometheus Books, 2007).

Vervaeke, J., and Kennedy, J. M., 'Metaphors in Language and Thought: Falsification and Multiple Meanings', *Metaphor and Symbolic Activity* 11, no. 4 (1996), pp. 273–84.

Walen, S., Digiuseppe, R. and Dryden, W. (eds), *A Practitioner's Guide to Rational-Emotive Therapy*, 2nd edn (Oxford: Oxford University Press, 1992).

Watson, J. C., and Greenberg, L. S., 'Empathic Resonance: A Neuroscience Perspective', in J. Decety and W. Ickes (eds), *The Social Neuroscience of Empathy* (Cambridge, MA: The MIT Press, 2009) pp. 125–38.

Wehr, G., *Martin Buber: Leben - Werk – Wirkung*, Kindle Edition (Gütersloh: Gütersloher Verlagshaus, 2010).

Weil, S., *Waiting on God* (London: Routledge & Kegan Paul, 1951).

Weil, S., *First and Last Notebooks,* trans. R. Rees (London: Oxford University Press, 1970).

Weil, S., *The Notebooks of Simone Weil*, trans. A. Willis, vol. 2 (London: Routledge & Kegan Paul, 1976).

Weil, S., *Grace and Gravity* (London: Routledge, 2002).

Weinandy, T., *Does God Suffer?* (Edinburgh: T&T Clark, 2000).

Weingarten, K., 'Witnessing, Wonder, and Hope', *Family Process* 39, no. 4 (2000), pp. 389–402.

Weingarten, K., 'Cancer, Meaning Making, and Hope: The Treatment Dedication Project', *Families, Systems, and Health* 23, no. 2 (2005), pp. 155–60.

Weingarten, K., 'Hope in a Time of Global Despair', unpublished paper delivered at the International Family Therapy Association Conference, Reykjavik, Iceland, 4–7 October, 2006.

Whitehead, A. N., *Process and Reality* (New York: Harper & Row, 1960).

Whitehead, J. D. and Whitehead, E. E., *Method in Ministry: Theological Reflection and Christian Ministry* (New York: Seabury Press, 1980).

Whitehead, J. D. and Whitehead, E. E., *Method in Ministry: Theological Reflection and Christian Ministry*, rev. edn (London: Sheed & Ward, 1995).

Williams, D. T., '*Perichoresis* and the South African Ideal', *Koers – Bulletin for Christian Scholarship 78*, 1. Art #2118, 2013, 7 pages. Accessed from http://dx.doi.org/10.4102/koers.v78i1.2118.

Wimberly, E. P., *Using Scripture in Pastoral Counseling* (Nashville, TN: Abingdon Press, 1994).

Wimmer, H. and Perner, J., 'Beliefs about Beliefs: Representation and Constraining Function of Wrong Beliefs in Young Children's Understanding of Deception', *Cognition* 13 (1983), pp. 103–8.

Winnicott, D., 'Hate in the Countertransference', in *Collected Papers through Paediatrics to Psychoanalysis* (New York: Basic Books, 1958), pp. 194–203.

Wyrostok, N., 'The Ritual as a Psychotherapeutic Intervention', *Psychotherapy 32*, no. 3 (1995), pp. 397–404.

Yalom, I., *Existential Psychotherapy* (New York: Basic Books, 1980).

Yalom, I., *Love's Executioner and Other Tales of Psychotherapy* (New York: Basic Books, 2012).

Young, F., *Face to Face* (Edinburgh: T&T Clark, 1990).

Young, I. M., *Justice and the Politics of Difference* (Princeton, NJ: Princeton University Press, 1990).

Young, I. M., *Responsibility for Justice* (New York: Oxford University Press, 2011).

Zepf, S. and Hartmann, S., 'Some Thoughts on Empathy and Countertransference', *Journal of the American Psychoanalytic Association 56*, no. 3 (2008), pp. 741–68.

Index of Names and Subjects